Advanced Manufacturing and Precision Machining

Advanced Manufacturing and Precision Machining

Guest Editor

Wei Li

Basel • Beijing • Wuhan • Barcelona • Belgrade • Novi Sad • Cluj • Manchester

Guest Editor
Wei Li
College of Mechanical and
Vehicle Engineering
Hunan University
Changsha
China

Editorial Office
MDPI AG
Grosspeteranlage 5
4052 Basel, Switzerland

This is a reprint of the Special Issue, published open access by the journal *Applied Sciences* (ISSN 2076-3417), freely accessible at: https://www.mdpi.com/journal/applsci/special_issues/6HW113RF50.

For citation purposes, cite each article independently as indicated on the article page online and as indicated below:

Lastname, A.A.; Lastname, B.B. Article Title. *Journal Name* **Year**, *Volume Number*, Page Range.

ISBN 978-3-7258-3021-3 (Hbk)
ISBN 978-3-7258-3022-0 (PDF)
https://doi.org/10.3390/books978-3-7258-3022-0

© 2025 by the authors. Articles in this book are Open Access and distributed under the Creative Commons Attribution (CC BY) license. The book as a whole is distributed by MDPI under the terms and conditions of the Creative Commons Attribution-NonCommercial-NoDerivs (CC BY-NC-ND) license (https://creativecommons.org/licenses/by-nc-nd/4.0/).

Contents

About the Editor vii

Wei Li
Advanced Manufacturing and Precision Machining
Reprinted from: *Appl. Sci.* **2024**, *14*, 11642, https://doi.org/10.3390/app142411642 1

Xinmin Feng, Xiwen Fan, Jingshu Hu and Jiaxuan Wei
Research on Cutting Temperature of GH4169 Turning with Micro-Textured Tools
Reprinted from: *Appl. Sci.* **2023**, *13*, 6832, https://doi.org/10.3390/app13116832 5

Xin Song, Feifan Ke, Keyi Zhu, Yinghui Ren, Jiaheng Zhou and Wei Li
Study on Preparation and Processing Properties of Mechano-Chemical Micro-Grinding Tools
Reprinted from: *Appl. Sci.* **2023**, *13*, 6599, https://doi.org/10.3390/app13116599 21

Shuning Liang, Bo Xiao, Chunyang Wang, Lin Wang and Zishuo Wang
A Polishing Processes Optimization Method for Ring-Pendulum Double-Sided Polisher
Reprinted from: *Appl. Sci.* **2023**, *13*, 7893, https://doi.org/10.3390/app13137893 37

Wei Tang, Jie He, Yunya Xiao, Weiwei Qu, Jiying Ye, Hui Long and Chaolin Liang
Design of a Quick-Pressing and Self-Locking Temporary Fastener for Easy Automatic Installation and Removal
Reprinted from: *Appl. Sci.* **2023**, *13*, 3004, https://doi.org/10.3390/app13053004 56

Zhipeng Liang and Huawei Zhou
Investigation of Spatial Symmetry Error Measurement, Evaluation and Compensation Model for Herringbone Gears
Reprinted from: *Appl. Sci.* **2023**, *13*, 8340, https://doi.org/10.3390/app13148340 71

Jian Li, Huankun Li, Pengbo He, Liping Xu, Kui He and Shanhui Liu
Flexible Job Shop Scheduling Optimization for Green Manufacturing Based on Improved Multi-Objective Wolf Pack Algorithm
Reprinted from: *Appl. Sci.* **2023**, *13*, 8535, https://doi.org/10.3390/app13148535 85

Li Li, Zhaoyun Wu and Liping Lu
Research on Visualization Technology of Production Process for Mechanical Manufacturing Workshop
Reprinted from: *Appl. Sci.* **2023**, *13*, 9754, https://doi.org/10.3390/app13179754 102

Shijie Wang, Jing Zhou and Guolin Duan
Optimization of Pin Type Single Screw Mixer for Fabrication of Functionally Graded Materials
Reprinted from: *Appl. Sci.* **2024**, *14*, 1308, https://doi.org/10.3390/app14031308 118

Hyeonmin Lee, Youngbae Ko and Woochun Choi
Stability Analysis of the Rapid Heating Multilayer Structure Mold by the Contact Error and Thickness of Layers
Reprinted from: *Appl. Sci.* **2024**, *14*, 2813, https://doi.org/10.3390/app14072813 140

Yazhou Wang, Zhen Wang, Gang Wang and Huike Xu
Prediction of Tooth Profile Deviation for WEDM Rigid Gears Based on ISSA-LSSVM
Reprinted from: *Appl. Sci.* **2024**, *14*, 4596, https://doi.org/10.3390/app14114596 153

About the Editor

Wei Li

Wei Li is a professor and doctoral supervisor, as well as the Vice Dean of the College of Mechanical and Vehicle Engineering, Hunan University. He holds several prestigious titles, including National High-Level Talent (Youth), Hunan Province Outstanding Youth. His primary research focuses on precision machining and intelligent manufacturing. He has led over 10 major research projects, including national key R&D programs. Additionally, he has directed nearly 20 enterprise-commissioned research projects. He has published more than 50 high-level academic papers, co-authored two English academic books, and filed 31 national invention patents. He serves as an editorial and youth editorial board member for 20 prestigious national and international journals, and is a reviewer for numerous journals. He has also achieved many awards including the First-Class China Mechanical Industry Technology Invention Award and the Second-Class Hunan Province Teaching Achievement Award.

Editorial

Advanced Manufacturing and Precision Machining

Wei Li [1,2]

1. College of Mechanical and Vehicle Engineering, Hunan University, Changsha 410082, China; liwei@hnu.edu.cn
2. Greater Bay Area Institute for Innovation, Hunan University, Guangzhou 511300, China

1. Introduction

The field of advanced manufacturing represents a core technological domain vital for the evolution of modern manufacturing industries, acting as a critical driver for industrial transformation and the enhancement of international competitiveness. Building upon traditional manufacturing techniques, it deeply integrates interdisciplinary technologies such as electronic information, computer science, materials engineering, and intelligent control. By employing efficient, flexible, energy-saving, and environmentally friendly production methods, advanced manufacturing substantially improves the precision and efficiency of manufacturing systems. The rapid growth of this field not only reflects continuous innovation in manufacturing technologies but also signals major directions for the future development of the manufacturing industry. As a crucial component of advanced manufacturing, precision machining provides indispensable support for the production of critical components such as precision screws, gears, worm gears, guides, and bearings, which are extensively used in high-tech industries like aerospace [1,2], medical devices [3,4], and semiconductors [5,6]. With machining precision ranging from 10 to 0.1 μm and surface roughness below 0.1 μm, advancements in precision machining technologies significantly enhance the manufacturing precision and efficiency of complex components. Furthermore, these advancements bolster the performance stability and service life of critical parts, offering essential technical support for the safe and efficient operation of major devices and equipment.

The fields of advanced manufacturing and precision machining continue to face numerous challenges. On one hand, balancing manufacturing precision with efficiency remains a key technical hurdle. As demand for high-performance components grows, extreme manufacturing conditions, such as micro/nano machining and ultra-precision processing scenarios [7,8], place new demands on process control technologies [9], error compensation techniques [10], and equipment performance. Simultaneously, global manufacturing is undergoing a rapid transition toward greener, smarter, and more sustainable practices. Within this context, advanced manufacturing and precision machining, as core technologies of the industry, shoulder the dual mission of driving manufacturing transformation. This includes improving resource utilization, reducing energy consumption and carbon emissions, and meeting the dual requirements of flexibility and precision in intelligent manufacturing. Achieving a digital and intelligent upgrade across the entire process—from design to production—requires not only the collaborative optimization of high-performance equipment and advanced processes [11,12] but also the integration of key technologies, such as intelligent sensing, data-driven decision-making, and adaptive control [13–15]. As research in this field deepens, the developmental trajectory of advanced manufacturing and precision machining is becoming increasingly evident. This trajectory involves addressing current technological bottlenecks through interdisciplinary integration, theoretical innovation, and technological convergence [16], achieving efficient manufacturing processes driven by demand while satisfying the precision requirements of complex components [17], and establishing environmentally friendly and resource-efficient

Citation: Li, W. Advanced Manufacturing and Precision Machining. *Appl. Sci.* **2024**, *14*, 11642. https://doi.org/10.3390/app142411642

Received: 10 December 2024
Accepted: 11 December 2024
Published: 13 December 2024

Copyright: © 2024 by the author. Licensee MDPI, Basel, Switzerland. This article is an open access article distributed under the terms and conditions of the Creative Commons Attribution (CC BY) license (https://creativecommons.org/licenses/by/4.0/).

manufacturing models with green manufacturing as the ultimate goal [18]. Research advancements in advanced manufacturing and precision machining will significantly drive technological progress in this domain, delivering substantial economic and social value to global manufacturing and providing critical support to meet complex industrial demands.

In the future, the precision and efficiency of manufacturing will continue to advance, with higher-level application scenarios and innovative development models emerging through deeper integration with intelligent manufacturing systems. The transformation and progression of these fields will propel the manufacturing industry toward high-end, digital, and sustainable practices, further solidifying its role as a cornerstone of social and economic development.

2. An Overview of the Published Articles

In recent years, significant progress has been made in the fields of advanced manufacturing and precision machining, with innovative research focusing on the development of novel tools, the design of micro-structured cutting tools, process optimization, and intelligent control systems. These advancements have further driven the evolution of high-performance, high-precision manufacturing technologies, offering crucial technological support to meet the demands of complex machining.

To meet the high-precision machining requirements of hard and brittle materials such as single-crystal silicon, researchers have developed a novel micro-grinding tool based on mechano-chemical action, achieving efficient and low-damage machining results. Simulation and experimental studies revealed that a grinding tool composed of 25% cerium oxide abrasive and calcium oxide additives significantly activated solid–solid phase chemical reactions at the tool interface through the synergistic effects of mechanical force and grinding temperature. The softening reaction products generated by this chemical interaction were removed via mechanical friction between the abrasive particles and the silicon wafer surface, enabling low-damage processing. Machining test results demonstrated that the surface roughness of single-crystal silicon reached Ra 1.332 nm using the mechano-chemical grinding tool, a substantial improvement compared to the Ra 96.363 nm achieved with traditional diamond abrasives. Additionally, the tool exhibited significant advantages in material removal efficiency, greatly enhancing the material removal rate while reducing machining damage. This research offers a promising solution for the high-precision, high-surface-quality manufacturing of semiconductors and optical components, marking a significant advancement in machining technologies for hard and brittle materials [19].

Another innovative study focused on the efficient machining of the nickel-based superalloy GH4169, a material well-known for its machining challenges. Researchers developed micro-structured cutting tools by incorporating surface features such as micro-pits, micro-grooves, and elliptical textures, significantly enhancing cutting performance. Using finite element simulations and experimental analysis, the research systematically evaluated the effects of various micro-structure morphologies on the cutting process, examining their influence on friction, heat distribution, and stress during machining. The findings revealed that, compared to untextured tools, micro-structured tools demonstrated superior cutting performance, with reduced cutting temperatures and significantly lower friction coefficients. Moreover, these micro-structures improved the contact behavior between the tool and the chip, enhancing heat dissipation during machining and further improving machining quality. This research provides valuable technical insights into the machining of complex aerospace components and establishes a clear direction for the development of high-performance cutting tools tailored for difficult-to-cut materials [20].

Researchers have also explored advancements in the precision machining of optical components. To meet the high-precision polishing requirements of optical elements, a robust model predictive control (RMPC) system was developed, utilizing a ring-pendulum double-sided polisher. By optimizing the dynamic performance of the radial-feed system, this approach enhanced the stability and precision of the polishing process. The system's effectiveness was validated through simulations and experiments. The experimental results demonstrated that the RMPC system effectively suppressed disturbances in the radial-feed system, significantly improving machining precision. Specifically, the peak-to-valley (PV) error of the polished optical elements decreased from 1.49 λ PV to 0.99 λ PV, while the root mean square (RMS) error was reduced from 0.257 λ RMS to 0.163 λ RMS. Additionally, the method optimized polishing efficiency, offering a reliable solution for the mass production of large-aperture optical components. The proposed control strategy substantially enhances polishing precision and dynamic stability, providing both theoretical and technical support for the efficient machining of optical elements. This research also advances optical polishing processes toward greater intelligence and reliability [21].

In addition to the aforementioned research, published studies also delve into technologies such as error detection and real-time compensation, novel material processing, and flexible job shop scheduling, underscoring the pivotal role of advanced manufacturing and precision machining in meeting the complex demands of modern industry. These advancements are driving technological breakthroughs, laying a solid foundation for the realization of an efficient, low-energy, and sustainable modern manufacturing system. Moreover, these innovations are paving new pathways for the production of high-precision, high-value components, poised to profoundly influence technological upgrades and industrial transformation in the future of manufacturing.

3. Conclusions

Through in-depth exploration of key technologies in advanced manufacturing and precision machining—such as novel tool development, micro-structured cutting tool design, process optimization, and intelligent control systems—relevant research has offered new insights and solutions that drive the field forward. These innovations have resulted in notable improvements in manufacturing efficiency, precision, and system stability. They have also laid a strong foundation for addressing complex manufacturing challenges while guiding the sustainable and reliable development of future manufacturing processes. In summary, the key technological advancements in this domain are propelling the green, intelligent, and sustainable evolution of advanced manufacturing and precision machining. These efforts contribute to building a more efficient, low-energy, and environmentally friendly modern manufacturing system while providing essential technical support for diverse industrial applications.

Funding: This research was funded by the National Natural Science Foundation of China, grant number 52275421, the Excellent Youth Project of Educational Committee of Hunan Province, grant number 2022JJ10010, the Guangdong Basic and Applied Basic Research Foundation, grant number 2023A1515011193, and the subtask of Strategic Priority Research Program of the Chinese Academy of Sciences, grant number XDA25020317-05.

Conflicts of Interest: The author declares no conflicts of interest.

References

1. Li, Z.; Zeng, Z.; Yang, Y.; Ouyang, Z.; Ding, P.; Sun, J.; Zhu, S. Research progress in machining technology of aerospace thin-walled components. *J. Manuf. Process.* **2024**, *119*, 463–482. [CrossRef]
2. Zheng, Y.; Liu, W.; Zhang, Y.; Ding, H.; Li, J.; Lu, Y. Laser in-situ measurement in robotic machining of large-area complex parts. *Measurement* **2025**, *241*, 115718. [CrossRef]
3. Tan, R.; Jin, S.; Wei, S.; Wang, J.; Zhao, X.; Wang, Z.; Liu, Q.; Sun, T. Evolution mechanism of microstructure and microhardness of Ti-6Al-4V alloy during ultrasonic elliptical vibration assisted ultra-precise cutting. *J. Mater. Res. Technol.-JMRT* **2024**, *30*, 1641–1649. [CrossRef]
4. Akhtar, W.; Rahman, H.U.; Lazoglu, I. Machining process monitoring using an infrared sensor. *J. Manuf. Process.* **2024**, *131*, 2400–2410. [CrossRef]
5. Liu, J.; Zhu, J.; Yu, Z.; Feng, X.; Li, Z.; Zhong, L.; Zhang, J.; Gu, H.; Chen, X.; Jiang, H.; et al. Quasi-visualizable detection of deep sub-wavelength defects in patterned wafers by breaking the optical form birefringence. *Int. J. Extrem. Manuf.* **2025**, *7*, 015601. [CrossRef]
6. Tan, Y.; Yip, W.S.; Zhao, T.; To, S.; Zhao, Z. Subsurface damage and brittle fracture suppression of monocrystalline germanium in ultra-precision machining by multiple ion implantation surface modification. *J. Mater. Process. Technol.* **2024**, *334*, 118640. [CrossRef]

7. Liu, H.; Yan, Y.; Cui, J.; Geng, Y.; Sun, T.; Luo, X.; Zong, W. Recent advances in design and preparation of micro diamond cutting tools. *Int. J. Extrem. Manuf.* **2024**, *6*, 062008. [CrossRef]
8. Li, Y.; Zhang, G.; Zhang, J.; Song, D.; Guo, C.; Zhou, W.; Fu, Z.; Zhu, X.; Wang, F.; Duan, Y.; et al. Advanced multi-nozzle electrohydrodynamic printing: Mechanism, processing, and diverse applications at micro/nano-scale. *Int. J. Extrem. Manuf.* **2025**, *7*, 012008. [CrossRef]
9. Hu, F.; Zou, X.; Hao, H.; Hou, P.; Huang, Y. Research and application of simulation and optimization for CNC machine tool machining process under data semantic model reconstruction. *Int. J. Adv. Manuf. Technol.* **2024**, *132*, 801–819. [CrossRef]
10. Sun, H.; Qiao, Y.; Zhang, Z.; Dong, Y.; Deng, S.; Jin, X.; Zhang, C.; Zheng, Z. Research on geometric error compensation of ultra-precision turning-milling machine tool based on macro–micro composite technology. *Int. J. Adv. Manuf. Technol.* **2024**, *132*, 365–374. [CrossRef]
11. Xing, Y.; Liu, Y.; Yin, T.; Li, D.; Sun, Z.; Xue, C.; Yip, W.S.; To, S. Magnetic and ultrasonic vibration dual-field assisted ultra-precision diamond cutting of high-entropy alloys. *Int. J. Mach. Tools Manuf.* **2024**, *202*, 104208. [CrossRef]
12. Su, Q.; Zhang, N.; Gilchrist, M.D. Precision injection moulding of micro components: Determination of heat transfer coefficient and precision process simulation. *Int. J. Mech. Sci.* **2024**, *269*, 109065. [CrossRef]
13. Sun, T.; Feng, B.; Huo, J.; Xiao, Y.; Wang, W.; Peng, J.; Li, Z.; Du, C.; Wang, W.; Zou, G.; et al. Artifcial Intelligence Meets Flexible Sensors: Emerging Smart Flexible Sensing Systems Driven by Machine Learning and Artifcial Synapses. *Nano-Micro Lett.* **2024**, *16*, 14. [CrossRef]
14. Yan, D.; Li, Y.; Zhou, W.; Qian, Z.; Wang, L. A one-step integrated forming and curing process for smart thin-walled fiber metal laminate structures with self-sensing functions. *J. Mater. Process. Technol.* **2025**, *335*, 118648. [CrossRef]
15. Rahman, M.A.; Saleh, T.; Jahan, M.P.; McGarry, C.; Chaudhari, A.; Huang, R.; Tauhiduzzaman, M.; Ahemad, A.; Al Mahmud, A.; Bhuiyan, M.S.; et al. Review of Intelligence for Additive and Subtractive Manufacturing: Current Status and Future Prospects. *Micromachines* **2023**, *14*, 508. [CrossRef] [PubMed]
16. Szejka, A.L.; Junior, O.C.; Mas, F. Knowledge-based expert system to drive an informationally interoperable manufacturing system: An experimental application in the Aerospace Industry. *J. Ind. Inf. Integr.* **2024**, *41*, 100661. [CrossRef]
17. Zhong, B.; Wu, W.; Wang, J.; Zhou, L.; Hou, J.; Ji, B.; Deng, W.; Wei, Q.; Wang, C.; Xu, Q. Process Chain for Ultra-Precision and High-Efficiency Manufacturing of Large-Aperture Silicon Carbide Aspheric Mirrors. *Micromachines* **2023**, *14*, 737. [CrossRef]
18. Zhu, W.; Yang, G. Analysis of the spatiotemporal evolution and influencing factors of green development level in the manufacturing industry. *Heliyon* **2024**, *10*, e30156. [CrossRef]
19. Feng, X.; Fan, X.; Hu, J.; Wei, J. Research on Cutting Temperature of GH4169 Turning with Micro-Textured Tools. *Appl. Sci.* **2023**, *13*, 6832. [CrossRef]
20. Song, X.; Ke, F.; Zhu, K.; Ren, Y.; Zhou, J.; Li, W. Study on Preparation and Processing Properties of Mechano-Chemical Micro-Grinding Tools. *Appl. Sci.* **2023**, *13*, 6599. [CrossRef]
21. Liang, S.; Xiao, B.; Wang, C.; Wang, L.; Wang, Z. A Polishing Processes Optimization Method for Ring-Pendulum Double-Sided Polisher. *Appl. Sci.* **2023**, *13*, 7893. [CrossRef]

Disclaimer/Publisher's Note: The statements, opinions and data contained in all publications are solely those of the individual author(s) and contributor(s) and not of MDPI and/or the editor(s). MDPI and/or the editor(s) disclaim responsibility for any injury to people or property resulting from any ideas, methods, instructions or products referred to in the content.

Article

Research on Cutting Temperature of GH4169 Turning with Micro-Textured Tools

Xinmin Feng, Xiwen Fan, Jingshu Hu * and Jiaxuan Wei

Key Laboratory of Advanced Manufacturing Intelligent Technology, Ministry of Education,
Harbin University of Science and Technology, Harbin 150080, China; sxfxmin@163.com (X.F.);
17780924565@139.com (X.F.)
* Correspondence: hjs4600@163.com; Tel.: +86-15846009563

Abstract: The GH4169 superalloy has the characteristics of high strength, strong thermal stability, large specific heat capacity, small thermal conductivity, etc., but it is also a typical hard-to-cut material. When cutting this material with ordinary cutting tools, the cutting force is large, and the cutting temperature is high, which leads to severe tool wear and short service life. In order to improve the performance of tools when cutting GH4169, reduce the cutting temperature, and extend the service life of the tool, micro-textured tools were used to cut GH4169 in spray cooling. The effects of micro-texture morphology and dimensional parameters on cutting temperature were analyzed. Firstly, tools with micro-textures of five different morphologies were designed near the nose on the rake face of the cemented carbide tools. The three-dimensional cutting models of the micro-textured tools with different morphologies were established by using ABAQUS, and a simulation analysis was carried out. Compared with the non-textured tools, the micro-texture morphology with the lowest cutting temperature was selected according to the simulation results of the cutting temperature. Secondly, based on the optimized morphology, tools with micro-textures of different size parameters were designed. When cutting GH4169, the cutting temperature of the tools was simulated and analyzed, and the size parameters of the micro-textured tools with the lowest cutting temperature were selected as well. Finally, the designed micro-textured tools were processed and applied in cutting experiments. The simulation model was verified in the experiments, and the influence of size parameters of micro-textures on the cutting temperature was analyzed. This paper provides a theoretical reference and basis for cutting GH4169 and the design and application of micro-textured tools.

Keywords: micro-texture; cutting parameters; temperature; finite element simulation; GH4169

1. Introduction

The nickel-based superalloy GH4169 has strong thermal strength, thermal stability, and thermal fatigue properties. It is widely used in the aerospace field [1,2]. However, GH4169 is a typical difficult-to-machine material. In the process of cutting GH4169, the commonly used tools are often accompanied by harsh working conditions. In the cutting process, the cutting temperature of the tool is very high, so it will change the friction coefficient of the rake face and the performance of the workpiece material, and affect the size of the built-up edge. All of these aspects will directly influence the service life of the tool. In addition, it can also cause problems such as an unsatisfactory surface quality of the processed workpiece and a failure to achieve the expected accuracy [3].

To solve the problem of high tool temperature in cutting, many scholars have used different cooling technologies to cool down the cutting environment, such as low-temperature cooling technology [4], high-pressure cooling technology [5,6], and spray cooling technology [7].

In addition, with the continuous development of science and technology, a micro-textured tool with excellent cutting performance has been favored by scholars in recent

years, which can reduce the cutting temperature, cutting force, and friction coefficient, and improve the surface quality of the machined workpiece.

Micro-textured tools originate from bionic tribology [8]. They are tools with a rake face/flank that is designed and manufactured with micro-grooves, micro-pits, or other surface textures of reasonable shape and arrangement by means of micro-machining techniques such as the electric spark, lithography, and laser techniques. In the process of cutting, the insertion of the structure reduces the contact length between the tool and the chips and increases the heat dissipation area of the tool surface, thereby reducing the friction coefficient, cutting temperature, and cutting force. Moreover, it also improves the machined surface quality of the workpiece, prolongs tool life, and reduces energy consumption [9–11].

In recent years, many scholars have conducted a lot of research on micro-textured tools with different morphologies and size parameters to improve cutting performance and reduce cutting temperature:

Some scholars have studied the effect of micro-textures on the cutting performance of tools. For instance, Rao et al. investigated the influence of micro-textured tools on the cutting performance of Ti-6Al-4V titanium alloy with finite element simulation and experiments. Through the research, it was found that in the same cutting conditions, the cutting temperature of the micro-textured tools decreased by 30% [12]. Zhang et al. studied the cutting performance of the micro-textured tools when cutting Ti-6Al-4V. Through theoretical analysis and experiments, it was verified that the micro-textured tools can effectively improve the lubrication performance and reduce the cutting temperature in machining [13]. Liu et al. studied the cutting performance of the micro-textured WC-10Ni3Al tools when cutting Ti-6Al-4V. It was found that, compared with the non-textured tools, micro-textured WC-10Ni3Al tools can store lubricating oil and promote lubricating oil penetration in the process of cutting, thus significantly reducing the cutting temperature in the process of processing [14]. WU et al. conducted a comparative study on the cutting performance of non-textured and micro-textured tools in cutting Ti-6AL-4V using ABAQUS finite element simulation and experiments. They found that the cutting temperature of micro-textured tools decreased by 5–25% during cutting [15].

Moreover, scholars also studied the influence of micro-textured tools with different morphologies on cutting performance. Sun et al. studied the influence of micro-pit and micro-groove composite textures on the cutting performance of WC/Co-based cemented tools when cutting pure iron, and the experimental results found that the cutting temperatures of micro-textured tools were significantly lower than that of non-textured tools, and compared with a single micro-texture, the cutting temperatures of composite micro-textures were reduced by 7.1~33.3% [16]. Feng et al. designed ceramic micro-textured tools with different morphologies (MST-0, MST-1, MST-2), and conducted finite element simulation on the cutting of Al2O3-TiC composite materials using micro-textured tools with AdvantEdge. After comparison and verification with experiments, it was found that the cutting temperature of MST-2 micro-textured tools was the lowest compared with traditional non-textured tools (MST-0) [17]. AlaaOleak et al. designed micro-textured tools with different morphologies, and based on three-dimensional finite element simulation, studied the impact of micro-textures with different morphologies on the cutting performance of tools when cutting titanium alloys. Otherwise, it was found that pit micro-textured tools have the best cooling effect, and compared with non-textured tools, the high-temperature area of micro-textured tools is significantly less than that of non-textured tools [18].

In addition, some scholars have studied the influence of micro-textured tools with different size parameters on cutting performance. For example, Yang et al. studied the cutting temperature of micro-textured ball end milling cutters with different size parameters when milling the titanium alloy by combining finite element simulation and experimental verification. The optimal parameters of the micro-circular pit texture were obtained as follows: the diameter of the micro-circular pit was 40 microns, pit spacing was 225 microns, the distance from the cutting edge was 100 microns, and the radius of the blunt edge was 60 microns [19]. Li et al. analyzed the influence of width, spacing, edge distance, and depth of micro-texture on the main cutting force and cutting temperature of the tool when cutting Ti-6AL-4V. The results showed that when the width of the micro-texture was 40 µm, the edge distance was 80 µm, the spacing was 70 µm, the depth was 20 µm, and the cutting temperature of the tool was the lowest [20].

There are also some scholars that have conducted relevant research on the distribution mode of micro-textures. D et al. simulated the cutting process of cutting Ti-6Al-4V with micro-textured WC/Co tools by using DEFORM 3D finite element simulation with SAE 40 as a semi-solid lubricant, and studied the influence law of cutting Ti-6Al-4V with micro-textured tools. Finally, combined with the turning experiment, it was found that the cutting temperature of micro-textured tools decreased to different degrees during the cutting process. This effect was more apparent when cutting with micro-textured tools of the vertical shape [21]. Wang et al. simulated the cutting of medium carbon steel AISI 1045 with micro-textured tools. It was found that the cooling effect of the lateral micro-textured tool was more apparent compared with non-textured tools, and it showed good chip fragility in the process of cutting [22].

To conclude, reasonable shapes, structures, and arrangements of micro-textures on the surface of the tool can reduce the cutting temperature in the actual cutting process. However, for research on the cutting performance of micro-textured tools, the cooling effect of micro-textured tools with different morphologies and size parameters is also different when cutting different materials. At present, most research on cutting materials is focused on titanium alloy, with only a small number of pure iron and medium carbon steel. There is little research on the cutting of GH4169 using micro-structured tools in spray cooling conditions, and there is even less research on the influence of the morphology, size parameters, and arrangement of micro-structured tools on the cutting temperature when cutting GH4169.

Based on the above problems, the cutting temperature of GH4169 with micro-textured tools of different morphologies and size parameters was studied by a combination of simulations and experiments in spray cooling. Firstly, five types of micro-textures with different morphologies were designed on the rake face of the tools. The simulation models of the micro-textured tools cutting GH4169 were established and simulated in ABAQUS, and the morphology of the micro-texture with the lowest cutting temperature was selected. Secondly, based on the optimal micro-texture morphology, an orthogonal simulation scheme for micro-texture size parameters was designed, and a cutting simulation was conducted to analyze and select the combination of micro-texture size parameters with the lowest cutting temperature. Finally, the micro-textured tools were processed using a femtosecond laser, and cutting experiments were conducted in spray cooling, which verified the previous simulation analysis results and ultimately obtained the influence of the micro-texture parameters on the cutting temperature. These studies will provide guidance for the efficient machining of GH4169 and the design and application of micro-textured tools.

2. Finite Element Modeling of Micro-Textured Tool for Cutting GH4169

2.1. The Establishment of Geometric Models

In the process of cutting, the cutting heat is mainly focused on the tool nose. In this study, only the part of the carbide tool that was in contact with the chips was established to simplify the geometric model of the tool. To ensure that the processing of micro-textures was not affected by grooves, a flat insert was selected. Then, a matching shank was selected. The insert was installed on the shank, with a rake angle of $-5°$ and a clearance angle of $5°$ in cutting, so the tool rake angle was set as $-5°$ and the tool clearance angle was set as $5°$ in this study. The parameters related to the YG8 tool are shown in Table 1.

Table 1. Material properties of cutting tools.

Tool Material	Density (g/cm³)	Young's Modulus (Gpa)	Poisson's Ratio	Linear Expansivity (m/m°C)	Specific Heat (J/kg·°C)	Thermal Conductivity (W/m²·K)
Carbide	14.6	640	0.22	4.5×10^{-7}	220	75.4

Due to the severe friction, high temperatures were generated on the rake face and flank face of the tools when cutting GH4169. In order to study the influence of the existence of micro-textures on the cutting temperature distribution of the tool and the temperature variation in the contact area between the tool and the chips, the micro-texture distribution was set in the range of 500 μm from the tool nose in this paper. The area occupancy of the micro-texture was 20%, and the depth was 20 μm. Based on the flow characteristics of the chips during cutting, five types of morphologies of micro-textures were designed, as shown in Figure 1. T1, a micro-pit textured tool, has micro-pits arranged in a circular arc shape on the rake surface near the tool nose, similar to the surface microstructure of a dung beetle shell; T2, a micro-pyramid textured tool, has micro-grooves on the rake face near the tool nose, similar to the rib-like texture of a shark's skin; T3, a micro-groove-parallel textured tool, has linear micro-grooves that are approximately parallel to the arc of the tool nose, similar to the surface groove structure of clam shells; T4, a micro-groove-vertical textured tool, has a micro-groove structure that is approximately perpendicular to the arc of the tool nose, similar to the surface groove structure of a clam shell rotated 90°; T5, a micro-elliptical textured tool, has circular grooves on the rake face near the tool nose, similar to the microstructure of pangolin scales.

The size parameters of the micro-texture shapes are shown in Table 2, namely: the distance from the micro-pits (micro-groove) to the tool nose arc (edge distance A), the distance between the micro-pits (micro-groove) (spacing B), and other dimensions (diameter, long/short axis, length/width) (parameter C). The micro-texture shapes designed in this section are shown in Figure 1.

Table 2. Micro-texture size parameters of different morphologies.

Tool Number	A/μm	B/μm	C (c1, c2, C1, C2)/μm
T1	120	90	40
T2	120	70	80, 40
T3	120	70	50, 450
T4	120	70	450, 50
T5	120	30	120, 240, 300, 600

2.2. Material Constitutive Model

In response to the high-thermoplastic, creep, thermal stability, and stress-strengthening characteristics of GH4169, this paper adopts the Johnson–Cook material constitutive model, whose mathematical expression is as follows [23]:

$$\sigma = [A + B\varepsilon^n]\left[1 + C\ln\frac{\dot{\varepsilon}}{\dot{\varepsilon}_0}\right]\left[1 - \left(\frac{T - T_r}{T_m - T_r}\right)^m\right] \quad (1)$$

where A is the yield strength (Mpa) of the material; B is the hardening modulus (Mpa) of the material; C is the strain rate strength coefficient; M is the thermal softening coefficient; N is the strain-strengthening coefficient; ε is equivalent plastic strain; $\bar{\varepsilon}$ is the equivalent plastic strain rate; $\bar{\varepsilon}_0$ is the quasi-static strain rate; T_r is the melting point temperature of the material; and T_0 is the ambient temperature. Meanwhile, the plastic parameters A, B, n, c, and m of the material can be obtained from the SHPB split Hopkinson bar experiment and quasi-static experiment of smooth specimens, and the equivalent strain rate can be obtained by fitting the average values of the compression bar, tension, and torsion experiments.

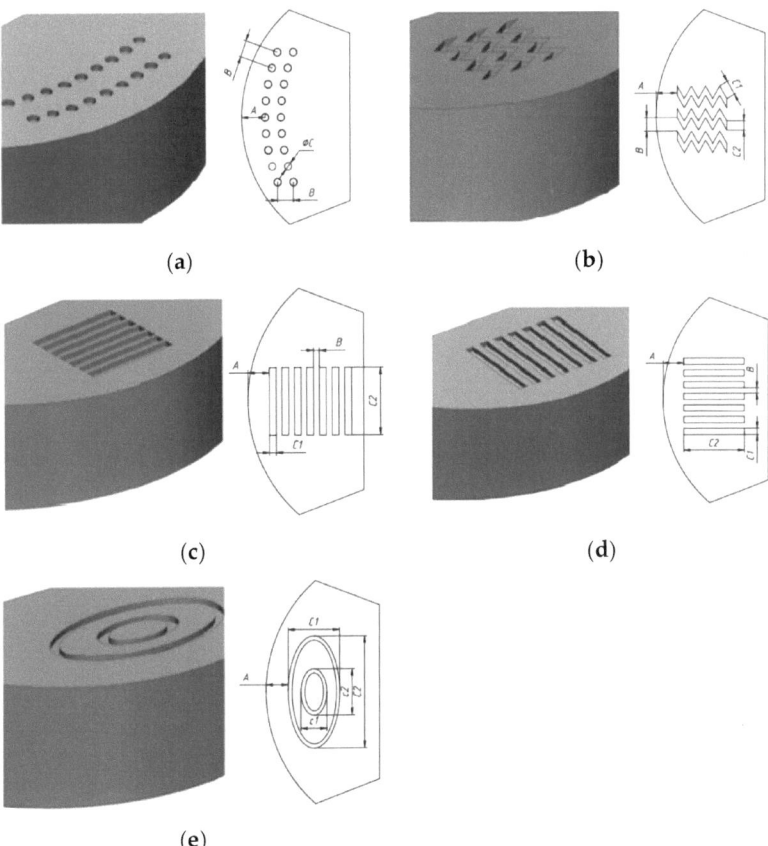

Figure 1. Schematic diagram of micro-texture shapes and parameters: (**a**) micro-pit; (**b**) micro-pyramids; (**c**) micro-groove-parallel; (**d**) micro-groove-vertical; (**e**) micro-elliptical.

Johnson–Cook constitutive model parameters of GH4169 are shown in Table 3.

Table 3. J–C constitutive model parameters of GH4169.

Materials	A/Mpa	B/Mpa	m	c	n	$T_m/°C$
GH4169	860	683	1	0.01	0.47	1260

Johnson–Cook shear failure criterion was adopted as the failure criterion. The values of parameters defined in the Johnson–Cook dynamic failure model are shown in Table 4 [24].

Table 4. J–C failure parameters of GH4169.

Failure Criterion	d_1	d_2	d_3	d_4	d_5
Value	0.11	0.75	−1.45	0.04	0.89

2.3. Mesh

The meshing method used in this paper was a combination of free mesh and sweeping mesh, and the linear reduced integral element was selected as the solid element(C3D8R) [25]. To ensure accuracy, reduce the number of dividing units, and meet the mesh density and unit type, the micro-texture structure was divided into N regions. The unit type was the temperature–displacement coupling. Hexahedral units (Hex), which can ensure the accuracy of the model, stability of the model, and computational efficiency and are easy to generate and process, were used for dividing, and the neutral axis algorithm, which is easier to obtain a regular shape mesh, was selected. The mesh is shown in Figure 2.

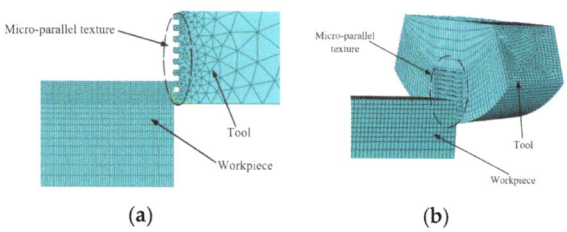

Figure 2. Meshing of the cutting model: (**a**) meshing (two-dimensional cutting model); (**b**) meshing (three-dimensional cutting model).

2.4. Setting Coefficient of Heat Transfer

The experiment was carried out in spray cooling. In order to consider the effect of spray cooling, the coefficient of heat transfer was introduced in the simulation model. Combining with ANSYS, DEFORM, and previous research, the range of heat transfer coefficient h was 2400–2700 (W/m^2·K) when cutting GH4169 in a constant spray pressure and the flow rate [26].

3. Simulation Analysis of Cutting Temperature for Micro-Textured Tools with Different Morphologies

According to the previous experiment for GH4169, in order to minimize the cutting force, the cutting parameters set in the cutting simulation model were as follows: the cutting speed v was 50 m/min, the feed rate f was 0.2 mm/r, the cutting depth a_p was 0.2 mm, and the environmental temperature was set as 25 °C. Under the set cutting parameters, the cutting simulation of GH4169 using micro-textured tools with different morphologies was carried out.

Figure 3 shows the distribution of temperature of the tool and workpiece in the turning process under the same working conditions. It was easily found that the high-temperature area is concentrated in the contact area of the tool–chip and diffuses step by step from the tool nose. It can be seen from the tool nose that the temperature of tool T3 is significantly lower than that of the non-textured tool, and it may have also formed C-shaped chips earlier. In other words, the micro-textured tool with a parallel groove to the tool nose can increase the unit curl degree of chips, and the effect of the chips breaking should be better.

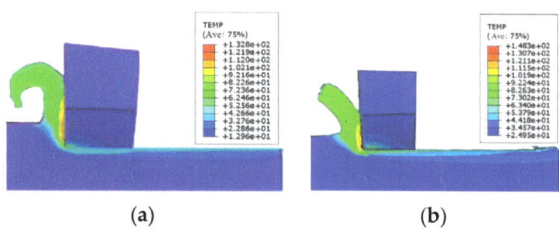

Figure 3. Temperature field of tool and workpiece: (**a**) micro-pit tool; (**b**) non-textured tool.

Figure 4 shows that when the cutting temperature was stable, the temperature field distribution of the rake face of the five micro-textured tools was extracted by the post-processing of ABAQUS. The maximum temperature of the tool was concentrated in the local deformation area near the tool nose because this area was where plastic deformation and tool–chip friction were relatively concentrated. As the cutting temperature accumulates with the plastic deformation and friction of the workpiece, the temperature center shifts from the tool nose to the micro-texture. Through the comparative analysis, the micro-texture has a significant impact on the cutting temperature of the tool. Therefore, it could be seen that the maximum temperature of the non-textured tool is concentrated within 0.4 mm from the tool nose during the stable cutting; the maximum temperature reached 148 °C; the maximum cutting temperature of the micro-groove-parallel textured tool was 125.9 °C; and this temperature is the lowest among these cutting tools. Compared with the non-textured tool T0, the temperature of the tool T1 was reduced by 10.1%, while the temperatures of the tools T2, T3, T4, and T5 decreased by 12.2%, 14.9%, 6.8%, and 11.5%, respectively. Through the above analysis, it could be found that the reason for this may be that the micro-texture of the T3 tool is perpendicular to the direction of chip outflow, which reduces the length of tool–chip contact and friction and results in a decrease in cutting temperature.

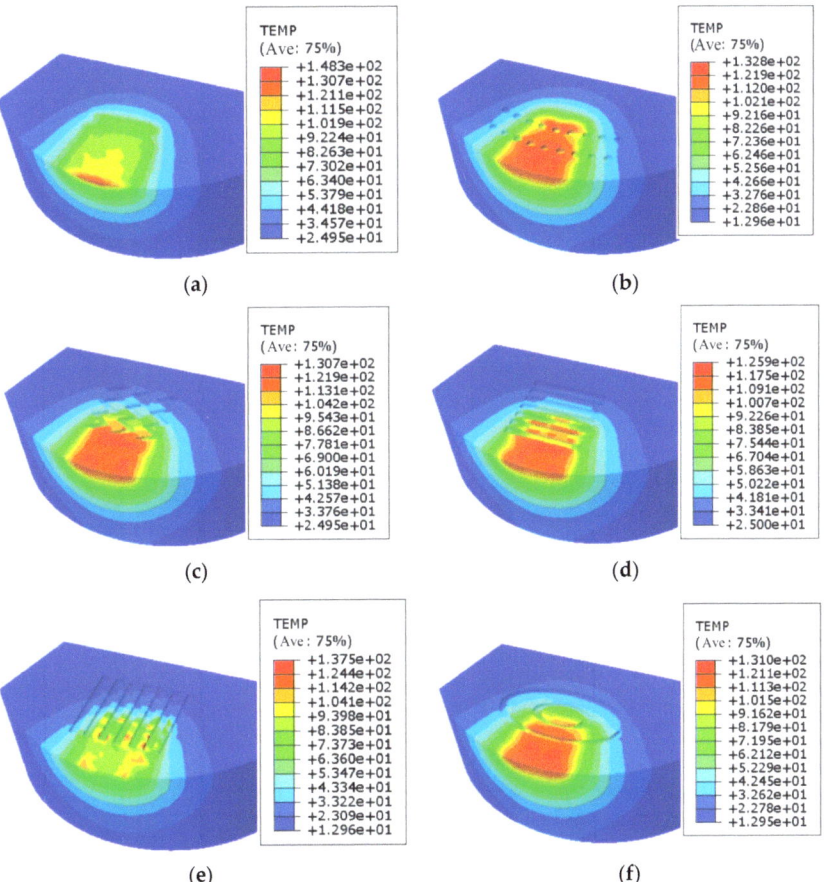

Figure 4. Distribution diagram of tool temperature field in the stable stage of the cutting temperature: (**a**) non-textured tool T0; (**b**) micro-pit texture tool T1; (**c**) micro-pyramids textured tool T2; (**d**) micro-groove-parallel textured tool T3; (**e**) micro-groove-vertical textured tool T4; and (**f**) micro-elliptical textured tool T5.

Figure 5 shows the changing curves of the temperatures of the tool nose when the analysis steps were 10, 20, 30, and 40 for the non-textured tool and the five micro-textured tools with different morphologies. In a complete analysis step of cutting, the cutting temperature of the tool nose tended to be stable after rising, and the temperature of the non-textured tool increased instantaneously after contacting the workpiece. With the increase in the analysis step, the curvature changed, and the rate slowed down between 25–40 steps; however, the heating speed was still faster than that of the micro-textured tool. The heating curves of the T1, T2, and T5 tools were roughly the same. Because of the small cutting parameters, the cutting area of the micro-texture placed on the rake face was roughly the same, the temperature change was not obvious, and the rising rate of the temperature was roughly distributed as T0 > T4 > T5 > T1 > T2 > T3. In step 40, it could be seen that the temperature did not increase or decrease linearly but oscillated around a stable value.

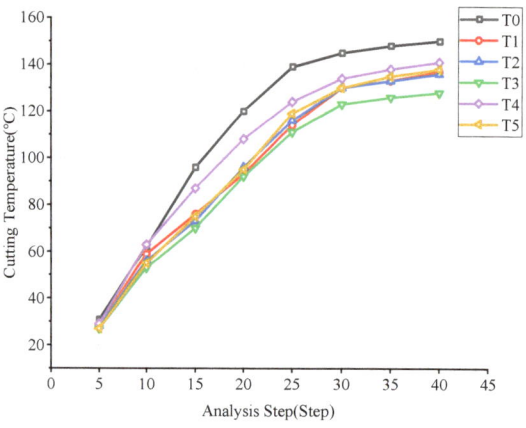

Figure 5. Temperature under different simulation analysis steps.

The overall local temperatures of the micro-textured tool were lower than those of the non-textured tool. The reason for the decrease in the temperature could be analyzed from the chip shape and the friction reduction mechanism of the micro-texture. On the one hand, the reduction in temperature was due to the increase in the unit chip curl rate, which was caused by the micro-textured tool. Compared with the non-textured tool, the chip was separated from the rake face of the tool earlier, which reduced the contact area of the friction pair. On the other hand, in the close contact area of the chips, the micro-texture made the chips form vacuum contact in their existing area, which was also an important factor in reducing the cutting temperature of the micro-textured tool. Being involved in the complexity of material failure and friction conditions in the actual cutting process, the simulation results were acceptable.

According to the cutting principle, the formation of the cutting heat was positively correlated with the contact length between the tool and chips, and the micro-grooves of tool T3 played two important roles in the formation of the chip. Firstly, continuous chips were divided into short segments, and the close contact only occurred at the peak of the micro-groove. Secondly, the micro-groove acted on the initial position of the chips flowing across the surface, making the micro-groove reduce the cutting heat caused by chip flow. Due to the small cutting parameters, the chips would immediately curl after flowing through the first deformation area of the micro-groove. When placed in parallel, the width of the micro-groove was small, and thus the contact area was smaller, which may be the reason why the micro-grooves parallel to the tool nose have better cooling performance.

4. Simulation Analysis of Cutting Temperature for Micro-Groove-Parallel Texture with Different Parameters

From the results of the simulation of different micro-texture morphologies above, the cooling effect of tool T3 was the most obvious. To further study the performance of tool T3 with different size parameters and select the micro-texture size parameters with the lowest cutting temperature, an orthogonal simulation scheme for the size parameters of tool T3 was designed and analyzed through simulation. The groove parameters of tool T3 were as follows: edge distance A, spacing B, width $C1$, and length $C2$ (meaning of parameters shown in Figure 1). During the simulation, the cutting parameters were set as follows: cutting speed v was 50 m/min, cutting depth a_p was 0.2 mm, and feed rate f was 0.2 mm/r. The simulation scheme of the relevant size parameters and tool nose temperature are shown in Table 5.

Table 5. Orthogonal simulation scheme of the tool T3.

Number	A/μm	B/μm	$C1$/μm	$C2$/μm	Cutting Temperature/°C
1	50	60	20	300	130
2	80	80	30	300	134
3	110	100	40	300	131
4	140	120	50	300	128
5	80	100	20	350	138
6	50	120	30	350	138
7	140	60	40	350	142
8	110	80	50	350	135
9	110	120	20	400	133
10	50	100	30	400	129
11	140	80	40	400	133
12	80	60	50	400	132
13	140	80	20	450	135
14	110	60	30	450	143
15	80	120	40	450	141
16	50	100	50	450	141

From Table 5, tool NO.4 has the lowest temperature and, therefore, the best cooling effect. Its size parameters are as follows: A is 140 μm, B is 120 μm, $C1$ is 50 μm, and $C2$ is 300 μm.

5. Turning Experiment

In this section, the micro-textured tools were used to cut GH4169 in spray cooling to verify the accuracy of the simulation of ABAQUS.

In the experiment, the CKA6140 machine tool was used for cutting, and the cutting material was a GH4169 bar with a size of Φ120 × 300 mm. The designed carbide micro-texture tools (micro-texture was processed on the rake face of inset CNMA120408-KR-3225 produced by Sandvik, coated with CVD TiCN+Al2O3+TiN) were used, the temperature-measuring equipment adopts artificial thermocouple method, standard thermocouple (WPNK-191) was used, and the cooling mode was spray cooling. The model of the composite spray cooling equipment is OoW129S. A specific cutting fluid was prepared for the experiment. The cutting fluid was added to the cutting fluid tank of OoW129S. The cutting fluid was vaporized under high pressure produced by an extra-linked air pump and sprayed into the cutting area, which cooled the cutting area. The nozzle flow rate of the spray device is 3.16 L/h, and the inlet pressure is 0.2 Mpa. In the experiment, the micro-textured tools listed in Table 2 were processed using a femtosecond laser, and the tool nose was partially enlarged, as shown in Figure 6.

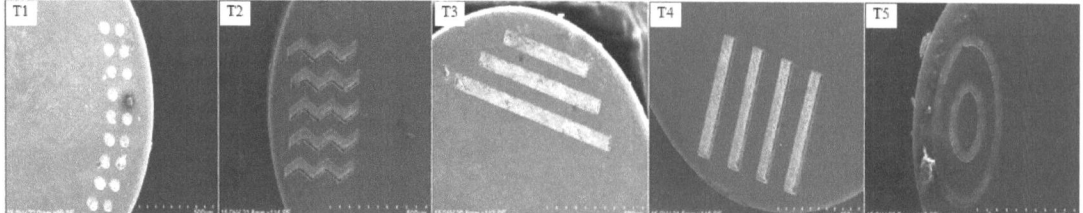

Figure 6. Enlarged views of micro-texture shapes of five tool noses.

5.1. Actual Temperature of the Cutting Area

5.1.1. Temperature Measuring Method and Processing Method

The measurement methods of temperature in the turning process are usually divided into contact and non-contact measurement methods. The specific measurement methods include the thermocouple method [27], infrared thermal imager method [28], radiation pyrometer method [29], and enhanced CCD method [30], in which thermocouple also includes artificial, semi-artificial, and natural thermocouple.

Since the cutting in this paper was carried out in spray cooling, and spray would cause the interference of the infrared ray and lead to inaccurate temperature measurement, the natural thermocouple method was used in this experiment to measure temperature.

Considering the influence of the strength of the micro-textured tool, the electric discharge machining [31] was used to drill the hole in the bottom side of the tool to measure the temperature near the rake face of the tool. As shown in Figure 7a, the distance between the thermocouple measuring area and the cutting area was 1 mm, and the diameter of the hole was 0.5 mm. Standard thermocouples were inserted into the hole and maintained the insulation between the thermocouples and the hole wall. In cutting, the thermocouples felt the temperature of the measuring point, and the potential value was measured by the instrument. Then, the temperature of the measuring point was obtained based on the thermocouple calibration curve. In the experiment, the sensing wire of the thermocouple can be directly inserted into the blind hole inside the tool and fixed by the resin coating. Figure 7b shows the drilling position of the micro-textured tool.

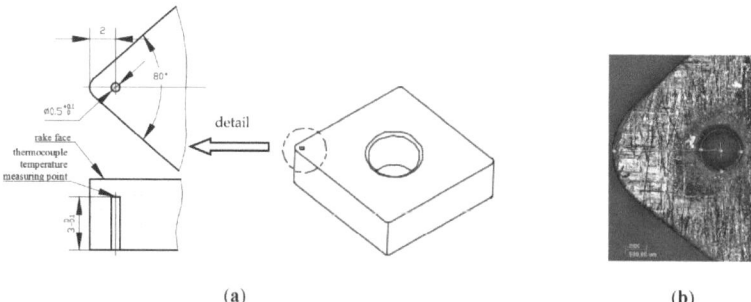

(a) (b)

Figure 7. Position of the temperature measurement point: (**a**) hole of the thermocouple; (**b**) the hole machined by EDM of the tool.

5.1.2. Derivation of Tool Nose Temperature

Because the thermocouple temperature measurement can only measure the temperature at a certain point the certain distance from the rake face, in order to eliminate this limitation of thermocouple temperature measurement, the inverse heat conduction method was used to find out the relationship between the temperature measured by the thermocouple and the actual temperature of the tool nose. The specific flow chart of the inverse heat conduction method is shown in Figure 8.

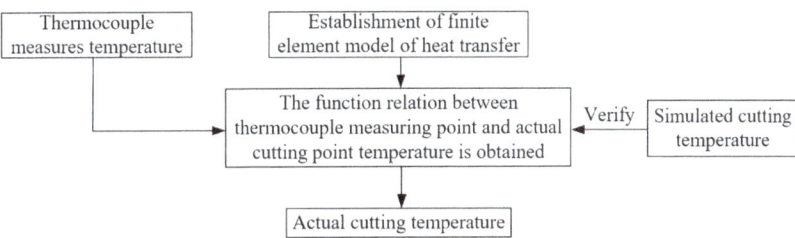

Figure 8. Flow chart of heat conduction inverse method.

The heat transfer model was established in ANSYS. As shown in Figure 9, only the tool nose and its adjacent area participated in the whole cutting process, and the cube of 0.7 mm × 0.7 mm × 1 mm was divided at the tool nose. The upper surface of the cube was used as the cutting area, the lower surface was used as the measurement area of the thermocouple, and the temperature obtained in the cutting area was the cutting temperature.

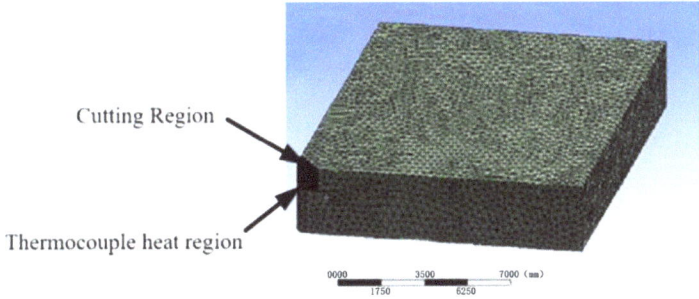

Figure 9. Heat-transfer model.

In the analysis of the heat-transfer process, the main step was the temperature transfer of the small cube cut from the tool nose. Then, the meshes of the small cube part were refined to improve the accuracy of the calculation. The properties of the carbide material are shown in Table 6. After applying the cutting temperatures of 200 °C, 250 °C, 300 °C, and 350 °C in the cutting area, the temperatures in the thermocouple measurement area can be obtained, respectively. Table 7 shows the comparison between the measured temperatures of the thermocouple and the actual cutting temperatures.

Table 6. Properties of cemented carbide.

Materials	Carbide
Thermal Conductivity (W/M·°C)	71
Density (Kg/m^3)	15,600
Specific Heat(J/Kg·°C)	452

Table 7. Heat transfer results.

Number	Tool Nose Temperature Y	Measuring Temperature X
1	200	123.98
2	250	167.47
3	300	214.97
4	350	256.90

The data in Table 7 were fitted by MATLAB, and the final equation of the relationship between the actual temperature of the tool nose and the measured temperature is as follows:

$$Y = 0.00021873X^2 + 1.0366X + 68.6841 \quad (2)$$

where X was the temperature of the measurement area of the thermocouple, and Y was the temperature of the tool nose in the cutting area. Experiments showed that the temperature measured by the thermocouple in dry cutting was 136 °C; substituting this into the above formula, X obtained that Y was equal to 213.71 °C, which was the temperature of the tool nose. Under the same cutting parameters, the cutting temperature of the simulation was 197 °C by using DEFORM. Compared with the results of DEFORM, the results obtained by substituting the temperature measured by the thermocouple into the formula and the error of the simulation results relative to the experimental results is 7.51%, which was within the acceptable range. In conclusion, the fitted quadratic function is more accurate.

5.2. Cutting Experiments with Different Micro-Texture Shapes

Figure 10 shows the machining site of the micro-textured tools when cutting GH4169 in spray cooling. The morphologies and size parameters of the micro-textured tools used in the experiments were consistent with those in the simulation.

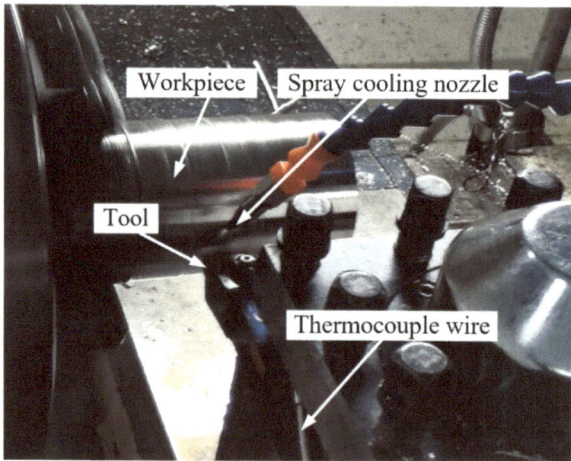

Figure 10. Experimental setup of cutting GH4169 in spray cooling.

As shown in Figure 11, the actual temperature curves of the tool noses were obtained when cutting GH4169 under the conditions of cutting parameters that v was 50 m/min, f was 0.2 mm/r, and a_p was 0.2 mm. It can be seen from the curves that the cutting temperatures of the five micro-textured tools were lower than that of the non-textured tool, and the cooling effects of different micro-textured tools were different for the five micro-textured tools. At the beginning of the cutting, the temperature rose rapidly, and the temperature curves in the later period showed a trend of smooth rising. Among them, the highest cutting temperatures of T0, T1, T2, T3, T4, and T5 were 82 °C, 68 °C, 75 °C, 63 °C, 65 °C, and 69 °C, respectively. Compared with the non-textured tool, the cooling rates of the micro-textured tools were 17%, 9%, 23%, 21%, and 15%, respectively. The micro-textured tool T3 had the best cooling effect.

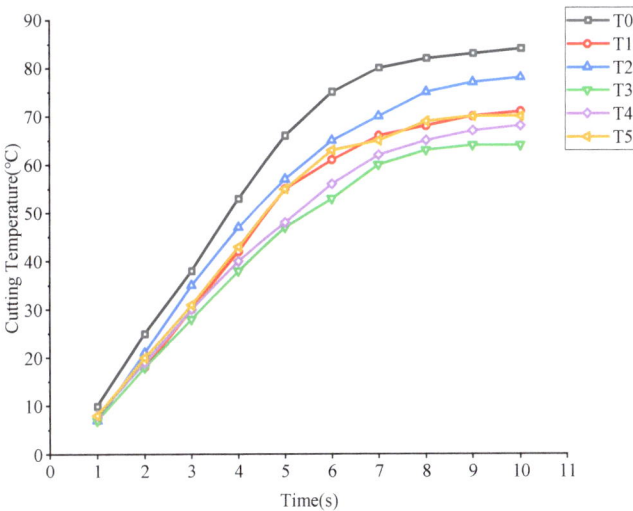

Figure 11. Temperature of tool noses with different shapes at different time points.

5.3. Cutting Experiment of Micro-Groove-Parallel Texture Tools with Different Size Parameters

In order to verify the accuracy of the simulation model of cutting GH4169 with the micro-textured tools designed in Table 5 and to explore the influence of the parameters *A*, *B*, *C*1, and *C*2 of the micro-texture of tool T3 on the cutting temperature, the tools designed in Table 5 were processed, and several tool noses were locally enlarged, as shown in Figure 12. The cutting experiments on GH4169 were carried out using these tools, with the same cutting parameters as the simulation; that is, v was 50 m/min, f was 0.2 mm/r, and a_p was 0.2 mm.

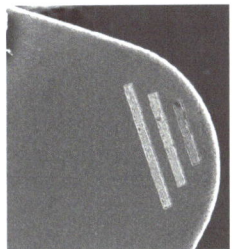 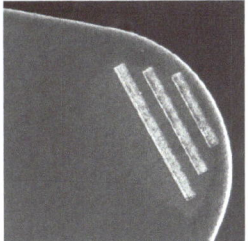 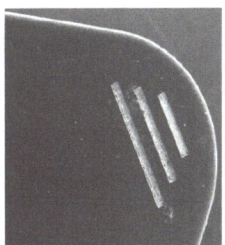 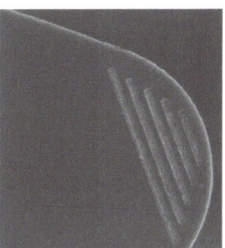

Figure 12. Micro-groove-parallel textured tools with different size parameters.

Figure 13 shows the tool nose temperature measurement of the T3 tool under the different micro-texture size parameters. From Figure 13, it can be seen that under the condition of spray cooling, the cutting temperature of tool No. 4 is the lowest, with a value of 56 °C. The size parameter *A* of tool No. 4 is 140 μm, and *B* is 120 μm. *C*1 is 50 μm, and *C*2 is 300 μm. The results are consistent with the optimization of simulation data, proving the accuracy of the simulation model. It was also proven that the optimal size parameter combination of the groove which parallels the tool nose of the micro-textured tools is as follows: the distance from the groove to the tool nose is 140 μm, the space between grooves is 120 μm, the width of the groove is 50 μm, and the length of the groove is 300 μm.

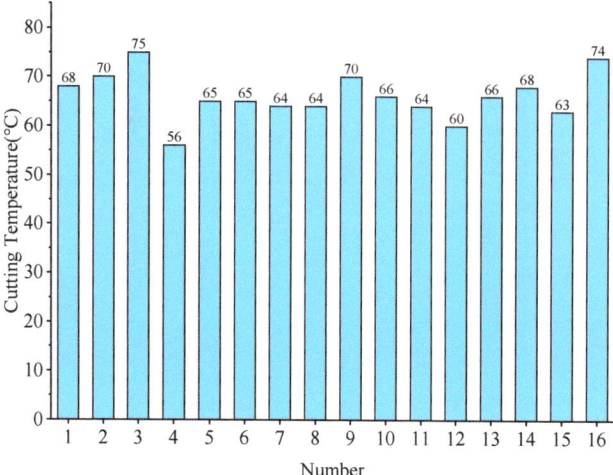

Figure 13. Temperature of tool nose with different size parameters of micro-groove-parallel textured tools.

In cutting GH4169, micro-textured tools can reduce cutting temperature. The best cooling morphology is T3. Firstly, in reference [16], when cutting AISI 1045, compared with the non-textured tools, the cutting temperature of the micro-textured tools was reduced by 21.7%, while the cutting temperature of tool T3 (linear groove parallel to the tool nose) in cutting GH4169 was reduced by 23% in this paper. Secondly, in reference [20], when cutting Al7076-T6, the parameters of micro-grooves are 80 μm, 110 μm, and 10 μm, while the optimal parameters A, B, and $C1$, in this paper for T3 cutting GHH4169, are 140 μm, 120 μm, and 50 μm, respectively. Finally, the same cutting parameters were adopted in both the simulation and experiment of this paper, and further research can be conducted on the optimal match between micro-textures and cutting parameters.

6. Conclusions

This paper studied the cutting temperature of micro-textured tools when cutting GH4169 in spray cooling. The research was conducted in finite element simulations and experiments. The influence of micro-textures with different morphologies and size parameters on the cutting temperature was revealed. The optimized morphology and size parameters of micro-textures were obtained. The following conclusions were drawn:

(1) Compared with non-textured tools, the use of micro-textured tools in cutting reduced both the average cutting temperature and the temperature at the tool nose. This results from two factors. On the one hand, the micro-textured tools increase the curl rate of the unit chip, which leads to an earlier separation of the chip from the rake face of the tool, thus reducing the contact area of the friction pair and lowering the cutting temperature. On the other hand, in the area where the chips are in close contact with the rake face, the micro-texture forms a vacuum contact, and it also means the existence of the vacuum contact becomes an important factor in cutting temperature reduction;

(2) Furthermore, the morphology of micro-textures has an effect on temperature reduction. Among the five designed morphologies, the comprehensive cooling performance of T3 (linear groove parallel to the tool nose) is significantly superior to the other morphologies. Compared with the non-textured tools, the temperature reduction in T3 is 23%, and those of T1, T2, T4, and T5 are 17%, 9%, 21%, and 15%, respectively;

(3) In addition, the size parameters of micro-textures have an effect on temperature reduction as well. Among the 14 combinations of dimensional parameters designed

for T3, the best combination with the lowest cutting temperature is as follows: A is 140 μm, B is 120 μm, $C1$ is 50 μm, and $C2$ is 300 μm;

(4) Experiments were conducted in the same working conditions as the simulation. Since the experimental results conformed to those of the simulation analysis, it can verify the accuracy and reliability of the simulation model.

Author Contributions: Methodology, X.F. (Xinmin Feng); software, X.F. (Xiwen Fan); validation, J.H.; writing—original draft preparation, X.F. (Xinmin Feng); writing—review and editing, J.W. All authors have read and agreed to the published version of the manuscript.

Funding: This research was financially supported by the National Science Foundation of China (Grant No. 51675144).

Data Availability Statement: Not applicable.

Conflicts of Interest: The authors declare no conflict of interest.

References

1. Hao, Z.; Yang, S.; Fan, Y.; Lu, M. Machining characteristics of cutting Inconel 718 with carbide tool. *Int. J. Mater. Prod. Technol.* **2019**, *58*, 275–287. [CrossRef]
2. Shi, L.; Zhang, C. Experimental research on turning of superalloy GH4169 under high pressure cooling condition. *Integr. Ferroelectr.* **2020**, *207*, 75–85. [CrossRef]
3. Pan, L.; Wu, Z.R.; Fang, L.; Song, Y.D. Investigation of surface damage and roughness for nickel-based superalloy GH4169 under hard turning processing. *Proc. Inst. Mech. Eng. Part B J. Eng. Manuf.* **2020**, *234*, 679–691. [CrossRef]
4. Li, J.; Wang, X.; Qiao, Y.; Fu, X.; Guo, P. Experimental and simulation of low-temperature cutting of nickel based alloy Inconel 718 using liquid nitrogen cooling. *J. Mech. Eng.* **2020**, *56*, 61–72.
5. Li, L.; Wu, M.; Liu, X.; Cheng, Y.; Yu, Y. Experimental study of the wear behavior of PCBN Inserts during cutting of GH4169 superalloys under high-pressure cooling. *Int. J. Adv. Manuf. Technol.* **2018**, *95*, 1941–1951. [CrossRef]
6. Zhang, Y.; Wu, M.; Liu, K. Optimization research of machining parameters for cutting GH4169 based on tool vibration and surface roughness under high-pressure cooling. *Materials* **2021**, *14*, 7861. [CrossRef]
7. Shu, S.; Zhang, Y.; He, Y.; Zhang, H. Design of a novel turning tool cooled by combining circulating internal cooling with spray cooling for green cutting. *J. Adv. Mech. Des. Syst. Manuf.* **2021**, *15*, 1–11. [CrossRef]
8. Xie, F.; Lei, X. The influence of bionic micro-texture's surface on tool's cutting performance. In *Key Engineering Materials*; Trans Tech Publications Ltd.: Wollerau, Switzerland, 2016; pp. 1155–1162.
9. Ozturk, E. FEM and statistical-based assessment of AISI-4140 dry hard turning using micro-textured insert. *J. Manuf. Process.* **2022**, *81*, 290–300. [CrossRef]
10. Yu, X.; Wang, Y.; Lv, D. Study on machining characteristics with variable distribution density micro-texture tools in turning superalloy GH4202. *Int. J. Adv. Manuf. Technol.* **2022**, *123*, 187–197. [CrossRef]
11. Zhang, K.; Li, Z.; Wang, S.; Wang, P.; Zhang, Y.; Guo, X. Study on the cooling and lubrication mechanism of magnetic field-assisted Fe_3O_4@CNTs nanofluid in micro-textured tool cutting. *J. Manuf. Process.* **2023**, *85*, 556–568. [CrossRef]
12. Rao, C.M.; Rao, S.S.; Herbert, M.A. Development of novel cutting tool with a micro-hole pattern on PCD insert in machining of titanium alloy. *J. Manuf. Process.* **2018**, *36*, 93–103. [CrossRef]
13. Zhang, J.; Yang, H.; Chen, S.; Tang, H. Study on the influence of micro-textures on wear mechanism of cemented carbide tools. *Int. J. Adv. Manuf. Technol.* **2020**, *108*, 1701–1712. [CrossRef]
14. Liu, X.; Liu, Y.; Li, L.; Tian, Y. Performances of micro-textured WC-10Ni (3) Al cemented carbides cutting tool in turning of Ti6Al4V. *Int. J. Refract. Met. Hard Mater.* **2019**, *84*, 104987. [CrossRef]
15. Wu, Z.; Bao, H.; Liu, L.; Xing, Y.; Huang, P.; Zhao, G. Numerical investigation of the performance of micro-textured cutting tools in cutting of Ti-6Al-4V alloys. *Int. J. Adv. Manuf. Technol.* **2020**, *108*, 463–474. [CrossRef]
16. Sun, J.; Zhou, Y.; Deng, J.; Zhao, J. Effect of hybrid texture combining micro-pits and micro-grooves on cutting performance of WC/Co-based tools. *Int. J. Adv. Manuf. Technol.* **2016**, *86*, 3383–3394. [CrossRef]
17. Feng, Y.; Zhang, J.; Wang, L.; Zhang, W.; Tian, Y.; Kong, X. Fabrication techniques and cutting performance of micro-textured self-lubricating ceramic cutting tools by in-situ forming of Al_2O_3-TiC. *Int. J. Refract. Met. Hard Mater.* **2017**, *68*, 121–129. [CrossRef]
18. Olleak, A.; Özel, T. 3D Finite element modeling based investigations of micro-textured tool designs in machining titanium alloy Ti-6Al-4V. *Proced. Manuf.* **2017**, *10*, 536–545. [CrossRef]
19. Yang, S.; Su, S.; Liu, X.; Han, P. Study on milling temperature of titanium alloy with micro-textured ball end milling cutter under radius of blunt edge. *Appl. Sci.* **2020**, *10*, 587. [CrossRef]
20. Li, K.; Du, J.; Liu, L.; Shen, F.; Ma, L.; Pang, M. Effect of texture parameters on main cutting Force and temperature of cutting tools. *Tool Eng.* **2019**, *53*, 42–46.
21. Arulkirubakaran, D.; Senthilkumar, V.; Kumawat, V. Effect of micro-textured tools on machining of Ti-6Al-4V alloy: An experimental and numerical approach. *Int. J. Refract. Met. Hard Mater.* **2016**, *54*, 165–177. [CrossRef]

22. Wang, B.; Zhang, J.Y.; Wu, C.L.; Deng, W.J. A numeric investigation of rectangular groove cutting with different lateral micro textured tools. In *Key Engineering Materials*; Trans Tech Publications Ltd.: Wollerau, Switzerland, 2016; Volume 693, pp. 697–703.
23. Moakhar, S.; Hentati, H.; Barkallah, M.; Louati, J.; Haddar, M. Parametric study of aluminum bar shearing using Johnson-Cook material modeling. *Proc. Inst. Mech. Eng. Part B J. Eng. Manuf.* **2021**, *235*, 1399–1411. [CrossRef]
24. Wang, Z.; Lv, Y. Simulation Study on cutting force of high temperature alloy GH4169 based on ABAQUS. *Light Ind. Mach.* **2019**, *37*, 42–45.
25. İynen, O.; Ekşi, A.K.; Akyıldız, H.K.; Özdemir, M. Real 3D turning simulation of materials with cylindrical shapes using ABAQUS/Explicit. *J. Braz. Soc. Mech. Sci. Eng.* **2021**, *43*, 374. [CrossRef]
26. Feng, X.; Dong, Q.; Hu, J. Simulation and experiment analysis of the cutting force of high-speed turning GH4169 with spray cooling. *J. Mach. Des.* **2021**, *38*, 74–79.
27. Zhou, M.; Kulenovic, R.; Laurien, E.; Kammerer, M.C.; Schuler, X. Thermocouple measurements to investigate the thermal fatigue of a cyclic thermal mixing process near a dissimilar weld seam. *Nucl. Eng. Des.* **2017**, *320*, 77–87. [CrossRef]
28. Qi, Z.; Guohe, L.; Yong, S.; Fei, S. Experimental study on emissivity setting before precise temperature measurement of SiCp/Al cutting by infrared thermal imager. *Infrared Laser Eng.* **2022**, *51*, 179–188.
29. De Lucas, J.; Segovia, J.J. Measurement and Analysis of the Temperature Gradient of Blackbody Cavities, for Use in Radiation Thermometry. *Int. J. Thermophys.* **2018**, *39*, 57. [CrossRef]
30. Luo, T.; Zhang, Q. Application of CCD non-contact detection technology in industrial production. *New Technol. New Prod. China* **2021**, 69–71. [CrossRef]
31. Rex, N.A.; Vijayan, K. Machining of microholes in Ti-6Al-4V by hybrid electro-discharge machining process. *J. Braz. Soc. Mech. Sci. Eng.* **2022**, *44*, 129. [CrossRef]

Disclaimer/Publisher's Note: The statements, opinions and data contained in all publications are solely those of the individual author(s) and contributor(s) and not of MDPI and/or the editor(s). MDPI and/or the editor(s) disclaim responsibility for any injury to people or property resulting from any ideas, methods, instructions or products referred to in the content.

Article

Study on Preparation and Processing Properties of Mechano-Chemical Micro-Grinding Tools

Xin Song [1,2], Feifan Ke [1], Keyi Zhu [1,*], Yinghui Ren [1], Jiaheng Zhou [1] and Wei Li [1]

1. College of Mechanical and Vehicle Engineering, Hunan University, Changsha 410082, China; feifanke@hnu.edu.cn (F.K.); rebecca_ryh@163.com (Y.R.); zjheng1997@163.com (J.Z.); liwei@hnu.edu.cn (W.L.)
2. CSSC Intelligent Technology Shanghai Co., Ltd., Shanghai 200011, China; songxin716@126.com
* Correspondence: keyizhu@hnu.edu.cn

Abstract: The application of hard and brittle materials such as single-crystal silicon in small parts has expanded sharply, and the requirements for their dimensional accuracy and processing surface quality have been continuously improved. This paper proposes using mechano-chemical micro-grinding tools to process single-crystal silicon, which can realize the high-quality and efficient processing of such tiny parts through mechano-chemical composite action. The microstructure composition of the mechano-chemical micro-grinding tools was designed, the theoretical analysis model of grinding force was established and verified by experiments, and the temperature field distribution during mechano-chemical micro-grinding of single-crystal silicon was simulated and studied, which provided a theoretical basis for mechano-chemical action. Special micro-grinding tools were developed, and mechano-chemical micro-grinding processing tests were carried out. The results show that the coupling synergy of grinding force and grinding temperature improves the chemical activity of the micro-grinding tools, thereby promoting the solid–solid phase chemical reaction of abrasives and additives at the sharp points of the surface of the micro-grinding tools. And when the content of cerium oxide abrasive is 25%, it is more conducive to the solid–solid phase chemical reaction, and calcium oxide can be used as an additive to promote the active agent of solid–solid phase chemical reaction, improve the degree of chemical reaction, and thus improve the removal rate of materials. Soft reactants that are easy to remove are generated on the surface of monocrystalline silicon and are removed by the mechanical friction between the abrasive grain and the surface of the silicon wafer, and finally achieve low-damage processing with a surface roughness of Ra1.332 nm, which is much better than the surface roughness of Ra96.363 nm after diamond abrasive processing.

Keywords: mechano-chemical; micro-grinding tools; micro-grinding; grinding performance; grinding force

Citation: Song, X.; Ke, F.; Zhu, K.; Ren, Y.; Zhou, J.; Li, W. Study on Preparation and Processing Properties of Mechano-Chemical Micro-Grinding Tools. *Appl. Sci.* **2023**, *13*, 6599. https://doi.org/10.3390/app13116599

Academic Editor: Mark J. Jackson

Received: 5 May 2023
Revised: 24 May 2023
Accepted: 26 May 2023
Published: 29 May 2023

Copyright: © 2023 by the authors. Licensee MDPI, Basel, Switzerland. This article is an open access article distributed under the terms and conditions of the Creative Commons Attribution (CC BY) license (https://creativecommons.org/licenses/by/4.0/).

1. Introduction

The application of small parts of hard and brittle materials such as single-crystal silicon is increasingly extensive, such as the manufacture of complex surface structure silicon microchannel plates, aspheric microlens molds, and other devices. However, such parts are usually processed with small feature sizes, and the surface quality and dimensional accuracy requirements are very high, usually requiring the surface of the silicon wafer to achieve nanometer roughness while also requiring no damage to the subsurface [1–4]. Although the current micro-grinding technology can process silicon-based small and complex structural parts, it easily produces cracks, chipping, missing corners, and other damage [5–7]. Therefore, conducting in-depth research on the efficient and high-precision machining of small parts of complex structures is necessary.

Mechano-chemical grinding (MCG) technology is an ultra-precision machining method that couples mechanical action and chemical reaction, which was first proposed by the team of Zhou Libo of Ibaraki University in Japan [8]. With the proper grinding parameters,

MCG technology can produce ultra-high quality surfaces with a surface roughness of Ra < 1 nm [9,10], and its ground surface quality is comparable to chemical-mechanical polishing (CMP) technology. Zhou et al. [11–13] observed silicon wafers processed by mechanochemical grinding with TEM and found no subsurface damage, proving that MCG can achieve subsurface damage processing under suitable parameters. Wu et al. [14] believed that MCG was a chemical and mechanical interaction process, and only when the two interactions reached a certain equilibrium could a surface without subsurface damage be obtained. When the mechanical action was stronger than the chemical action, a subsurface damage layer of a certain thickness would be produced. Tian et al. [15] used grinding wheels to process silicon wafers with MCG technology, observed the change process of grinding surface morphology and the material removal mechanism of MCG processing, and studied the relationship between material removal rate and surface roughness. The results showed that the MCG process could eliminate the scratches caused by the ordinary grinding process, and the material removal rate decreases with surface roughness. Additionally, MCG technology can eliminate surface defects such as scratches left by diamond grinding wheels on the surface of the workpiece in the previous process. Therefore, it is possible to use diamond grinding wheels for efficient machining with a large margin, and then high-quality machining with MCG to obtain a high-precision surface.

Although MCG technology can solve the problems of large edge damage and poor surface quality in the processing of small parts, it is mainly used for the backside thinning processing of large-size silicon wafers, and most of the existing research is to analyze the removal mechanism of MCG. It needs more research on micro-grinding tools for mechanochemical micro-grinding. Therefore, according to the principle of mechano-chemical grinding and the material characteristics of single-crystal silicon, this paper designed and developed mechano-chemical micro-grinding tools, established a theoretical analysis model of grinding force and verified it by experiment, and studied the processing technology and grinding performance of mechano-chemical micro-grinding tools, which made up for the shortcomings of existing research in the field of micro-grinding.

2. Design of Mechano-Chemical Micro-Grinding Tools

Unlike traditional grinding processing, which uses an abrasive higher than the hardness of the material to be processed to remove the brittleness or plasticity of single-crystal silicon, mechanochemical grinding achieves material removal through the solid–solid phase chemical reaction between the abrasive and additives and the surface of the material, as well as the synergistic effect of mechanical stress [16]. Therefore, the design of micro-grinding tools usually needs to meet four conditions:

(1) The hardness of the abrasive is lower than that of the material being processed;
(2) The abrasive can undergo a solid–solid phase chemical reaction with the processed material;
(3) Abrasive additives can directly react with the material to be processed or can promote solid–solid phase chemical reactions;
(4) Abrasive additives can adjust the porosity ratio of the abrasive.

Based on the above conditions, this paper made a reasonable selection of the microstructure components of the abrasive in three aspects: abrasives, binders, and additives, and reflected the microstructure of the abrasives through the content ratio. Cerium oxide was selected as an abrasive, which has a lower hardness than single-crystal silicon, has an excellent grinding effect, and is not easy to clog [17]. The phenolic resin was selected as the binder. The micro-grinding tools made of it usually have good elasticity and self-sharpening, and it is easy to obtain a good processing surface. Sodium bicarbonate, zinc sulfate, calcium oxide, and copper powder were selected as additives, which can enhance the chemical activity of the abrasive, thereby improving the grinding performance of mechano-chemical micro-grinding tools to achieve the purpose of high-quality processing [18]. The main functions of each component of the additive are as follows.

(1) Sodium bicarbonate: Sodium bicarbonate will decompose under hot pressing conditions of about 190 °C to produce carbon dioxide gas and sodium carbonate. Carbon

dioxide gas can make certain pores in the micro-grinding tools, thereby ensuring the self-sharpening of the micro-grinding tools. The sodium carbonate produced by decomposition can be used as an active agent to weaken the adhesion between the cerium oxide abrasive and the binder, thereby enhancing the self-sharpening of the micro-grinding tools;

(2) Zinc sulfate: Adding zinc sulfate to the abrasive can make the additive particles adsorb around the abrasive. After the abrasive particles adsorb the particles, they are more likely to be broken in the mechanical collision during grinding, thereby increasing the specific surface area of the abrasive particles and improving the chemical activity;

(3) Calcium oxide: Calcium oxide acts as a curing agent in additives and can promote the curing of the resin. Furthermore, because of its good heat resistance and high bonding strength, it can play a hygroscopic role in micro-grinding tools;

(4) Copper powder: Because copper powder has good thermal conductivity, the heat generated by the interaction between the abrasive and the workpiece during the grinding process can be conducted through the copper powder, improving the overall heat resistance of the micro-grinding tools.

The design size of the individual micro-grinding tool is 10 mm in diameter and 8 mm in height, and the composition ratio is shown in Table 1.

Table 1. The composition ratio of micro-grinding tools (*vol*%).

Cerium Oxide	Phenolic Resin	Sodium Bicarbonate	Zinc Sulfate	Calcium Oxide	Copper Powder
25	15	20	10	5	5

After calculating the amount of each ingredient added, follow these steps to make a micro-abrasive:

(1) Screening: After grinding the powder, use the #400 screen for screening, filter out larger particles, and improve the uniformity of the powder, so that the components can be mixed more evenly;

(2) Weighing: To prevent the loss of raw materials in the subsequent baking and mixing process, 120% of the theoretical feeding amount calculated by each component should be weighed after the screening;

(3) Drying: To prevent the powder's moisture from affecting the abrasive's performance, the weighed powder should be dried. In this experiment, each powder was placed in an electric constant temperature drying oven and kept warm at 50 °C for 30 min.

(4) Mixing powder: The ingredients are mixed according to the different proportions of the design, and the ingredients are evenly mixed by stirring;

(5) Hot pressing of filler: The abovementioned evenly mixed powder is filled into the mold sprayed with mold release agent according to the total theoretical mass and placed under the hot press machine for hot pressing operation. The hot pressing conditions are pressure 5 MPa, temperature 180 °C, and holding time of 40 min;

(6) Secondary curing: After the preliminary hot pressing operation, the cylindrical micro-grinding tool has a certain hardness and strength but is not fully cured. The electric constant temperature drying oven is used to carry out the secondary curing operation of the micro-grinding tool. At the same time, to make the micro-grinding tool heat evenly, it needs to be buried in quartz sand for heating;

(7) Preservation of micro-grinding tools: The micro-grinding tools made after the above steps are kept in a sealed bag after they are lowered to room temperature. The overall preparation process of the micro-grinding tools is shown in Figure 1.

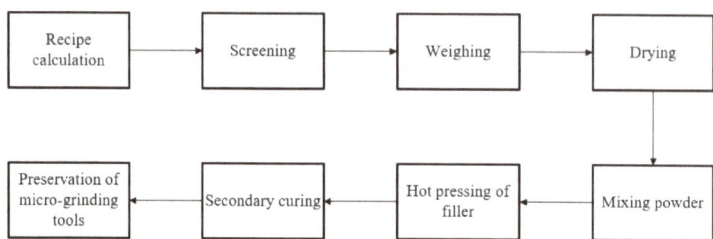

Figure 1. Preparation flow chart of micro-grinding tools.

Using the MKC2945C continuous trajectory coordinate grinding machine as the processing platform, the cylindrical mechanochemical micro-grinding tool shown in Figure 2 was ground and processed experimentally. The micro-grinding tool was fixed on the fixture, and the micro-grinding tool was driven by the rotation of the electric spindle of the machine tool, and then the single-crystal silicon was ground. The processing site is shown in Figure 3.

Figure 2. The physical object of micro-grinding tools.

Figure 3. The grinding of the micro-grinding tool.

3. Analysis of Micro-Grinding Force

3.1. Theoretical Analysis of Grinding Force

Since the soft layer generated by the reaction will undergo a certain degree of elasto-plastic deformation under the normal force of the micro-grinding tool, a coefficient ε of the contact geometry deformation of the reaction abrasive and silicon wafer is introduced in this paper, and the grinding force formula can be expressed as

$$\vec{F} = \vec{F_n} + \vec{F_t} \tag{1}$$

$$F_n = \varepsilon\left(F_{nf} + F_{nc}\right) \tag{2}$$

$$F_t = \varepsilon\left(F_{tf} + F_{tc}\right) \tag{3}$$

where F_n is the normal grinding force of the abrasive grain, F_t is the tangential grinding force of the abrasive grain, F_{nf} is the normal friction force, F_{nc} is the normal cutting force, F_{tf} is the tangential friction force, and F_{tc} is the tangential cutting force.

Figure 4 is a schematic diagram of the force on the abrasive grain.

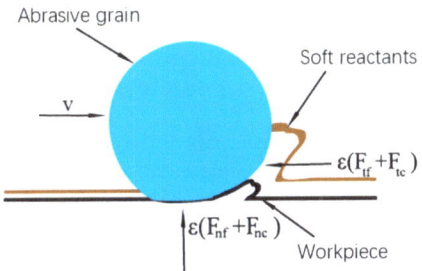

Figure 4. Schematic diagram of abrasive grain stress.

3.1.1. Grinding Depth Model of the Abrasive

When the micro-grinding tool processes, the scratches on the surface of the workpiece can reflect the motion state of the abrasive, and the volume of the removed single-crystal silicon can be expressed by the product of the length of the abrasive mark and the average cutting area of the abrasive. When grinding, the silicon wafer is in a stationary state, and the grinding width is the radius of the soft abrasive, that is, the center of the abrasive disc moves on the edge of the silicon wafer. To obtain the length of the wear mark, the coordinate system shown in Figure 5 is established with O point as the origin of the coordinate system, OD on the geometric center line of the silicon wafer, O' as the geometric center of the micro-grinding tool, and the apex A in the contact zone between the micro-grinding tool and the silicon wafer is assumed to be l away from AO, and let l be the variable.

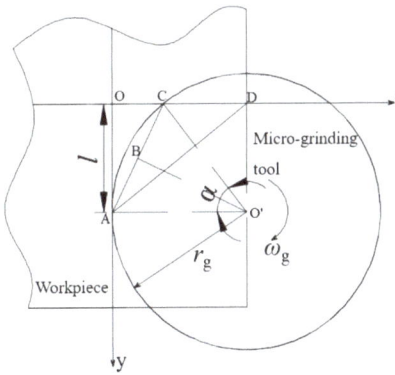

Figure 5. Schematic diagram of material removal.

The geometric relationship can be deduced from the relationship between the rotation angle of the micro-grinding tool α and l, as shown in Equation (4).

$$\alpha = arccos\sqrt{1 - \left(\frac{l}{r_g}\right)^2} \tag{4}$$

where r_g is the radius of the micro-grinding tool, and l is the distance between the contact area's vertex and the silicon wafer's centerline.

The abrasive mark length $L(l)$ can be expressed as the product of the micro-grinding tool's angle and the micro-grinding tool's radius, as shown in Equation (5).

$$L(l) = r_g \cdot \alpha = r_g \cdot arccos\sqrt{1 - \left(\frac{l}{R_g}\right)^2} \tag{5}$$

The instantaneous amount of material removed dV from the geometric centerline l of the silicon wafer is shown in Equation (6).

$$dV = S \cdot L(l) \cdot \beta \cdot N \tag{6}$$

where $L(l)$ is the length of the wear mark at the geometric centerline l of the silicon wafer, S is the material removal area of a single abrasive grain, β is the repetitive cutting coefficient of the abrasive grain, and the value is 0.66 [19]; N is the number of effective abrasive grains from the center of the end face geometry of the micro-grinding tool.

The instantaneous removal volume of the material can be calculated as shown in Equation (7).

$$dV = r_g \cdot \gamma \cdot \left[\frac{2(r_a - z_g)}{r_a}\right]^{2.5} \cdot \left(1 - \frac{l^2}{r_g^2}\right)^{-0.5} \cdot \beta dl \tag{7}$$

Among them, γ is the volume ratio of the abrasive, and $r_a - z_g$ is the maximum grinding depth of the abrasive.

The average depth of cut can be further calculated as shown in Equation (8).

$$d_a = \frac{1}{2}(r_a - z_g) = \frac{r_a}{4}\left(\frac{2\pi \cdot l \cdot a_p}{\omega_g r_g \cdot \beta \cdot \gamma}\sqrt{1 - \frac{l^2}{r_g^2}}\right)^{0.4} \tag{8}$$

where ω_g is the speed of the abrasive, and a_p is the depth of cut for a given micro-grinding tool.

As can be seen from the results of Equation (8), factors such as the size of the micro-grinding tool and the size of the abrasive grain will impact the material removal volume of the micro-grinding tool. It can also be seen that even under the condition of a macroscopic depth of cut, a change in the grinding position causes a change in the depth of the cut.

3.1.2. The Friction and Cutting Force of a Single Abrasive Grain

The micro-grinding tool is in mechanical contact with the surface of the silicon wafer by mechanical action during the grinding process. The normal force caused by friction can be expressed as a function of the depth of cut of the abrasive [20], as shown in Equation (9).

$$F_{nf} = \sqrt{\frac{16 d_a^3 \cdot r_a \cdot E^{*2}}{9}} \tag{9}$$

where E^* is the equivalent modulus of elasticity.

It can be further calculated to obtain

$$F_{nf} = \frac{r_a^2}{6((1-v_1^2)/\eta E_1 + (1-v_2^2)/E_2)}\left(\frac{2\pi \cdot l \cdot a_p}{\omega_g r_g \cdot \beta \cdot \gamma}\sqrt{1 - \frac{l^2}{r_g^2}}\right)^{0.6} \tag{10}$$

where E_1 and E_2 are the elastic moduli of single-crystal silicon and cerium oxide, respectively, and v_1 and v_2 are Poisson's ratios of monocrystalline silicon and cerium oxide abrasives, respectively.

The tangential force caused by friction can be obtained by multiplying the normal force by μ friction coefficient (the friction coefficient between the micro-grinding tool and the silicon wafer at room temperature μ = 0.327).

For the grinding force model of a single abrasive grain, the normal grinding force is formed during the grinding process due to the generation of chips, which is proportional to the corresponding cross-sectional area. It is obtained by calculation that

$$F_{nc} = \frac{4 r_a^2 \cdot k}{15}\left(\frac{2\pi \cdot l \cdot a_p}{\omega_g r_g \cdot \beta \cdot \gamma}\sqrt{1 - \frac{l^2}{r_g^2}}\right)^{0.6} \tag{11}$$

where *k* is the chip thickness coefficient, which is related to the properties of the material being processed.

When chips are generated during the grinding process, the resulting normal and tangential forces are proportional [21]. For (100) crystal-oriented single-crystal silicon, the scale factor $\delta = 0.58$. Combined with the self-introduced geometric deformation coefficient, the expression of the total normal grinding force and tangential grinding force during the grinding is shown in Equations (12) and (13).

$$F_n = \varepsilon\left(F_{nf} + F_{nc}\right) = \varepsilon\left[\frac{r_a^2}{6\left(\frac{1-v_1^2}{\eta E_1} + \frac{1-v_2^2}{E_2}\right)} + \frac{4r_a^2 \cdot k}{15}\right] \cdot \left(\frac{2\pi \cdot l \cdot a_p}{\omega_g r_g \cdot \beta \cdot \gamma}\sqrt{1 - \frac{l^2}{r_g^2}}\right)^{0.6} \quad (12)$$

$$F_t = \varepsilon\left(F_{tf} + F_{tc}\right) = \varepsilon\left[\frac{\mu r_a^2}{6\left(\frac{1-v_1^2}{\eta E_1} + \frac{1-v_2^2}{E_2}\right)} + \frac{4r_a^2 \cdot k \cdot \delta}{15}\right] \cdot \left(\frac{2\pi \cdot l \cdot a_p}{\omega_g r_g \cdot \beta \cdot \gamma}\sqrt{1 - \frac{l^2}{r_g^2}}\right)^{0.6} \quad (13)$$

It can be seen from Equations (12) and (13) that the characteristics of the micro-grinding tool itself, including changes in the abrasive diameter, modulus of elasticity, abrasive volume ratio, and other factors, will affect the grinding force. At the same time, changes in grinding parameters such as speed and cutting depth will also affect the change in grinding force.

3.2. Experimental Study of Grinding Force

To verify the model's accuracy, the grinding force of the surface of the silicon wafer ground by the micro-grinding tool was measured experimentally. The experiment was performed on the MKC2945C continuous trajectory coordinate grinder. The experimental silicon wafer is commercially purchased (100) crystalline single-crystal silicon with a size of 15 × 10 × 3 mm; The sensor is a KISTLER load cell. In this experiment, the end-face grinding method is adopted, and Figure 6 is the diagram of the experimental device.

Figure 6. Device diagram of the grinding force experiment.

In the experiment, the fixture of the silicon wafer was first designed and fixed to the sensor with a countersunk bolt, and the silicon wafer was fixed on the fixture for the grinding force test. The grinding force on the silicon wafer is transmitted to the sensor through the fixture, resulting in force signal data in three spatial coordinate directions. After the tool was set between the tool and the workpiece, a single 1 μm axial feed was carried out, followed by a reciprocating lateral feed, and the above process was repeated to complete the grinding process. The processing parameters are shown in Table 2.

Table 2. Processing parameters of the grinding experiment.

Project	Parameter
Speed (r/min)	1500
Axial feed speed (μm/min)	1
Processing time (h)	1
No feed light grinding times	10
Transverse feed speed (mm/min)	10
Grinding method	Dry grinding

After the grinding state was stable, the data was collected. Figure 7 shows the normal and tangential grinding forces under different cutting depth conditions after filtering treatment, and the sensor data acquisition time is 10 s. The variable for this grinding force measurement experiment is the depth of cutting.

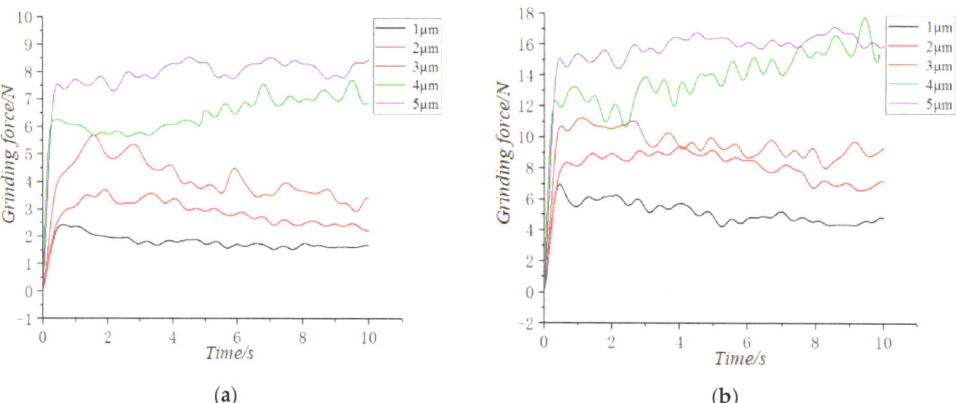

Figure 7. The grinding force under different depths of cut conditions. (a) Tangential grinding force. (b) Normal grinding force.

From the grinding force measurement results in Figure 7, it can be seen that after filtering, both the normal grinding force and the tangential grinding force will show fluctuations within a certain range. The cause of this phenomenon may be fluctuations in force caused by the system's vibration. In addition, from the grinding force measurement results of Figure 7a,b, it can be seen that when the grinding depth is 1~3 μm, the grinding force will decrease to a certain extent as the grinding process progresses. Illustrating that at a given cutting depth, material removal occurs at the contact surface of the micro-grinding tool and silicon wafer, decreasing the contact pressure between the two contact surfaces. When the cutting depth is 4~5 μm, the grinding force does not show a decreasing trend, which may be due to the average particle size of cerium oxide abrasive grain being 5 μm; when the cutting depth reaches 4~5 μm, it has exceeded the cutting edge height of cerium oxide abrasive grain. At this time, the deformation degree of the abrasive grain is large, and there is a more serious extrusion phenomenon between the micro-grinding tool and the silicon wafer, so the measured grinding force is large.

To reflect the grinding force more realistically, the average data points within 0.5~4 s after the rising stage of each force measurement result were compared, and the results after adjusting the selected interval are shown in Figure 8.

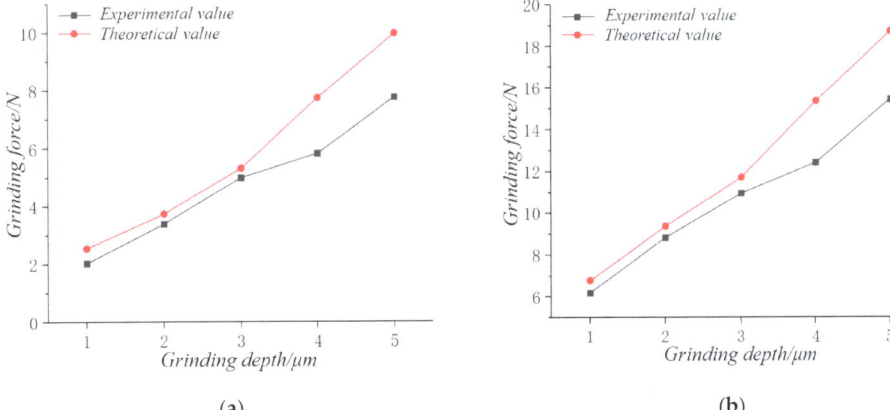

Figure 8. Comparison of experimental and theoretical grinding force values in the initial stage. (**a**) Tangential grinding force. (**b**) Normal grinding force.

It can be seen from the results of Figure 8 that after changing the sampling time range of the grinding force, the experimental value and theoretical value of the grinding force at a cutting depth of 1~3 μm were greatly reduced, both of which were about 10%. In contrast, the error at a cutting depth of 4~5 μm increased. This phenomenon may be because the average particle size of the abrasive grain used was 5 μm. Its hardness is close to the hardness of the processed single-crystal silicon, and the cutting depth of 4~5 μm exceeded the cutting edge height of the abrasive grain.

From the above-shown results, it can be seen that the prediction error of normal grinding force is small in terms of the error between the theoretical and experimental values of the model. Without changing the size of the micro-grinding tool and silicon wafer, the change of the speed and axial feed speed will affect the grinding force, and the grinding force increases with the increase of the feed speed and decreases with the increase of the speed.

4. Simulation Analysis of Grinding Temperature

To study the temperature distribution of silicon materials processed by mechanochemical micro-grinding tools, ABAQUS software (https://en.wikipedia.org/wiki/Abaqus#External_links) was used for finite element simulation analysis. When analyzing the grinding temperature, since both contact surfaces satisfy the heat transfer equation, the study object can be discretized to study the tiny cells.

4.1. Material Parameters and Model Building

The material property parameters required for triboscopic heat generation and heat transfer analysis are density, Poisson's ratio, Young's modulus, coefficient of thermal expansion, thermal conductivity, and specific heat. The material property parameters are shown in Table 3.

Table 3. Properties of materials.

Material	Density g/cm³	Young's Modulus GPa	Poisson's Ratio	Coefficient of Thermal Expansion K^{-1}	Thermal Conductivity $W \cdot (m \cdot K)^{-1}$	Specific Heat $J \cdot (kg \cdot K)^{-1}$
Single-crystal silicon	2.329	131	0.28	2.6×10^{-6}	150	700
Cerium dioxide	7.132	165	0.5	10×10^{-6}	20	359

For the micro-grinding tools and silicon wafers, the areas affected by mechano-chemical grinding are all thin layers of contact surfaces, so to reduce the number of invalid calculations, the model is simplified to 1 mm for both the abrasive and silicon wafers, and the size of the silicon wafers is reduced appropriately to 3 mm × 3 mm, and the part module of the software is used for modeling.

Define material properties and test boundary conditions, and mesh the model via the software's Mesh module. Since only the temperature is analyzed in this paper, and the geometry of the abrasive and the processed silicon wafer is regular, the hexahedral mesh and C3D8T cell type, three-way linear displacement, and three-way linear temperature are selected. Figure 9 shows the result of meshing, where the simplified abrasive contains 30,317 grid elements, and the simplified silicon wafer contains 6250 mesh elements.

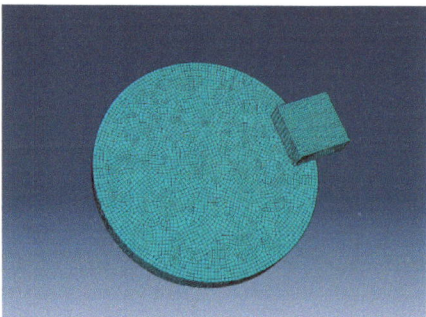

Figure 9. Simplified finite element model of micro-grinding tool and silicon wafer.

4.2. Temperature Distribution Characteristics

The grinding temperature comes from the mutual friction between the two contact surfaces. Due to the fast friction speed, the temperature rise rate is higher than the heat loss rate caused by the heat conduction of the silicon wafer and the micro-grinding tool itself. Figure 10 shows the temperature distribution of the abrasive surface, and the grinding time is 1 s, 2 s, 3 s, and 5 s, respectively. As can be seen from Figure 10, the maximum temperature of the contact point between the silicon wafer and the abrasive is 57.4 °C, 70.5 °C, 88.0 °C, and 144 °C. The simulation results show that as the grinding time increases, the temperature generated by the contact surface of the abrasive and the silicon wafer also increases. Moreover, it can also be seen from Figure 10 that the heat source is mainly concentrated on the edge of the abrasive, which is mainly due to the high linear velocity at the edge of the abrasive and the longer friction distance at the same time. As a result, the temperature at the edge of the abrasive is higher than in the internal area, and material removal is more likely to occur.

Due to the low hardness and small particles of the abrasives and additives, they are prone to crushing and heat generation during grinding. The instantaneous maximum heat generated by the powder crushing caused by friction between the two contact surfaces can be calculated by Equation (14).

$$Q = \frac{0.236\mu WV}{l\left[K_A + 0.88K_B\left(\frac{Vl}{K_B}\right)^{0.5}\right]} \tag{14}$$

where μ is the sliding friction coefficient, W is the vertical weight of the contact point, V is the sliding speed, l is the perimeter of the contact area, and K_A and K_B are the thermal conductivity of the two contact objects.

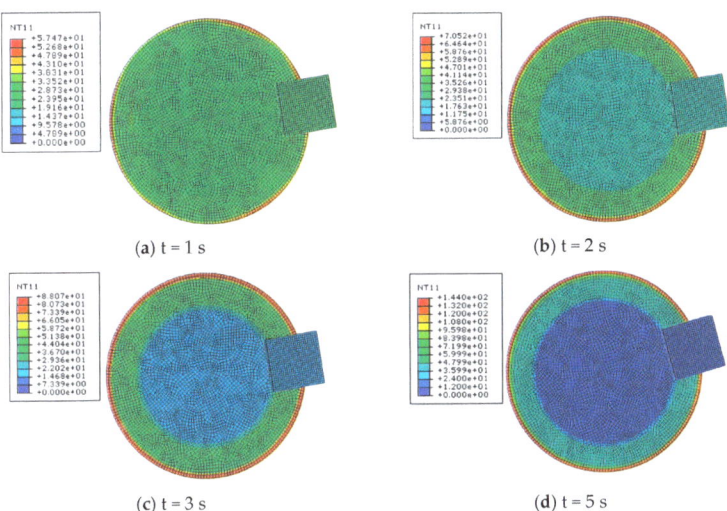

(a) t = 1 s (b) t = 2 s (c) t = 3 s (d) t = 5 s

Figure 10. Simulated temperature distribution cloud.

Substituting the relevant data into the calculation Equation (14) shows that a high temperature of more than 1000 K can be generated during grinding, and the temperature threshold for solid phase reaction between cerium oxide and single-crystal silicon can be reached [16]. Therefore, based on the above analysis, it can be preliminarily concluded that under the test conditions in this paper, the self-made micro-grinding tools can undergo solid–solid phase chemical reactions when grinding silicon wafers.

5. Performance Analysis of the Micro-Grinding Tools

5.1. Microscopic Topography

Scanning electron microscopy (SEM) was used to observe the end topography of the micro-grinding tool, as shown in Figure 11. Because the micro-grinding tool is made by hot pressing at higher pressure, the overall compactness of the structure is high, and the abrasive grain distribution is uniform. Since sodium bicarbonate is decomposed by heat to produce gas, there are pores in the matrix of the micro-grinding tool for chip removal and heat dissipation.

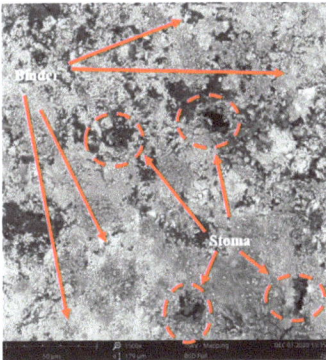

Figure 11. Surface micromorphology of the micro-grinding tool.

5.2. Micro-Grinding Performance

5.2.1. Experimental Conditions

The experimental conditions for the grinding performance of mechano-chemical micro-grinding tools are the same as those for grinding force measurement. After grinding, a white light interferometer (ZYGO New View 7100) is used to measure the surface roughness after grinding.

The silicon wafer processed by mechano-chemical micro-grinding tools and diamond grinding tools is shown in Figure 12, the left side is the silicon wafer processed by mechano-chemical micro-grinding tools, and the right side is the silicon wafer processed by diamond grinding tools. It can be seen that the self-made micro-grinding tool can grind the single-crystal silicon into a smooth surface with a specular reflection effect. The surface of the diamond grinding tool with the same mesh number is relatively rough under the same process conditions, does not show mirror luster, and there are obvious scratches.

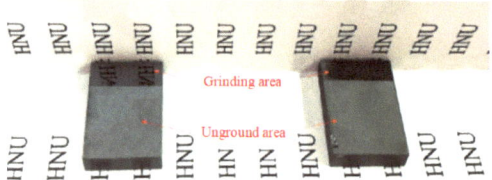

Figure 12. Actual view of the silicon wafer after processing.

5.2.2. Results and Discussion

In this experiment, the self-made micro-grinding tools, diamond grinding tools of the same mesh and size, and commercially purchased silicon wafers processed by CMP were compared under the same process conditions, and the surface morphology was observed. Figure 13 shows the micromorphology comparison of the grinding area and the unground area of the silicon wafer processed under the ultra-depth microscope. It can be seen that the self-made micro-grinding tool can process the originally rough surface of the single-crystal silicon very smoothly. Figure 14 shows the surface topography of a silicon wafer ultra-depth of field microscope after using a diamond grinding tool, a self-made micro-grinding tool, and CMP processing. From the observation of Figure 14, it can be seen that the surface of the silicon wafer after diamond grinding tool processing shows very obvious processing traces and processing defects such as crushing and pits. The surface of the silicon wafer processed by self-made micro-grinding tools and CMP has no obvious processing scratches and no processing defects such as crushing, scratches, and pits.

Figure 13. Micromorphology of single-crystal silicon grinding zone and unground area.

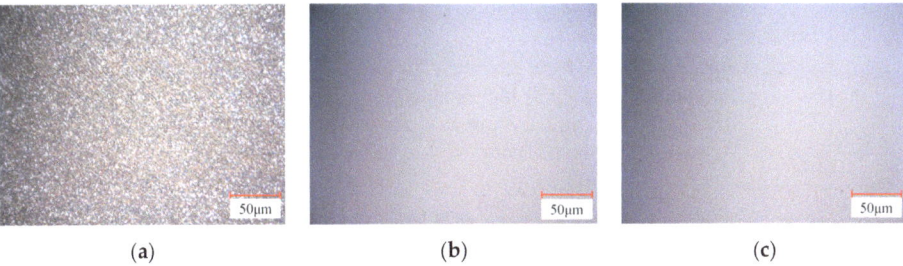

(a) (b) (c)

Figure 14. Micromorphology of silicon wafer processed by different processing methods. (**a**) Diamond grinding tools processing. (**b**) Self-made micro-grinding tools processing. (**c**) CMP processing.

The measurement results of surface roughness are shown in Figure 15. The measurement results showed that the surface of the silicon wafer, after the processing of self-made micro-grinding tools and diamond grinding tools, had a recognizable directional grinding texture. The measurement results showed that the surface roughness of silicon wafers after grinding self-made micro-grinding tools was Ra = 1.332 nm. In contrast, the surface roughness of silicon wafers after grinding diamond grinding tools was Ra = 96.363 nm, and the grinding effect of self-made micro-grinding tools was much better than that of diamond grinding tools. Analyzing the above phenomenon, it was found that the self-made micro-grinding tool was a soft reaction layer through the chemical reaction between the abrasive and the surface material of the silicon wafer. Then, the surface material was removed through the mechanical action between the abrasive and the silicon wafer to form an ultra-smooth and ultra-low damage silicon wafer surface.

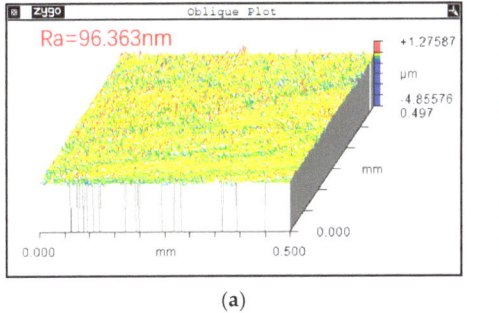 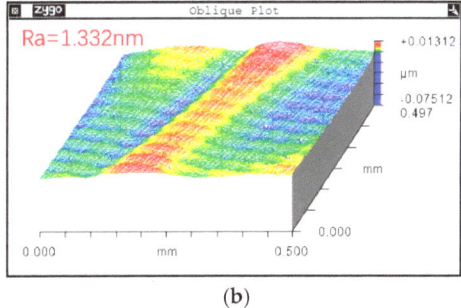

(a) (b)

Figure 15. Results of measuring surface roughness by a white light interferometer. (**a**) The machined surface of diamond grinding tools. (**b**) The machined surface of micro-grinding tools.

To explain the cause of the above phenomenon from a microscopic perspective, a scanning electron microscope picture of the abrasive was taken, as shown in Figure 16. The powder crushing that occurs during the abrasive grinding process causes the bonds of the crystals on the surface of the powder to break. Due to the formation of unsaturated atomic valence states, chemical reactions occur between two solids or the solid and the surrounding gases. The factors affecting the degree of solid–solid phase chemical reaction mainly include (1) the crystal lattice distortion or defect formation of solid under the action of mechanical force. (2) Through mechanical crushing into a fine powder, the solid surface energy is changed, and the specific surface area is increased by producing a new solid surface to improve the degree of the chemical reaction. (3) Under applied force, some atomic groups will be generated on the newly formed surface of the solid due to structural fragmentation, thereby improving the degree of the chemical reaction. The role of calcium oxide is to act as a curing agent to promote resin curing, and it has high bonding strength and heat resistance; adding an appropriate amount of calcium oxide can better bond abrasives and additives together, thereby facilitating the solid–solid phase chemical reaction of the surface convex of the silicon wafer. The addition of zinc sulfate to the abrasive can make the adsorbent around the abrasive [21]; when the solid particles adsorb the medium, due to its increased volume, it is more likely to be broken when subjected to grinding collision, releasing a large amount of energy to increase the temperature of the contact zone, which is conducive to the solid–solid phase chemical reaction.

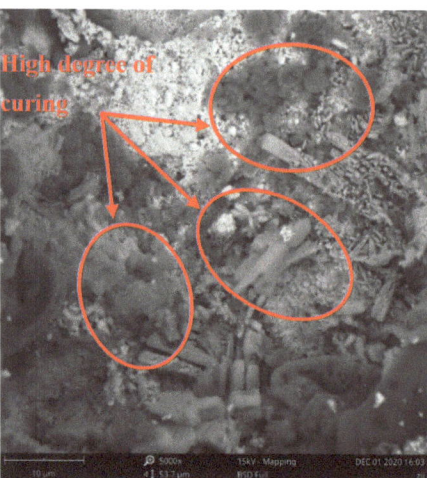

Figure 16. Scanning electron microscopy of the micro-grinding tool.

6. Conclusions and Outlook

In this paper, the development of micro-grinding tools and the research on their mechano-chemical grinding mechanism was carried out. The results showed that when the self-made micro-grinding tools grind single-crystal silicon, the chemical activity of the particles was first improved under the cumulative action of grinding force and grinding temperature. Then, the solid–solid phase chemical reaction occurred between the abrasives, additives, and the sharp points on the surface of the silicon wafer, and then the soft reactants generated were removed under the mechanical grinding of the micro-grinding tools to achieve high-quality and low-damage processing. This paper concluded as follows.

(1) The ε deformation coefficient of the contact geometry of the abrasive and silicon wafer was introduced. The grinding depth model was established by considering the geometric characteristics of the abrasive grain processing trajectory. Based on the established grinding depth model, the contact area grinding force model of single-crystal silicon grinding by the micro-grinding tools was established. The model showed that changes in the characteristics of the abrasive itself, including the abrasive diameter, elastic modulus, abrasive volume ratio, and other factors, would affect the grinding force. At the same time, changes in grinding parameters such as abrasive speed and cutting depth would also affect the change in grinding force;

(2) Self-made mechano-chemical micro-grinding tools could process single-crystal silicon into a very smooth mirror effect, and the surface roughness reached Ra1.332 nm. And the surface quality was close to that of the silicon wafer after chemical mechanical polishing (CMP) processing, and the surface was free of scratches, crushing pits, and other defects. The surface roughness of the silicon wafer after the diamond grinding tool processing was Ra96.363 nm, and there were obvious scratches on the surface and defects such as crushing. The processing effect of self-made mechano-chemical micro-grinding tools is much better than that of diamond grinding tools;

(3) In the process of grinding mechano-chemical micro-grinding tools, the instantaneous temperature of the surface of the silicon wafer could reach about 150 °C, which met the

temperature threshold conditions for solid–solid phase chemical reactions between cerium oxide and additives and single-crystal silicon. A soft compound was formed on the surface of the silicon wafer through a chemical reaction between silicon and cerium oxide abrasives and was removed by mechanical wear in the subsequent process, and ultra-low damage processing of single-crystal silicon was realized under the synergy of machinery and chemistry.

Author Contributions: Conceptualization, X.S. and Y.R.; methodology, X.S.; validation, K.Z.; formal analysis, F.K.; investigation, J.Z.; resources, W.L.; data curation, K.Z.; writing—original draft preparation, F.K.; writing—review and editing, X.S.; visualization, F.K.; supervision, W.L.; project administration, X.S. and Y.R. All authors have read and agreed to the published version of the manuscript.

Funding: The authors would like to appreciate the Special Sub-task of Strategic Leading Science and Technology of the Chinese Academy of Sciences (XDA25020317-05), Excellent Youth Project of Educational Committee of Hunan Province (2022JJ10010), Key Research and Development Program of Hunan Province (2022WK2003), the Natural Science Foundation of Hunan Province (2020JJ4193, 2021JJ40064) and the Natural Science Foundation of Changsha City (kq2014048).

Institutional Review Board Statement: Not applicable.

Informed Consent Statement: Not applicable.

Data Availability Statement: Not applicable.

Conflicts of Interest: The authors declare no conflict of interest.

References

1. Uhlmann, E.; Mullany, B.; Biermann, D.; Rajurkar, K.; Hausotte, T.; Brinksmeier, E. Process chains for high-precision components with micro-scale features. *CIRP Ann.* **2016**, *65*, 549–572. [CrossRef]
2. Chae, J.; Park, S.S.; Freiheit, T. Investigation of micro-cutting operations. *Int. J. Mach. Tools Manuf.* **2006**, *46*, 313–332. [CrossRef]
3. Dornfeld, D.; Min, S.; Takeuchi, Y. Recent Advances in Mechanical Micromachining. *CIRP Ann.* **2006**, *55*, 745–768. [CrossRef]
4. Robinson, G.; Jackson, M. A review of micro and nanomachining from a materials perspective. *J. Mater. Process. Technol.* **2005**, *167*, 316–337. [CrossRef]
5. Aurich, J.C.; Carrella, M.; Walk, M. Micro grinding with ultra small micro pencil grinding tools using an integrated machine tool. *CIRP Ann.* **2015**, *64*, 325–328. [CrossRef]
6. Wong, Y.S.; Rahman, M.; Asma, P.; Wong, Y.S. A study on microgrinding of brittle and difficult-to-cut glasses using on-machine fabricated poly crystalline diamond (PCD) tool. *J. Mater. Process. Technol.* **2012**, *212*, 580–593.
7. Haberland, R.; Schueler, G.M.; Engmann, J.; Haberland, R. Micro grinding tool for manufacture of complex structures in brittle materials. *CIRP Ann.* **2009**, *58*, 311314.
8. Zhou, L.B.; Kawai, S.; Honda, M. Research on mechano-chemical grinding (MCG) of Si wafer: 1st report: Development of MCG wheel. *Jpn. Soc. Precis. Eng.* **2002**, *68*, 1559–1663. [CrossRef]
9. Dai, H.Z.; Jiao, Z.H.; Wang, B. Mechano-chemical grinding for k9 optical glass. *Adv. Mater. Res.* **2014**, *1002*, 57–60. [CrossRef]
10. Huang, H.; Wang, B.L.; Wang, Y.; Zou, J.; Zhou, L. Characteristics of silicon substrates fabricated using nanogrinding and mechano-chemical grinding. *Mater. Sci. Eng. A* **2008**, *479*, 373–379. [CrossRef]
11. Zhou, L.B.; Shimizu, J.; Eda, H. A novel fixed abrasive process: Mechano-chemical grinding technology. *Int. J. Manuf. Technol. Manag.* **2005**, *7*, 441–454. [CrossRef]
12. Zhou, L.B.; Shimizu, J.; Eda, H.; Shimizu, J.; Eda, H.; Yakita, K. Research on mechano-chemical grinding (MCG) of Si wafer: 2nd report: Development of MCG wheel. *Jpn. Soc. Precis. Eng.* **2005**, *71*, 466–470.
13. Zhou, L.; Eda, H.; Shimizu, J.; Kamiya, S.; Iwase, H.; Kimura, S.; Sato, H. Defect-free fabrication for single crystal silicon substrate by mechano-chemical grinding. *CIRP Ann.-Manuf. Technol.* **2006**, *55*, 313–316. [CrossRef]
14. Wu, K.; Zhou, L.B.; Shimizu, J.; Onuki, T.; Yamamoto, T.; Ojima, H. Study on the potential of mechano-chemical grinding (MCG) process of sapphire wafer. *Int. J. Adv. Manuf. Technol.* **2017**, *91*, 1539–1546. [CrossRef]
15. Shimizu, J.; Tian, Y.B.; Zhou, L.B.; Tashiro, Y.; Kang, R.K. Elimination of surface scratch/texture on the surface of single crystal si substrate in mechano-chemical grinding (MCG) process. *Appl. Surf. Sci. A J. Devoted Prop. Interfaces Relat. Synth. Behav. Mater.* **2009**, *255*, 4205–4211.
16. Kang, R.K.; Gao, S.; Jin, Z.J.; Guo, D.M. Study on Grinding Performance of Soft Abrasive Wheel for Silicon Wafer. *Key Eng. Mater.* **2009**, *416*, 529–534. [CrossRef]
17. Dong, Z.G.; Gao, S.; Zhou, P.; Kang, R.K.; Guo, D.M. Grinding performance evaluation of the developed mechano-chemical grinding (MCG) tools for sapphire substrate. *Adv. Mater. Res.* **2012**, *565*, 105–110. [CrossRef]

18. Zhou, L.; Shiina, T.; Qiu, Z.; Shimizu, J.; Yamamoto, T.; Tashiro, T. Research on mechano-chemical grinding of large size quartz glass substrate. *Precis. Eng.* **2009**, *33*, 499–504. [CrossRef]
19. Sharp, K.W.; Scattergood, R.O.; Miller, M.H. Analysis of the grain depth-of-cut in plunge grinding. *Precis. Eng.* **2000**, *24*, 220–230. [CrossRef]
20. Wang, D.; Ge, P.; Bi, W.; Jiang, J. Grain trajectory and grain workpiece contact analyses for modeling of grinding force and energy partition. *Int. J. Adv. Manuf. Technol.* **2014**, *70*, 2111–2123. [CrossRef]
21. Younis, M.; Sadek, M.M.; El-Wardani, T. A New Approach to Development of a Grinding Force Model. *J. Eng. Ind.* **1987**, *109*, 306–313. [CrossRef]

Disclaimer/Publisher's Note: The statements, opinions and data contained in all publications are solely those of the individual author(s) and contributor(s) and not of MDPI and/or the editor(s). MDPI and/or the editor(s) disclaim responsibility for any injury to people or property resulting from any ideas, methods, instructions or products referred to in the content.

Article

A Polishing Processes Optimization Method for Ring-Pendulum Double-Sided Polisher

Shuning Liang [1], Bo Xiao [2,3], Chunyang Wang [1,2,*], Lin Wang [2,3] and Zishuo Wang [4]

[1] School of Electronic and Information Engineering, Changchun University of Science and Technology, Changchun 130022, China; 2020200113@mails.cust.edu.cn
[2] Xi'an Key Laboratory of Active Photoelectric Imaging Detection Technology, Xi'an Technological University, Xi'an 710021, China; xiaobo@xatu.edu.cn (B.X.); winnie_921@126.com (L.W.)
[3] School of Optoelectronic Engineering, Xi'an Technological University, Xi'an 710021, China
[4] School of Information and Control Engineering, Jilin Institute of Chemical Technology, Jilin 132022, China; wangzishuo2003@jlict.edu.cn
* Correspondence: wangchunyang19@163.com; Tel.: +86-13578898897

Abstract: This paper presents an optimization method that aims to mitigate disturbances in the radial-feed system of the ring-pendulum double-sided polisher (RDP) during processing. We built a radial-feed system model of an RDP and developed a single-tube robust model predictive control system to enhance the disturbance rejection capability of the radial-feed system. To constrain the system states inside the terminal constraint set and further enhance the system's robustness, we added the ε-approximation to approach the single-tube terminal constraint set. Finally, the effectiveness of the proposed method for the RDP radial-feed system was verified through simulations and experiments. These findings demonstrate the potential of the proposed method for improving the performance of the RDP radial-feed system in practical applications. The polish processing results demonstrated a substantial improvement in the accuracy of the surface shape measurements obtained by applying the STRMPC method. Compared to the MPC method, the PV value decreased from 1.49 λ PV to 0.99 λ PV, indicating an improvement in the convergence rate of approximately 9.78%. Additionally, the RMS value decreased from 0.257 λ RMS to 0.163 λ RMS, demonstrating a remarkable 35.6% enhancement in the convergence rate.

Keywords: optical polishing process; ring-pendulum double-sided polisher; radial-feed system; disturbance rejection control

1. Introduction

The ring-pendulum double-sided polisher (RDP) is a high-precision optical processing machine. It is designed for processing large-aperture planar optical components. These components are widely used in various essential scientific and technological fields, including space telescopes [1–3], high-energy laser weapons [4–6], laser nuclear fusion systems [7], and other essential scientific and technological fields [8–10].

In order to improve the precision optical element processing, numerous amounts of research have been carried out.

Numerous studies have been conducted to enhance precision optical element processing. Zhong et al. [11] systematically investigated the effects of four crucial process factors, namely polish pressure, pad rotational speed, polish head rotational speed, and slurry supply velocity, on chemically mechanically polished optical silicon substrates. Through meticulous CMP experiments, they successfully identified the optimal combination of these factors, resulting in a significant improvement in polishing efficiency. Ban et al. [12] introduced an advanced conditioning method called subaperture conditioning. By strategically removing and controlling specific regions of the pad surface using a smaller-sized conditioner tool, this method achieves a more uniform surface shape and higher polishing accuracy. Zhao et al. [13] investigated a polished trajectory interpolation scheme to ensure accuracy in trajectory runtime. The NURBS interpolation approach demonstrated a remarkable improvement in both interpolation and runtime error compared to linear interpolation. Moreover, the convergence rate of surface error for elements improved from 37.59% to 44.44%. Pirayesh et al. [14] examined the influence of slurry pH on the size of silica abrasives and their colloidal stability, and how these factors ultimately impacted the polish rate. Their findings provided strong evidence supporting the significant effects of slurry pH, abrasive concentration, and grain size on the polish rate. Notably, smaller abrasive particles with higher surface area showed improved performance in terms of polish rate. Chen et al. [15] investigated the impact of robot motion accuracy on element surface topography during polishing. They developed a material removal model that considers the normal error of the polishing tool, enabling predictions of surface morphology and form accuracy under varying normal-error conditions. This model offers guidance for achieving uniform material removal and improving polishing accuracy. Zhang et al. [16] proposed a material removal model to reduce surface roughness of optical elements. Through systematic analysis, they established a uniform polishing method that efficiently enhanced the surface roughness of hard-polished spherical optics. Zhang et al. [17] developed a material-removing model to analyze the effects of rotary table run-out error on polishing efficiency and accuracy at any given point on the element. Through an analysis and a series of polishing experiments using the KPJ1700 and KPJ1200 CMP machines, they obtained definitive evidence that reducing the run-out error leads to improved polishing efficiency and accuracy. Huang et al. [18] introduced an interpolation process for polishing trajectory using the equal proportional feed rate adjustment strategy. This approach significantly improved the accuracy of implementing dwell time in optical polishing. Simulations and experiments demonstrated that their proposed dwell time algorithm and spline interpolation method had a notable impact on enhancing the solution accuracy of dwell time and improving the convergence rate of form error during the polishing process.

These studies have led to significant advances in improving the accuracy and efficiency of the polishing process through the optimization of the process and the construction of material removal models from various perspectives. However, the uncertainty disturbances during the machining process can affect the polishing efficiency and the precision of the processed optical elements. Therefore, the disturbance rejection control of the RDP's radial-feed system requires further investigation.

Various control methods, such as proportional-integral-derivative (PID) control [19–21], sliding mode control [22–24], and model predictive control (MPC) [25–28], are commonly used in practical systems. PID control is known for its simplicity and ease of implementation, effectively suppressing small disturbances. However, its performance may be compromised when facing complex uncertainty perturbations. Sliding mode control excels at attenuating uncertainties but may introduce significant control oscillations, posing challenges in applications. MPC demonstrates excellent disturbance rejection capabilities by optimizing control actions based on a predictive model to minimize future errors. Despite its strengths in handling disturbances, MPC has limitations when dealing with substantial interferences that exceed the predictive model's capabilities. In comparison, robust model predictive control (RMPC) offers superior disturbance rejection capabilities [29–34]. By considering system uncertainties and employing robust optimization techniques, RMPC enhances its ability to withstand disturbances. However, it is important to note that even RMPC may have limitations when confronted with significant interferences, necessitating additional considerations during implementation.

This paper proposes an optimization method for the polishing process. The proposed method focuses on improving the radial-feed speed accuracy by establishing a single-tube RMPC system for the radial-feed system. By effectively mitigating disturbances during processing, this control system significantly enhances the performance of the radial-feed speed control in the RDP, resulting in improved polishing efficiency and accuracy for the RDP.

The subsequent sections of this paper are structured as follows. This paper is organized as follows. In Section 2, we establish the model for the radial-feed system of the RDP. In Section 3, we conduct the control structure of the RDP radial-feed system, highlighting the design of the single-tube robust model predictive control system. In Section 4, we present simulations and experiments that validate the effectiveness of our proposed method. Section 5 concludes the whole paper.

2. Model of Radial-Feed System of the RDP

The RDP is presented in Figure 1. It mainly comprises the lower-polishing disk with rotation pedestal, the element fixation disk, and the upper-polishing disk. The optical element is positioned on the element fixation disk, and the lower-polishing disk polishes the lower surface through rotation. The upper disk and the element-fixation disk polish the optical element's upper surface by rotational and radial-feed motion simultaneously.

Figure 1. The ring-pendulum double-sided polisher.

The radial-feed motion of the element fixation disk is less susceptible to uncertain disturbances compared to that of the upper-polishing disk. We establish a model for the radial-feed system of the latter. The upper-polishing disk radial-feed system of the RDP's structure is demonstrated in Figure 2. The radial-feed system is composed of a radial-feed permanent-magnet synchronous motor, a spherical screw drive, and an upper-polishing disk. The screw is driven by the motor to realize the radial-feed motion.

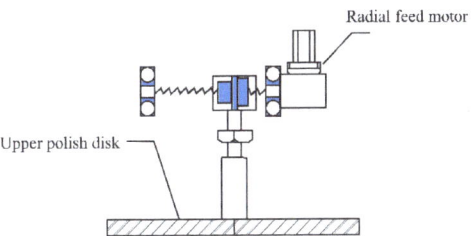

Figure 2. Schematic diagram of radial-feed system of ring pendulum double-sided polisher.

The second-order system model proposed in Equation (1) represents an open-loop transfer function of the radial feed's speed and current. The motor driving current $i_q(s)$ provides the input, while the radial-feed motor speed of the upper-polishing disk $\omega(s)$ represents the output. The remaining physical quantities in Equation (1) have the following meanings: T is the load torque, p_n is the number of motor poles, ψ_f is the flux of a permanent magnet, J is the motor's moment of inertia, and B is the viscous damping coefficient.

$$\frac{\omega(s)}{i_q(s)} = \frac{1.5p_n\psi_f}{(Ts+1)(Js+B)} = \frac{1.5p_n\psi_f}{JTs^2 + (J+TB)s + B} \quad (1)$$

Equation (2) shows the radial-feed system model with its parameters identified by the multi-innovation stochastic gradient descent parameter identification method [35,36].

$$\frac{\omega(z)}{i_q(z)} = \frac{-2.0491z^{-1} + 88.5127z^{-2}}{1 - 0.0788z^{-1} + 0.1852z^{-2}} \quad (2)$$

To facilitate the subsequent controller design, we transform the system transfer function into the state space in Equation (3), which adds the interferences of the system state and control quantity into the model.

$$\begin{aligned} x(k+1) &= Ax(k) + Bu(k) + w(k) \\ y(k) &= Cx(k) + v(k) \end{aligned} \quad (3)$$

where A = [0.0788, −0.1852; 1.0000, 0], B = [1; 0], and C = [−2.0491, 88.5127]. $x(k)$ is the system state variable and $u(k)$ is the system control quantity. $w(k)$ and $v(k)$ are system state disturbance and control quantity disturbance, respectively.

3. RDP Radial-Feed System Control Structure

3.1. Single-Tube RMPC

Figure 3 shows the control structure of the single-tube RMPC. x_i is the actual input. x_o is the actual output. The difference between the input and output is defined as actual state $x(k)$.

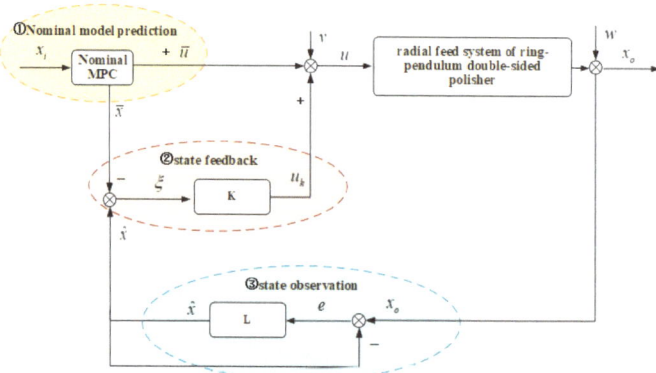

Figure 3. Single-tube RMPC structure.

The structure consists of three parts: nominal model predictive control, state estimation, and state feedback. The identification system model is utilized for the nominal MPC optimization. $\hat{x}(k)$ represents the estimated state of the system, which is obtained through the utilization of the estimation matrix L. The total control volume of the single-tube robust predictive controller consists of the nominal model predictive control (MPC) and the feedback control. Moreover, the system state gradually approaches the origin under the influence of the control quantity.

$$x \in \mathbb{X}, u \in \mathbb{U}, w \in \mathbb{W}, v \in \mathbb{V} \quad (4)$$

$$\overline{x}(k+1) = A\ \overline{x}(k) + B\overline{u}(k)$$
$$\overline{y}(k) = C\ \overline{x}(k) \qquad (5)$$

$x(k), u(k), w(k),$ and $v(k)$ in Equation (3) are constrained by Equation (4). $\mathbb{X}, \mathbb{U}, \mathbb{W},$ and $\mathbb{V}$ represent the constraint sets containing the origin. Equation (5) describes the nominal MPC system, which excludes the disturbances $w(k)$ and $v(k)$. $\overline{x}(k)$ is the nominal prediction state $\overline{x}(k)$. $\overline{u}(k)$ is the nominal model prediction control quantity.

$$\begin{aligned}
&\min_{\overline{x}(k),\overline{u}(k)^{0:N-1}} V_N\left(\overline{x}(k),\overline{u}(k|k)^{0:N-1}\right) = F(\overline{x}(N|k)) + \sum_{i=0}^{N-1} L(\overline{x}(i|k),\overline{u}(i|k)) \\
&F(\overline{x}(N|k)) = \overline{x}(N|k)^T P \overline{x}(N|k) \\
&L(\overline{x}(i|k),\overline{u}(i|k)) = \overline{x}(i|0)^T Q \overline{x}(i|k) + \overline{u}(i|k)^T R \overline{u}(i|k) \\
&\overline{x}(k) \in \mathbb{X} \quad \overline{u}(k)^{0:N-1} \in \mathbb{U} \quad \overline{x}(N) \in \mathbb{X}_f \\
&i = k, k+1, \cdots, k+N-1
\end{aligned} \qquad (6)$$

$x(k) = [\overline{x}(k|k), \overline{x}(k+1|k), \cdots \overline{x}(k+N|k)]$ is a sequence of the nominal system state and $u(k) = [\overline{u}(k|k), \overline{u}(k+1|k), \cdots \overline{u}(k+N-1|k)]$ is a sequence of the optimal control quantity at k = [0, … k]. The integer N represents the prediction horizon length. At current time k, $\overline{x}(k)$ is the nominal MPC system state and $\overline{u}(k) = \overline{u}^*(k|k)$ is the nominal MPC control quantity. $\mathbb{X}_f$ represents the nominal MPC reachable set, while R and Q are two weight matrices in nominal MPC cost function V_N.

$$u(k) = \overline{u}(k) + K(\hat{x}(k) - \overline{x}(k)) \qquad (7)$$

$$A_K = A + BK \qquad (8)$$

The feedback matrix K can eliminate the distance between the actual state and the estimated state. To ensure system stability, the feedback matrix K must satisfy the condition that the spectral radius of matrix A_K is below a value of 1.

$$\hat{x}(k+1) = A\hat{x}(k) + Bu(k) + L(C\hat{x}(k) - y(k)) \qquad (9)$$

$$A_L = A + LC \qquad (10)$$

$\hat{x}(k)$ in Equation (9) is the estimated state. The parameters in estimated matrix L must guarantee that the spectral radius of matrix A_L is below a value of 1, ensuring system stability. The estimated error $e(k)$ is defined as the difference between $x(k)$ and $\hat{x}(k)$. The prediction error $\xi(k)$ is defined as the difference between $\overline{x}(k)$ and $\hat{x}(k)$.

$$e(k) = x(k) - \hat{x}(k) \qquad (11)$$

$$\xi(k) = \hat{x}(k) - \overline{x}(k) \qquad (12)$$

Combining Equations (11) and (12), the actual state $x(k)$ can be presented as follows:

$$x(k) = \overline{x}(k) + \xi(k) + e(k) \qquad (13)$$

Combining Equations (7)–(12), we obtained the error system as follows:

$$e(k+1) = (A + LC)e(k) + w(k) + Lv(k) \qquad (14)$$

$$\xi(k+1) = (A + BK)\xi(k) - L(Ce(k) + v(k)) \qquad (15)$$

$A \oplus B := \{a + b | a \in F, b \in D\}$ is the Minkowski sum in the following formulas, where $\oplus$ represents the operation symbol. The terminal constraint set for $e(k)$ and $\xi(k)$ is designed by utilizing the minimal robust invariant set. According to Equations (14)–(16), we can obtain the constraint set $\mathbb{E}(k)$ for $e(k)$ and the constraint set $\Xi(k)$ for $\xi(k)$.

$$\mathbb{E}(k+1) = (A + LC)\mathbb{E}(k) \oplus \mathbb{W} \oplus L\mathbb{V} \tag{16}$$

$$\begin{aligned} \Xi(k+1) &= (A + BK)\Xi(k) \oplus \Phi(k) \\ \Phi(k) &= -LC \cdot \mathbb{E}(k) \oplus -L\mathbb{V} \end{aligned} \tag{17}$$

Combining the calculation of minimal robust invariant set in Reference [37] and Equations (14) and (15), we can obtain the minimal robust invariant sets $\mathbb{E}_\infty$ and Ξ_∞.

$$\mathbb{E}_\infty = (A + LC)\mathbb{E}_\infty \oplus \mathbb{W} \oplus L\mathbb{V} \tag{18}$$

$$\Xi_\infty = (A + BK)\Xi_\infty \oplus (-LC)\mathbb{E}_\infty \oplus (-L)\mathbb{V} \tag{19}$$

3.2. ε- Approximation of the Single-Tube Terminal Constraint Set

This section presents the computation of the single-tube terminal constraint set and approximates it by utilizing the ε-approximation method.

We define the single-tube constraint variable as $z(k)$. According to Equations (14)–(17), we obtain the calculation formulas of single-tube constraint reduction:

$$z(k+1) = Fz(k) + d(k), d(k) \in D(k) \tag{20}$$

$$F = \begin{pmatrix} A + LC & 0 \\ -LC & A + BK \end{pmatrix} \tag{21}$$

$$d(k) = \begin{bmatrix} I & L \\ 0 & -L \end{bmatrix} \begin{bmatrix} w(k) \\ v(k) \end{bmatrix} \tag{22}$$

$$\mathbb{Z}(k+1) = F\mathbb{Z}(k) \oplus D(k) \tag{23}$$

In order to extend the allowable range of system disturbances, the ε-approximation is designed for the single-tube terminal constraint set. We can utilize the following formula to calculate the single-tube constraint set $\mathbb{Z}_\infty$.

$$\mathbb{Z}_\infty = \bigoplus_{i=0}^{\infty} F^i D \tag{24}$$

For scalars $\alpha \in [0,1)$ and $\varepsilon > 0$, there exists a positive integer s that satisfies the condition $F^s = \alpha I$, which further satisfies $\mathbb{Z}_\infty = (1-\alpha)^{-1}\mathbb{Z}_s$. Then, we define $\mathbb{Z}_s$ as the ε-approximation of $\mathbb{Z}_\infty$.

$$\mathbb{Z}(\alpha, s) = (1-\alpha)^{-1}\mathbb{Z}_s \tag{25}$$

When $0 \in \text{int}(D)$, Equation (22) and $F^s W \subseteq \alpha W$ hold, so that $0 \in \text{int}(\mathbb{Z}(\alpha, s))$ and $\mathbb{Z}_\infty \subseteq \mathbb{Z}(\alpha, s)$. Based on Equations (24) and (25), $\mathbb{Z}(\alpha, s)$ can approach $\mathbb{Z}_\infty$, when we choose appropriate s or α.

$$\alpha(1-\alpha)^{-1}\mathbb{Z}_s \subseteq B_p^n(\varepsilon), \quad \alpha \in [0,1) \quad \varepsilon > 0 \tag{26}$$

Equation (26) shows that when condition $\varepsilon \geq \alpha(1-\alpha)^{-1}\max_{x \in F_s}\|z\|_p = \alpha(1-\alpha)^{-1}\min_\varepsilon$ $\{\mathbb{Z}_s \subseteq B_p^n(\varepsilon)\}$ holds, $\mathbb{Z}_\infty \subseteq \mathbb{Z}(\alpha, s) \subseteq \mathbb{Z}_\infty \oplus B_p^n(\varepsilon)$, and where $B_p^n(\varepsilon) = \{z \in R^n | \|z\|_p \leq \varepsilon\}$ represents a p-norm ball in R^n, then $\mathbb{Z}(\alpha, s)$ is an ε-approximation of the minimal robust invariant set $\mathbb{Z}_\infty$.

Table 1 presents an overview of the single-tube RMPC structure, which involves an offline computation phase and online computation phase. Steps 1 and 2 involve the former, while steps 3 and 4 are related to the latter. Step 2 computes $\mathbb{Z}(\alpha, s)$, which is utilized to constrain the system state. The control quantity $u(k)$ in step 4 facilitates the system state gradual convergence towards zero. For a more comprehensive understanding of the STRMPC control process, Figure 4 provides a visual representation.

Table 1. Steps of RDP radial-feed system control method.

Steps	Single-Tube RMPC Method
1	Define the predictive control step size N and the constraints $\mathbb{X}, \mathbb{U}, \mathbb{W}$, and $\mathbb{V}$. Set the system state $x(0)$ and matrixes L, K.
2	Compute $\mathbb{Z}(\alpha, s)$ as the single-tube constraint set by utilizing $\mathbb{Z}_\infty$.
3	Drive $\bar{x}(k)$ to the nominal MPC reachable set $\mathbb{X}_f$ by the nominal model prediction control quantity $\bar{u}(k)$.
4	Combine the $\bar{u}(k)$ and the feedback to obtain the general control law $u(k)$ and drive $x(k)$ into the single-tube constraint set.

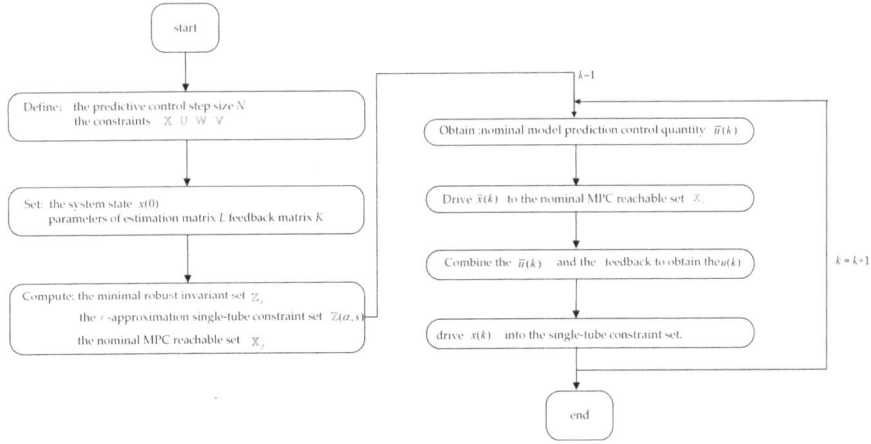

Figure 4. Flowchart of RDP radial-feed system control method.

3.3. Stability Analysis

As part of our analysis, we prove that the nominal MPC shows recursive feasibility. Moreover, we prove that $z(k)$ will be contained in the terminal constraint set $\mathbb{Z}_\infty$ and eventually approach zero.

Using Equation (6), we obtain the difference between the nominal predictive optimization cost functions $V_N(\bar{x}(k))$ and $V_{N-1}(\bar{x}(k+1))$ as follows:

$$\begin{aligned}
&V_{N-1}(\bar{x}(k+1)) - V_N(\bar{x}(k)) \\
&= L(\bar{x}(0\mid k+1), \bar{u}(0\mid k+1)) + \cdots + L\Big(\bar{x}(N-2\mid k+1), \bar{u}(N-2\mid k+1)_{N-2|k+1}\Big) \\
&+ F(\bar{x}(N-1\mid k+1)) - (L(\bar{x}(0\mid k), \bar{u}(0\mid k)) + \cdots + L(\bar{x}(N-1\mid k), \bar{u}(N-1\mid k)) + F(\bar{x}(N\mid k)))
\end{aligned} \quad (27)$$

Then, by combining Equation (27) and the condition $\bar{x}(i+1|k) = \bar{x}(i|k+1)$, $i \in [1, N-1]$, we obtain:

$$\begin{aligned}
V_{N-1}(\bar{x}(k+1)) - V_N(\bar{x}(k)) &= L(\bar{x}(1\mid k), \bar{u}(1\mid k)) + \cdots \\
&+ L(\bar{x}(N-1\mid k), \bar{u}(N-1\mid k)) + F(\bar{x}(N\mid k)) - (L(\bar{x}(0\mid k), \bar{u}(0\mid k)) + \cdots \\
&+ L(\bar{x}(N-1\mid k), \bar{u}(N-1\mid k)) + F(\bar{x}(N\mid k))) \\
&= -L(\bar{x}(0\mid k), \bar{u}(0\mid k)) = -\Big(\bar{x}(0\mid k)^T Q \bar{x}(0\mid k)\Big) - \Big(\bar{u}(0\mid k)^T R \bar{u}(0\mid k)\Big) \leq 0
\end{aligned} \quad (28)$$

The inequality of nominal model prediction optimization cost functions is extended as:

$$V_{N-2}(\overline{x}(k+2)) - V_{N-1}(\overline{x}(k+1)) = -L(\overline{x}(1\mid k+1), \overline{u}(1\mid k+1))$$
$$= -\left(\overline{x}(1\mid k)^T Q \overline{x}(1\mid k+1)\right) - \left(\overline{u}(1\mid k+1)^T R \overline{u}(1\mid k+1)\right) \leq 0 \quad (29)$$

Due to the nominal MPC ignoring the uncertain disturbance, we demonstrate that $V_N(\overline{x}(k))$ is a bounded and non-increasing sequence; therefore, the nominal MPC shows recursive feasibility.

As the nominal MPC shows recursive feasibility, when $k \geq 0$, $\overline{z}(k) \in \overline{\mathbb{Z}}$, and $\overline{u}(k) \in \overline{\mathbb{U}}$ are satisfied, $\overline{z}(k) \in \overline{\mathbb{Z}} \Rightarrow z(k) \in \mathbb{Z}$ and $\overline{u}(k) \in \overline{\mathbb{U}} \Rightarrow u(k) \in \mathbb{U}$. Then, using Equation (23), we can obtain $z(0) \in \mathbb{Z}$, $z(k) \in \mathbb{Z}$. For $k \geq 0$, we can derive $z(k) \in \mathbb{Z}$ from $z(0) \in \mathbb{Z}$; for $k \geq 0$, $x(k) = \begin{bmatrix} I & I \end{bmatrix} z(k) + \overline{x}(k)$ is satisfied. When $\overline{x}(k) \to 0$, we can obtain $e(k) + \xi(k) \to \mathbb{Z}_\infty$; then, $x(k) \to \mathbb{Z}_\infty$. As condition $\lim_{N \to \infty} x(k+N) = 0$, the system state is asymptotically stable. The system states will gradually approach zero and stabilize in the $\mathbb{Z}_\infty$.

4. Simulation and Experiment Verification

The parameters of single-tube RMPC (STRMPC) are as follows:

The constraints of the radial-feed control system state variable x_1 and its acceleration x_2 are defined as $\{\mathbb{X} : x_1 \in [-15, +15], x_2 \in [-15, +15]\}$, the constraint of the system input control quantity current is $\{\mathbb{U} : u \in [-5, +5]\}$, the constraint of the state disturbance is $\{\mathbb{W} : w_1 \in [-1, +1], w_2 \in [-1, +1]\}$, and the constraint of the control disturbance is $\{\mathbb{V} : v \in [-0.5, +0.5]\}$.

The nominal MPC parameters for the STRMPC are as follows:

The matrices $Q = [1, 0; 0, 1]$ and $R = [0.01]$. The observation matrix is set as $L = [0.0022; 0.0023]$. The feedback matrix is set as $K = [-0.0372, 0.0882]$ and the prediction horizon length is $N = 15$. The MPC method is provided as a comparison to the proposed method. The parameters of the matrices K, Q, and R in the MPC are identical to those in the nominal MPC.

As outlined in Section 3, the off-line calculation phase involved simulating the proposed algorithm and the MPC method to evaluate their performance, including a comprehensive analysis of the calculation costs. These simulations were conducted using MATLAB (R2019b) software on a computer system comprising an Intel Core i7-9750H CPU and 8 GB RAM. During the off-line computation phase, the MPC method exhibited a computation time of 0.54 s, whereas the STRMPC method required a slightly longer duration of 0.79 s. The slightly longer computation time of the proposed method during the off-line calculation phase does not affect the subsequent simulations and experiments outlined in this study, as these calculations are performed in advance.

4.1. Simulation

We set step, sine, and square wave with amplitudes of 10 rpm and periods of 16 s as input signals. We separately added noise and load disturbances to the system output to validate the proposed method's disturbance rejection capability. The initial system states for the STRMPC and MPC were defined as $x_0 = [-10, -3.5]$. We used the integral of the time-weighted absolute error (ITAE) performance index to evaluate the control performance.

(1) Load disturbance

To verify the system disturbance rejection performance with load disturbance, we superimposed a 1 rpm load disturbance onto the system output at 16 s and computed the ITAE indices.

In Figure 5, x_1 is presented on the horizontal axis as the system state and x_2 is presented on the vertical axis as the derivative of the system state. The green patches in Figure 5 represent the single-tube terminal constraint set $\mathbb{Z}(\alpha, s)$, while the gray patches denote the nominal MPC reachable set $\mathbb{X}_f$. The convergence results shows that the actual system state $x(k)$ follows $\overline{x}(k)$ and $\hat{x}(k)$, then eventually converges within the single-tube constraint set.

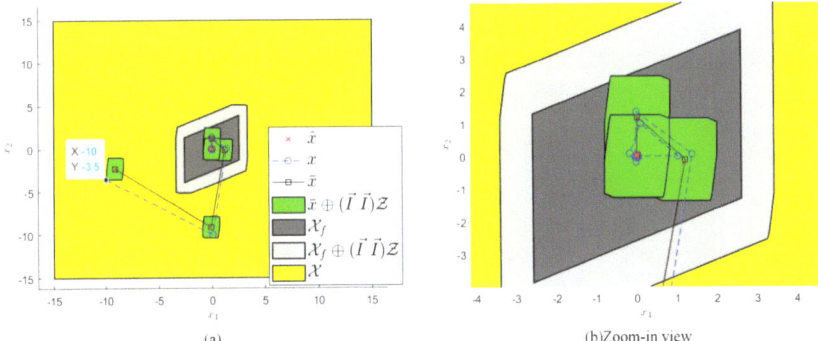

Figure 5. Convergence of system state and terminal constraint set with load disturbance.

Figures 6–8 show that the output curve without a controller is unable to resist the load disturbance. However, the MPC control method is able to resist load disturbance but still produces an overshoot. In comparison, the proposed method efficiently suppresses the disturbance and rarely produces an overshoot.

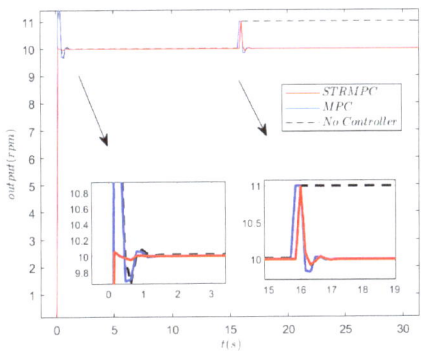

Figure 6. Step response with load disturbance.

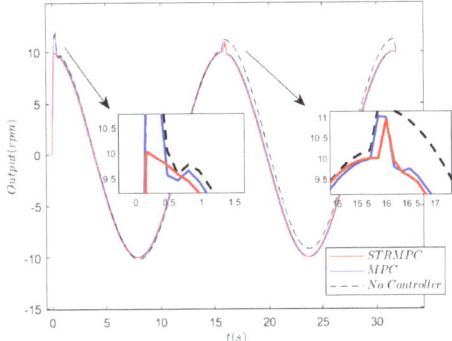

Figure 7. Sine wave tracking with load disturbance.

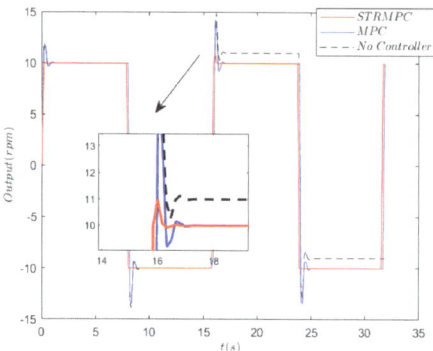

Figure 8. Square wave tracking with load disturbance.

Table 2 presents the ITAE indices obtained from the simulations. The STRMPC method achieves an ITAE index of 1.9203 in square wave tracking, which is approximately 89.87% lower than the MPC method and 94.63% lower than the no controller method. Similarly, for sine wave tracking and step response, the ITAE index of the STRMPC method is also 83.87% and 30.79% lower than the MPC method and 91.87% and 90.13% lower than the no controller method, respectively. The STRMPC method achieves higher control effectiveness compared to MPC and no controller. Compared with the results of the no controller and MPC method, the proposed STRMPC method has the smallest ITAE index, which indicates that the STRMPC method has better control performance.

Table 2. ITAE indices with load disturbance.

ITAE	Square	Sine	Step
No controller	35.7292	23.2893	18.4927
MPC	18.9680	11.7338	2.6376
STRMPC	1.9203	1.8931	1.8255

(2) Noise disturbance

The random white noise disturbance with the amplitude range of $[-0.5, 0.5]$ is set as the noise interference.

From Figure 9, the STRMPC method is able to maintain $x(k)$ in a terminal constraint set. Figures 10–12 demonstrate that the proposed STRMPC method is more effective in suppressing noise disturbance compared to the MPC method. Based on the simulation results in Table 3, it can be observed that the STRMPC method demonstrates higher control efficiency compared to the other methods. In square wave tracking, the STRMPC method has an ITAE index of 4.3713, which is approximately 83.29% lower than the MPC method and 84.86% lower than the no controller method. Similarly, for sine wave tracking and step response, the ITAE index of the STRMPC method is lower than the other two methods. It shows that the proposed method has the lowest index value, which also demonstrates its stability and tracking accuracy.

Table 3. ITAE indices with ±0.5 noise.

ITAE	Square	Sine	Step
No controller	28.8638	13.6897	10.4474
MPC	26.1636	4.4466	9.9588
STRMPC	4.3713	4.2557	4.1995

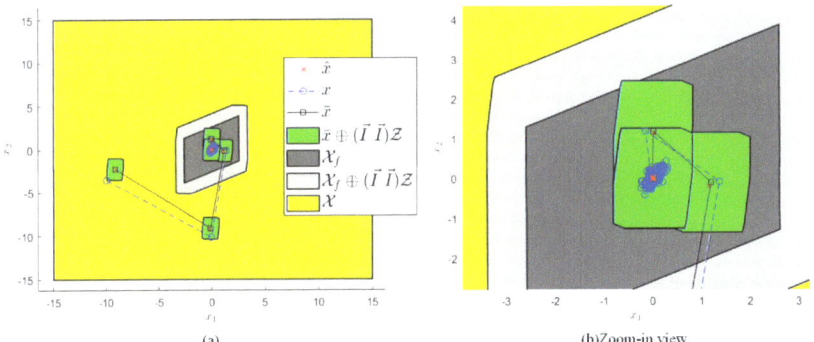

Figure 9. Convergence of system state and terminal constraint set with ± 0.5 noise disturbance.

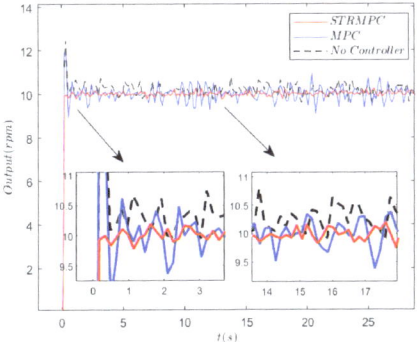

Figure 10. Step response with ±0.5 noise disturbance.

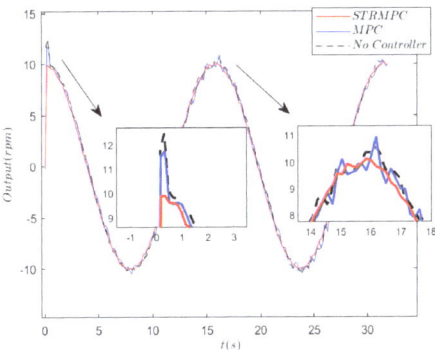

Figure 11. Sine wave tracking with ±0.5 noise disturbance.

To further verify the noise suppression capability of the proposed method, we expanded the noise range to $[-1, 1]$. The simulation results are presented below.

From Figure 13 it can be seen that the system actual states remain within the terminal constraint set. Therefore, this simulation result indicates that increasing noise interference has a rare effect on the system stability of the STRMPC method.

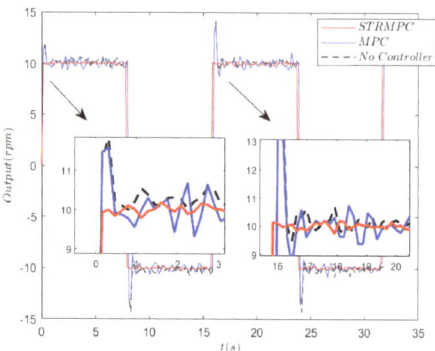

Figure 12. Square wave tracking with ±0.5 noise disturbance.

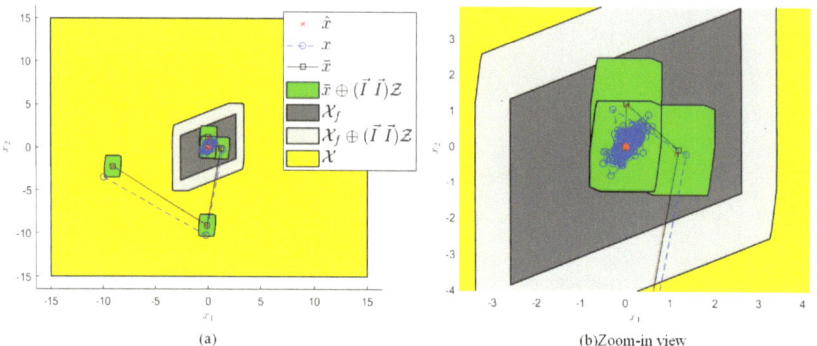

Figure 13. Convergence of system state and terminal constraint set with ±1 noise disturbance.

Figures 14–16 show the ability of the STRMPC method to effectively suppress the noise disturbance. The ITAE indices in Table 4 show that the STRMPC has a lowest value, indicating higher control accuracy compared to the other methods. The results demonstrate that the proposed method effectively suppresses interference, even in the presence of increased noise interference.

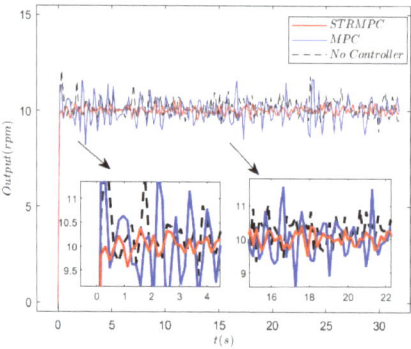

Figure 14. Step response with ±1 noise disturbance.

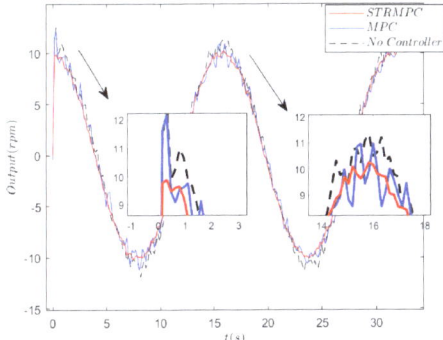

Figure 15. Sine wave tracking with ±1 noise disturbance.

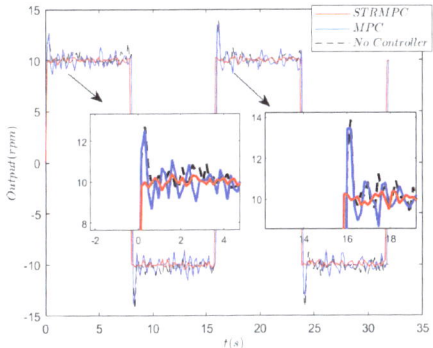

Figure 16. Square wave tracking with ±1 noise disturbance.

Table 4. ITAE indices with ±1 noise.

ITAE	Square	Sine	Step
No controller	32.7302	22.2239	17.3989
MPC	31.5702	19.6901	14.2556
STRMPC	7.0924	6.8015	6.7940

(3) Model parameters uncertainty

To verify the system robustness, we designed a model parameters uncertainty simulation with ±0.5 noise disturbance and load disturbance for the step response. The models with ±10% parameter fluctuations are laid out in Table 5.

Table 5. Comparison of the model parameters.

Model	A	B	C
f1 (90%)	[0.0709, −0.1667; 0.9, 0]	[0.9; 0]	[−1.8442, 79.6614]
f2 (95%)	[0.0749, −0.1759; 0.95, 0]	[0.95; 0]	[−1.9466, 84.0871]
f3 (100%)	[0.0788, −0.1852; 1, 0]	[1; 0]	[−2.0491, 88.5127]
f4 (105%)	[0.0827, −0.1945; 1.05, 0]	[1.05; 1.05]	[−2.1516, 92.9383]
f5 (110%)	[0.0867, −0.2037; 1.1, 0]	[1.1; 1.1]	[−2.2540, 97.3640]

The step response results in Figures 17–20 show that the output of different models is nearly identical and that the model parameters uncertainty has little influence on the system performance. The results in Table 6 demonstrate that the STRMPC method exhibits high control effectiveness and robustness against model parameter fluctuations, load changes, and noise interference. The ITAE index remains relatively stable for the load disturbance test, with a maximum value increase of only 0.1359 from f1 to f5. Similarly, for the noise interference test, the ITAE index shows minimal increase, with a maximum value increase of only 0.1255 from f1 to f5. These results highlight the ability of the STRMPC method to maintain accurate control performance, demonstrating its robustness and effectiveness in achieving high-precision control.

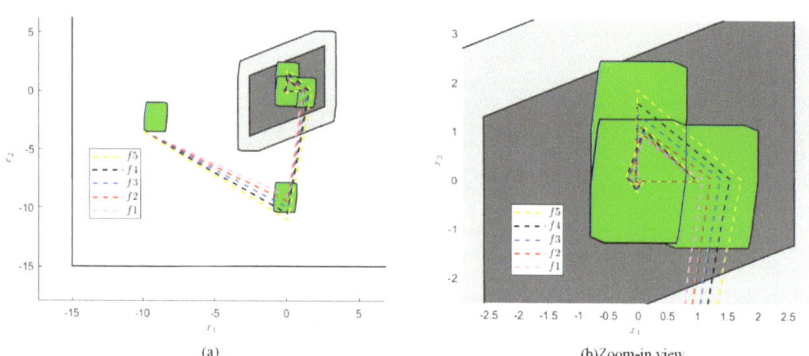

Figure 17. Convergence of system state and terminal constraint set with ±1 noise disturbance.

Based on the simulation results on disturbance rejection and robustness, we conclude that the proposed STRMPC method exhibits extraordinary ability in suppressing noise and load disturbances, thereby demonstrating its robustness.

Table 6. ITAE indices with ±1 noise.

ITAE	f1	f2	f3	f4	f5
Load	1.9932	2.0238	2.0566	2.0916	2.1291
Noise	3.9183	3.9439	3.9727	4.0065	4.0438

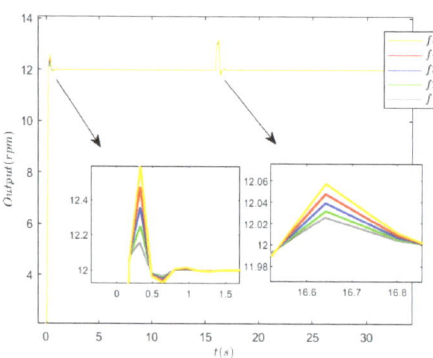

Figure 18. Step response of different models with load disturbance.

4.2. Experiment

To evaluate the effectiveness of the proposed method, we conducted experiments on the radial-feed motor speed and actual polishing process using MPC and STRMPC methods.

(4) Radial-feed motor speed

During the experiment on radial-feed motor speed, the sampling period was set to 0.002 s, and the radial-feed motor speed of the system with MPC method and system with no controller were given as comparisons to the proposed method. The radial-feed motor speed was set to 30 rpm, and, after the speed stabilized, we changed the reference to 18 rpm at a time of 20.84 s. The experiment's results are present in Figures 20 and 21.

The experimental results indicate that the STRMPC displays outstanding robustness in Figure 21; the speed of the system with STRMPC has fewer steady errors than the speed outputs of comparison, and hardly produces the overshoot. The better control performance can be attributed to the STRMPC's capability to restrict the output error through the single-tube terminal constraint set, as confirmed by the simulation results. The current curve in Figure 20 also verifies the robustness of the proposed method. Figure 22 demonstrates that when the speed changes abruptly, the proposed method has the more stable speed curves, which reflects its advantage in terms of robustness.

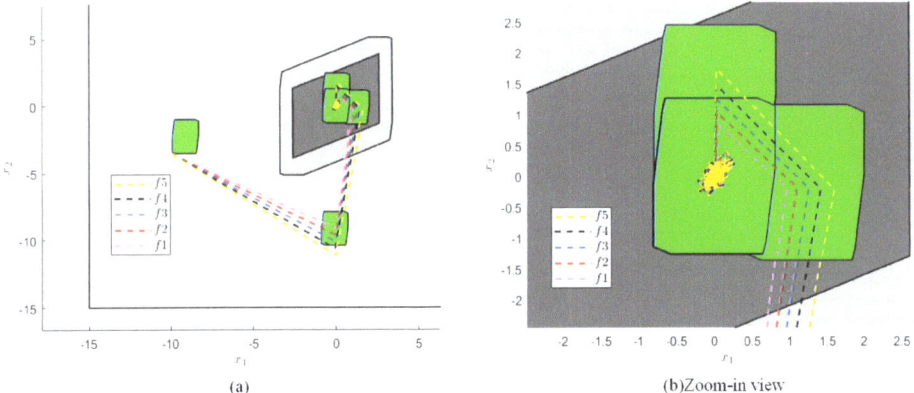

Figure 19. Convergence of system state and terminal constraint set of different models with ± 0.5 noise disturbance.

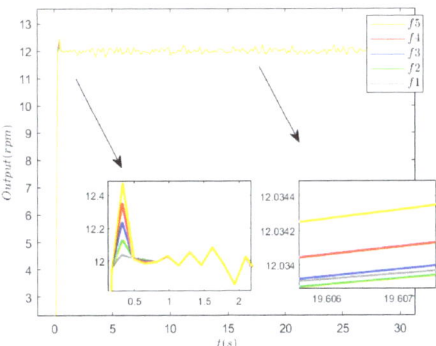

Figure 20. Step response of different models with ±0.5 noise disturbance.

(5) Actual polishing process

In the surface processing experiment, we chose a fused silica optical glass with dimensions of 430 × 430 mm and a thickness of 10 mm. The polishing pressure was set at 200 N, and the upper polishing disk had a radial displacement range of 20 mm relative to the center of the fused silica optical glass. Both the polishing disk and the glass were rotated at a speed of 15 rpm. Each piece of fused silica optical glass was then polished for a duration of 30 min.

Surface shape detection was performed before and after processing; the peak-to-valley (PV) and root-mean-square (RMS) indices are presented in Figures 23 and 24.

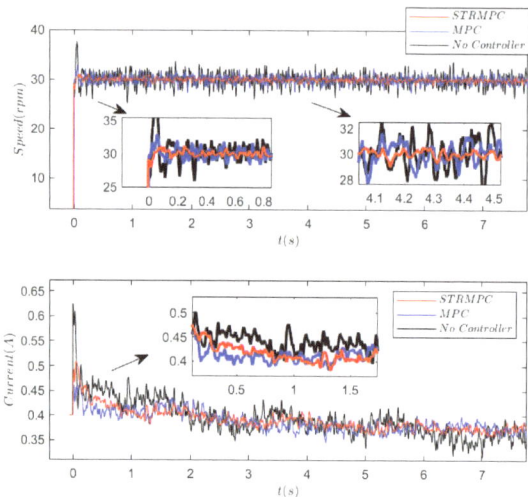

Figure 21. Step response of the RDP radial-feed system [ref. speed = 30 rpm].

The application of the MPC method yielded a 23.78% improvement in surface shape as evidenced by the reduction of the PV value from 1.43 λ to 1.09 λ. However, the reduction of RMS was reduced slightly from 0.218 λ RMS to 0.216 λ RMS, with a convergence rate of 0.9%. In contrast, the STRMPC method significantly enhanced both surface shape and roughness, reducing PV and RMS values from 1.49 λ PV and 0.257 λ RMS to 0.99 λ PV and 0.163 λ RMS, respectively. Compared with the MPC method, the STRMPC method achieved a higher convergence rate 33.56% and 36.57% for both PV and RMS. Specifically, the PV convergence rate was improved by 9.78%, while the RMS convergence rate increased by 35.6%. These findings suggest that the STRMPC method is more effective in improving surface shape and roughness accuracy than the conventional MPC method. Therefore, the STRMPC method's stable radial feed enables rapid and stable processing of the ring-pendulum double-sided polisher, resulting in a more uniform surface shape.

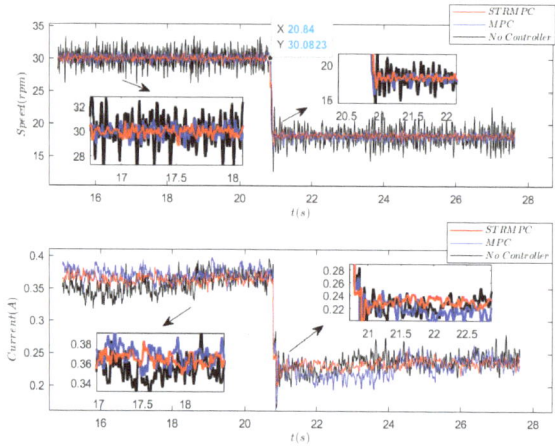

Figure 22. Step response of the RDP radial-feed system [ref. speed = 30 rpm and 18 rpm].

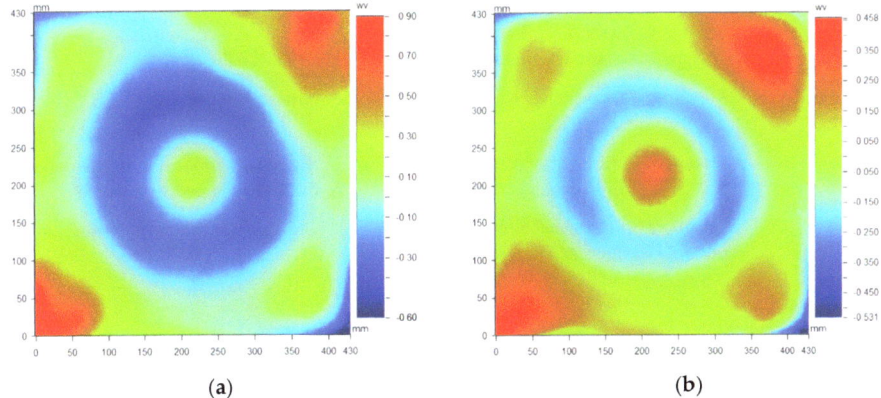

Figure 23. Surface shape processing by STRMPC: (**a**) surface shape before processing [PV = 1.49 λ, RMS = 0.257 λ]; (**b**) surface shape after processing [PV = 0.99 λ, RMS = 0.163 λ].

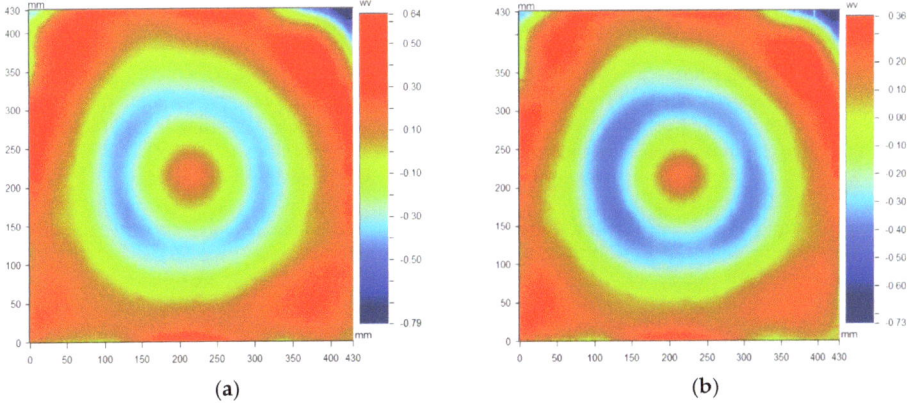

Figure 24. Surface shape processing by MPC: (**a**) surface shape before processing [PV = 1.43 λ, RMS = 0.218 λ]; (**b**) surface shape after processing [PV = 1.09 λ, RMS = 0.216 λ].

5. Conclusions

In this paper, we propose a single-tube RMPC method for the RDP's radial-feed system. The actual parameter identification model of the radial-feed system is presented. The single-tube RMPC structure is built to improve the disturbance suppression ability of the system. Further, the ε-approximation is conducted to enlarge the single-tube constraint sets, which improves the robustness of the system. Additionally, the stability analysis of the system is presented. Finally, the simulations and experiments have verified the efficacy of the proposed method in validating the disturbance rejection ability in the radial-feed system of RDP, and the uniformity of surface shape on optical elements processed by the RDP. Compared to the MPC method, the STRMPC method achieved higher convergence rates, a 9.78% improvement in PV convergence rate, and a 35.6% improvement in RMS convergence rate. These results demonstrate the superior performance of the STRMPC method in achieving faster and more accurate surface shape and roughness optimization.

However, this study includes the focus only on optimizing the radial-feed system motor speed control of the RDP, without focusing on its polish rotation system motor speed control. In the next step, the proposed method can be applied to rotation systems to achieve dual system linkage control, which further improves the polish efficiency and polish accuracy of the RDP.

Author Contributions: S.L.: Methodology, Writing—original draft. B.X.: Writing—review and editing. C.W.: Project administration, Funding acquisition. L.W.: Visualization. Z.W.: Validation. All authors have read and agreed to the published version of the manuscript.

Funding: This research was funded by the Equipment Advance Research Field Foundation, grant number: 80923010202.

Data Availability Statement: Data underlying the results presented in the paper are not publicly available at this time but may be obtained from the authors upon reasonable request.

Conflicts of Interest: The authors declare that there are no conflicts of interests; we do not have any possible conflicts of interest.

References

1. Hugot, E.; Ferrari, M.; Hadi, K.E.; Vola, P.; Hubin, N. Active Optics: Stress polishing of toric mirrors for the VLT SPHERE adaptive optics system. *Appl. Opt.* **2009**, *48*, 2932–2941. [CrossRef]
2. Zhao, W.; Wang, X.; Liu, H.; Lu, Z.; Lu, Z. Development of space-based diffractive telescopes. *Front. Inf. Technol. Electron. Eng.* **2020**, *21*, 884–902. [CrossRef]
3. Qu, Y.; Jiang, Y.; Feng, L.; Li, X.; Liu, B. Lightweight design of multi-objective topology for a large-aperture space mirror. *Appl. Sci.* **2018**, *8*, 2259. [CrossRef]
4. Zhan, R.; Lyu, C. Stop model development and analysis of optical collimation system for tactical high-energy laser weapon. *Appl. Opt.* **2021**, *60*, 3596–3603. [CrossRef]
5. Sprangle, P.; Hafizi, B.; Ting, A.; Fischer, R. High-power lasers for directed-energy applications. *Appl. Opt.* **2015**, *54*, F201. [CrossRef]
6. Nosov, P.A.; Shirankov, A.F.; Khorokhorov, A.M.; Zaytsev, K.I.; Yurchenko, S.O. Investigation of heating of optical elements during formation of high-power CW fiber laser radiation. *Russ. Phys. J.* **2019**, *61*, 2305–2312. [CrossRef]
7. Derkach, I.N.; Kudryashov, E.A.; Kachalin, G.N.; Kirdyaev, N.A.; Ladeishchikova, V.V.; Timaev, D.S. Damage of dusty optical elements in the field of continuous-wave laser radiation. *JETP Lett.* **2018**, *108*, 379–383. [CrossRef]
8. Xu, L.B.; Lu, X.Q.; Lei, Z.M. Influence of phase error of optical elements on optical path design of laser facilities. *Acta Phys. Sin. -Chin. Ed.* **2018**, *67*, 024201. [CrossRef]
9. Sun, X.; Zhang, X.; Liu, Z.; Fan, Q.; Liu, C.; Zhu, J. Stress and wavefront measurement of large-aperture optical components with a ptychographical iterative engine. *Appl. Opt.* **2022**, *61*, 7231–7236. [CrossRef]
10. Liu, Y.Q.; Ren, Z.; Shu, Y.; Wu, L.; Sun, J.; Cai, H.; Zhang, X.; Lu, L.; Qi, K.; Li, L.; et al. Broadband, large-numerical-aperture and high-efficiency microwave metalens by using a double-layer transmissive metasurface. *Appl. Phys. Express* **2021**, *15*, 014003. [CrossRef]
11. Zhong, Z.W.; Tian, Y.B.; Ang, Y.J.; Wu, H. Optimization of the chemical mechanical polishing process for optical silicon substrates. *Int. J. Adv. Manuf. Technol.* **2012**, *60*, a12. [CrossRef]
12. Ban, X.; Zhao, H.; Zhu, X.; Zhao, S.; Xie, R.; Liao, D. Improvement and application of pad conditioning accuracy in chemical mechanical polishing. *Opt. Eng.* **2018**, *57*, 095102-1. [CrossRef]
13. Zhao, D.; Guo, H. A trajectory planning method for polishing optical elements based on a non-uniform rational b-spline curve. *Appl. Sci.* **2018**, *8*, 1355. [CrossRef]
14. Pirayesh, H.; Cadien, K. The Effect of Slurry Properties on the CMP Removal Rate of Boron Doped Polysilicon. *ECS J. Solid State Sci. Technol.* **2016**, *5*, P233–P238. [CrossRef]
15. Chen, Y.T.; Liu, M.Y.; Cao, Z.C. Effect of Robot Motion Accuracy on Surface Form during Computer-Controlled Optical Surfacing Process. *Appl. Sci.* **2022**, *12*, 12301. [CrossRef]
16. Zhang, H.; Wang, P.; Li, Z.; Shen, Y.; Zhang, X. Uniform polishing method of spherical lens based on material removal model of high-speed polishing procedure. *Micromachines* **2020**, *11*, 938. [CrossRef]
17. Zhang, C.P.; Zhao, H.Y.; Xie, R.Q.; Zhao, Z.X.; Gu, Y.W.; Jiang, Z.D. Effect of motion accuracy on material removal during the cmp process for large-aperture plane optics. *Int. J. Adv. Manuf. Technol.* **2017**, *94*, 105–119. [CrossRef]
18. Huang, A.T.; Zhao, A.D.; Zhong, C.C. Trajectory planning of optical polishing based on optimized implementation of dwell time. *Precis. Eng.* **2020**, *62*, 223–231. [CrossRef]
19. Ren, T.J.; Chen, T.C.; Chen, C.J. Motion control for a two-wheeled vehicle using a self-tuning PID controller. *Control Eng. Pract.* **2008**, *16*, 65–75. [CrossRef]
20. Olivares, M.; Albertos, P. Linear control of the flywheel inverted pendulum. *ISA Trans.* **2014**, *53*, 1396–1403. [CrossRef]
21. Wang, J. Simulation studies of inverted pendulum based on PID controllers. *Simul. Model. Pract. Theory* **2011**, *19*, 440–449. [CrossRef]
22. Shtessel, Y.; Edwards, C.; Fridman, L.; Levant, A. *Sliding Mode Control and Observation*; Birkhauser: New York, NY, USA, 2014. [CrossRef]
23. Abbasi, S.J.; Kallu, K.D.; Lee, M.C. Efficient Control of a Non-Linear System Using a Modified Sliding Mode Control. *Appl. Sci.* **2019**, *9*, 1284. [CrossRef]

24. Bekiroglu, N.; Bozma, H.I.; Istefanopulos, Y. Model reference adaptive approach to sliding mode control. In Proceedings of the 1995 American Control Conference—ACC'95, Seattle, WA, USA, 21–23 June 1995; pp. 1028–1032. [CrossRef]
25. Mayne, D.Q.; Rawlings, J.B.; Rao, C.V.; Scokaert, P. Constrained model predictive control: Stability and optimality. *Automatica* **2000**, *36*, 789–814. [CrossRef]
26. Maciejonski, J. *Predictive Control with Constraints*; Prentice-Hall: Upper Saddle River, NJ, USA, 1999; ISBN 0-201-39823-0.
27. Garcia, C.E.; Prett, D.M.; Morari, M. Model predictive control: Theory and practice—A survey. *Automatica* **1989**, *25*, 335–348. [CrossRef]
28. Chen, H.; Allgöwer, F. A Quasi-Infinite Horizon Nonlinear Model Predictive Control Scheme with Guaranteed Stability. *Automatica* **1998**, *34*, 1205–1217. [CrossRef]
29. Pin, G.; Raimondo, D.M.; Magni, L.; Parisini, T. Robust model predictive control of nonlinear systems with bounded and state-dependent uncertainties. *IEEE Trans. Autom. Control* **2009**, *64*, 1681–1687. [CrossRef]
30. Limon, D.; Alamo, T.; Camacho, E.F. Input-to-state stable MPC for constrained discrete-time nonlinear systems with bounded additive uncertainties. In Proceedings of the 41st IEEE Conference on Decision and Control, Las Vegas, NV, USA, 10–13 December 2002. [CrossRef]
31. Pant, Y.V.; Abbas, H.; Mangharam, R. Robust model predictive control for non-linear systems with input and state constraints via feedback linearization. In Proceedings of the 2016 IEEE 55th Conference on Decision and Control (CDC), Las Vegas, NV, USA, 12–14 December 2016. [CrossRef]
32. Li, H.P.; Shi, Y. Robust distributed model predictive control of constrained continuous-time nonlinear systems: A robustness constraint approach. *IEEE Trans. Autom. Control* **2014**, *59*, 1673–1678. [CrossRef]
33. Chisci, L.; Rossiter, J.A.; Zappa, G. Systems with persistent disturbances: Predictive control with restricted constraints. *Automatica* **2001**, *37*, 1019–1028. [CrossRef]
34. Song, Y.; Wang, Z.D.; Wei, G.L. N-Step MPC for Systems With Persistent Bounded Disturbances Under SCP. *IEEE Trans. Syst. Man Cybern. -Syst.* **2020**, *50*, 4762–4772. [CrossRef]
35. Xu, C.; Mao, Y.W. Auxiliary Model-Based Multi-Innovation Fractional Stochastic Gradient Algorithm for Hammerstein Output-Error Systems. *Machines* **2021**, *9*, 247. [CrossRef]
36. Mao, Y.W.; Ding, F. Data Filtering-Based Multi-innovation Stochastic Gradient Algorithm for Nonlinear Output Error Autoregressive Systems. *Circuits Syst. Signal Process.* **2016**, *35*, 651–667. [CrossRef]
37. Rakovi, S.V.; Kouramas, K.I.; Kerrigan, E.C.; Allwright, J.C.; Mayne, D.Q. The Minimal Robust Positively Invariant Set for Linear Difference Inclusions and its Robust Positively Invariant Approximations. *Mathematics* **2005**. [CrossRef]

Disclaimer/Publisher's Note: The statements, opinions and data contained in all publications are solely those of the individual author(s) and contributor(s) and not of MDPI and/or the editor(s). MDPI and/or the editor(s) disclaim responsibility for any injury to people or property resulting from any ideas, methods, instructions or products referred to in the content.

Article

Design of a Quick-Pressing and Self-Locking Temporary Fastener for Easy Automatic Installation and Removal

Wei Tang [1], Jie He [2,*], Yunya Xiao [1], Weiwei Qu [3], Jiying Ye [1], Hui Long [1] and Chaolin Liang [1]

[1] School of Intelligent Engineering, Shaoguan University, Shaoguan 512023, China
[2] School of Mechanical Engineering, Dongguan University of Technology, Dongguan 523808, China
[3] College of Mechanical Engineering, Zhejiang University, Hangzhou 310027, China
* Correspondence: h971159345@163.com

Abstract: In the traditional pre-joining technology of aircraft panels, bolts are generally employed for pre-joining. Due to the length and width of panels, bilateral manual operations are required to operate bolts. In this case, there are problems such as low work efficiency, unstable quality, cumbersome operation, and inconvenient installation-removal. This paper takes a temporary fastener with one-side installation-removal as a research object and conducts in-depth research on three levels of quick-pressing: unloading, stable self-locking, and easy automatic installation. Firstly, by coordinating the ratchet and the spring, the restoring force of the spring is used to make the cylindrical top-rod rotary and realize the telescopic function to achieve quick loading and unloading of fasteners; subsequently, through the cooperation between the buckle and the spring, loading and unloading self-locking is attained; afterwards, through the threaded joining and the same cylinder design between the external profile components, the convenience of fasteners for automatic transportation is realized. When assembling two thin-walled parts of the aircraft, only continuous one-side pressing of fasteners is needed to carry out the tightening and unloading work, namely, one-pressing installation and one-pressing removal, which could solve the problems caused by the bilateral operation of traditional bolts and part tolerances. After the application of the fasteners into the pre-joining process of aircraft panels, the experiment results have shown that this temporary fastener provided a good clamping effect, could be quickly and efficiently installed and removed by continuous one-pressing, and avoided the problems of complexity and high cost for pre-joining processes.

Keywords: automatic installation; quick-pressing; self-locking; automatic removal

1. Introduction

In traditional aircraft manufacturing processes, numerous fasteners are used with parts in connection, and they play an important role in position and support. Traditional aircraft panel assembly often uses bolts for pre-joining, but the positioning accuracy and efficiency of bolts are not ideal. The clamping force cannot be accurately controlled by the intuitive judgment of workers, and the consistency of the clamping force cannot be guaranteed. At the same time, bilateral operations are required for bolts, which results in a cumbersome process and low efficiency. It is difficult to realize automated assembly for bolts, which directly affects the quality and efficiency of subsequent aircraft riveting assembly and has become a technological bottleneck in aircraft manufacturing processes.

Since the 1990s, scholars at home and abroad have conducted a number of studies on fasteners for thin-walled parts. Threaded connections are the most commonly used traditional technology [1,2]. Gong Hao et al. [3] summarized the reasons for and mechanisms of non-rotating and rotating loosening on threaded connections. Shan, ZW et al. [4] conducted a sample test on a direct fastening connection and proposed a modified expression for the yield strength of the connection. In order to solve the connection problem of steel pipe structures, some scholars [5,6] have developed special bolts, such as HSBB bolts, BOM bolts, and Ultra-Twist bolts, produced by the American company Huck International.

Citation: Tang, W.; He, J.; Xiao, Y.; Qu, W.; Ye, J.; Long, H.; Liang, C. Design of a Quick-Pressing and Self-Locking Temporary Fastener for Easy Automatic Installation and Removal. *Appl. Sci.* **2023**, *13*, 3004. https://doi.org/10.3390/app13053004

Academic Editor: Ricardo Branco

Received: 13 February 2023
Revised: 22 February 2023
Accepted: 22 February 2023
Published: 26 February 2023

Copyright: © 2023 by the authors. Licensee MDPI, Basel, Switzerland. This article is an open access article distributed under the terms and conditions of the Creative Commons Attribution (CC BY) license (https://creativecommons.org/licenses/by/4.0/).

Furthermore, in response to the problem of excessive connections in traditional panel assembly, Wei Tang et al. established a pre-joining optimization model and verified it through experiments, which could effectively reduce the number of pre-joining points [7–9]. However, they did not involve the design and optimization of pre-joining fasteners. In addition, C. Kim et al. [10–13] have conducted studies on the application of blind rivet nuts. Lele Sun [14] presented a novel form of T-shaped single-sided bolt connections for steel beams and hollow square steel tubes. Other researchers have proposed alternative connectors, such as the rotating slotted bolt connection [15], the high-strength single-sided bolt joint [16], and other fasteners for single-sided connections [17–19]. These above-mentioned fasteners can also be fitted on one side, but their structure is too complex to install on panels, or the operation must be tightened many times, making the operation laborious, inefficient, and difficult to process, so they are not ideal for connecting aircraft parts. To solve the traditional pre-joining process problems of large tightening torque and inconvenient bilateral tightening, W. Tang et al. [20] proposed a new temporary fastener that is labor-saving and reversible, which was performed by experiment. However, this fastener needs to be rotated back and forth during installation, and this installation process is not as simple as linear motion.

In order to overcome the shortcomings and deficiencies of traditional technology, this paper designs a quick-pressing temporary fastener with self-locking capabilities that is convenient for automatic installation and removal. When fastening or removing, it needs only one-side continuous pressing operation to carry out the above-mentioned work, that is, one-button installation and removal, which is conducive to the combination of the fasteners and automation, and is more compatible with automatic equipment loading and unloading to improve efficiency. Finally, this paper builds a model with 3D software, theoretically analyzes the critical state and final state of temporary fastener pressing, and designs an experiment to verify its actual effect.

2. Function and Principal Innovation

2.1. Function and Structure Innovation

In order to solve various installation problems caused by traditional bolt connections, some innovations for fasteners in function and structure have been proposed, as shown in Table 1.

Table 1. Functions and corresponding innovative structures.

Functional Innovation	Structure Innovation
Quick-press	The spring and cylindrical push rod closely cooperate with the ratchet.
Convenient for automated installation	The cylindrical-shape surface of the parts are the same.
Self-locking	Coordination between the mandrel retaining bar and the clamping jaw
Unilateral loading and unloading	Clamping jaws structure with elastic

The quick-pressing and self-locking temporary fastener is composed of a button, a transmission component, a shell, and a clamping component. The button is connected to one end of the transmission component; the other end of the transmission component has a sliding connection to the clamping component; and the transmission component is sleeved in the shell. The button and the clamping assembly pass through the shell; a spring is arranged between the shell and the button, and the end of the clamping assembly protruding out of the shell is provided with a barb. The overall structure is shown in Figure 1.

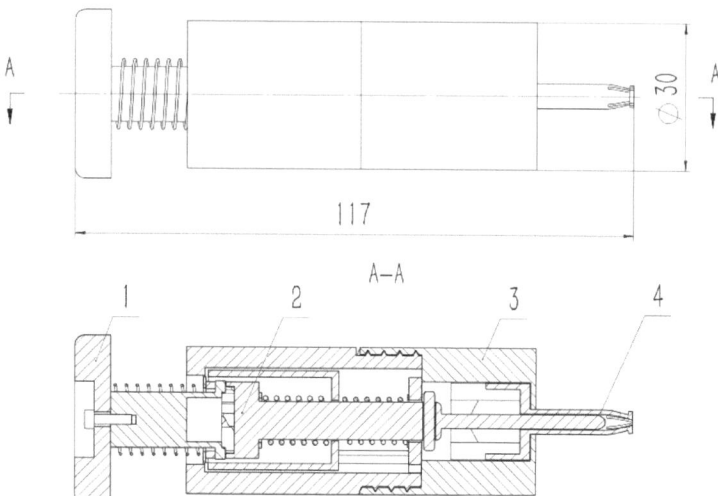

Figure 1. The overall structure of quick-press self-locking temporary fasteners. 1—Button, 2—Transmission assembly, 3—Shell, 4—Clamping assembly.

2.2. Working Principle of Fasteners and Steps of Loading and Unloading

2.2.1. Working Principle

First, the four-petal structure of the clamping jaw is used as the main part of the joining plates. This four-petal structure has the characteristics of elastic contraction and expansion. When working, the petal structure expands due to the external forces applied to fasten the connecting panels. When disassembling, the expanded shape of the petals contracts to loosen the connector. This design solves the problem of precise clamping to connection. Meanwhile, a ratchet mechanism is designed to carry out the unilateral operation of work and disassembly. Each time the round button is pressed, the cylindrical push rod rotates 90°, and this causes the mandrel to rotate to realize the fastening and loosening of the four-part clamping jaws, so as to achieve the work and disassembly without damaging the fastener itself. The design explosion diagram is shown in Figure 2.

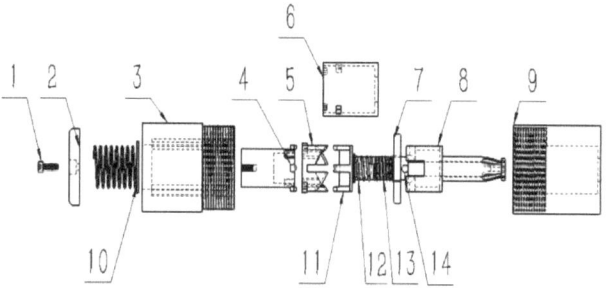

Figure 2. Exploded view of quick-press self-locking temporary fasteners. 1—Screw, 2—Round button, 3—Tail shell, 4—Cylindrical push rod, 5—Ratchet wheel, 6—Inner sleeve, 7—Baffle, 8—Clamping claw, 9—Head shell, 10—Return spring, 11—Cylindrical top rod, 12—Spring of ejector rod, 13—Supporting spring, 14—Mandrel retaining bar.

The head shell (9) and clamping jaw (8) have a square groove at one end; the clamping jaw (8) slides into the inner square; and the other end is a four-petal claw structure with a tapered barb shape. Simultaneously, the round button (2) and the cylindrical push rod (4) are screwed together; the cylindrical push rod (4) and cylindrical top rod (11) are installed in the ratchet (5) groove; and the spring of the ejector rod (12) and the supporting spring (13) are sleeved on the cylindrical top rod (11). At the same time, two springs are installed inside and outside of the inner sleeve (6); the baffle (7) is installed in the tail shell (3); and the head shell (9) and tail shell (3) are threaded together.

2.2.2. Fast Installation and Removing Method of Fasteners

The specific steps of the temporary fastener installation-removal method for aircraft assembly in Figures 3–8 are as follows:

(1) As shown in Figure 3, insert a temporary fastener into the round hole and push the round button (2) forward. Then, the transmission assembly will slide forward at the same time, and the ejector spring (12) and the support spring (13) will be squeezed and compressed by the cylindrical top rod (11) and the inner sleeve (6), respectively. Afterwards, the mandrel retaining bar (14) will slide into the inside of the square groove of the clamping jaw (8).

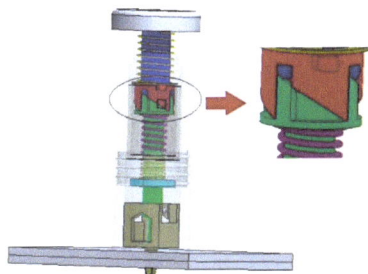

Figure 3. Schematic diagram of step 1.

(2) Continue to push the round button (2) forward. The ejector spring (12) will begin to compress, the ratchet wheel (5) will be stationary relative to the inner sleeve, and the top of the cylindrical push rod (4) will be against the inclined surface of the cylinder top on the rod (11) and will move forward. The cylindrical top rod (11) will push out the four-petal claw structure with the taper barb of the clamping jaw to enlarge the taper section of the jaw. Its schematic is shown in Figure 4.

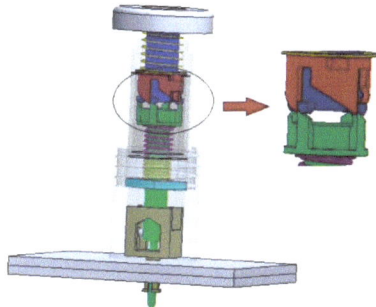

Figure 4. Schematic diagram of step 2.

(3) As illustrated in Figure 5, when the cylindrical top rod (11) moves beyond the groove of the ratchet wheel (5), it will begin to revolve. Hereafter, under the response force of the mandrel spring (12), it will rotate along the slope of the ratchet wheel (5), and the mandrel retention bar (14) will hook the clamping jaws (8) in the square grooves of the clamping jaws by turning.

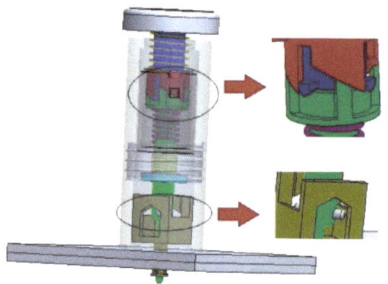

Figure 5. Schematic diagram of step 3.

(4) As shown in Figure 6, release the round button (2), and the inner sleeve (6) will slide backwards and pass through the mandrel retaining bar (14) on the cylindrical push rod (11). Drive the clamping jaws to slide back axially so that the barbs on the four-petal jaws contact the connecting panels. The mandrel retaining bar will rotate 90°, and the connecting panels will be clamped.

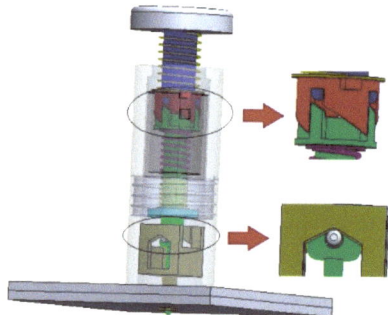

Figure 6. Schematic diagram of step 4.

(5) When removing the temporary fasteners, press the round button (2) again, and the internal parts of the fasteners will repeat the previous installation movement procedure until the cylindrical plunger (11) rotates 90° to remove the mandrel holding bar (14) to depart from the jaws, as depicted in Figure 7.

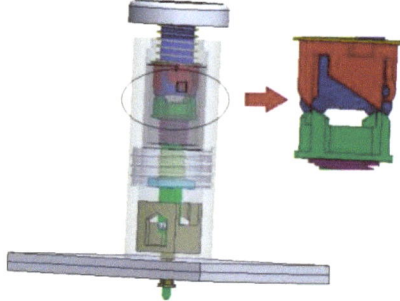

Figure 7. Schematic diagram of step 5.

(6) When the spring response force is applied, the moving components will return to their original positions, the clamping claw structure will shrink back to its original shape, and the barb structure will loosen the connecting panels, as shown in Figure 8.

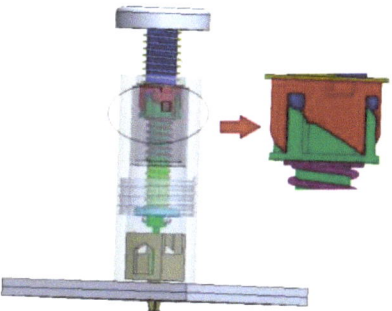

Figure 8. Schematic diagram of step 6.

(7) Repeat steps (1)–(6) for the installing and removing of other temporary fasteners.

3. Mechanical Relationship Analysis of Temporary Fasteners and Design of Key Parts

During the installation of the temporary fastener, the cylindrical top rod travels downward, owing to the application of the pressing force of the round button. When the rotation position of the cylindrical top rod occurs, the spring is squeezed to its maximum, which is the needed pressure force. Starting from the principle of mechanical equilibrium, to investigate the needed pressure force and clamping force, the critical point of the rotation of the cylindrical top rod and the final clamping condition are chosen for force analysis. Furthermore, the maximum force required to start the temporary fastener is calculated. The amount and magnitude of the clamping force is also calculated.

3.1. Critical State

When the interior of the temporary fastener reaches the critical rotational state, as shown in Figure 9, the cylindrical top rod is going to slip into the ratchet groove and spin due to the action of the big and small springs. Because the gravity of the component has a minor influence on the movement process, gravity is ignored for simplicity of analysis. For the cylindrical push rod, we performed the following analysis, as illustrated in Figure 10.

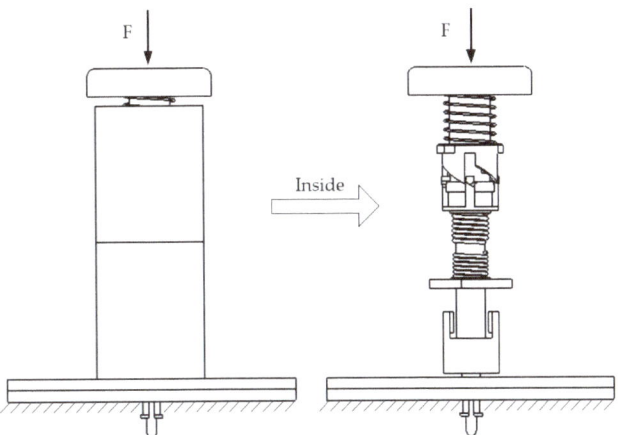

Figure 9. Critical state of temporary fastener.

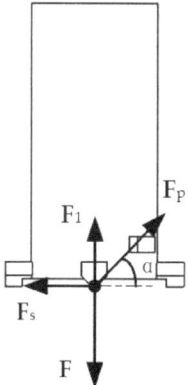

Figure 10. Force diagram of cylindrical push rod.

F—Pressure force,
F_1—The restoring force of the return spring,
F_p—The tip of the cylindrical push rod receives the reaction force of the cylindrical top rod,
F_s—Reaction force from ratchet chute,
α—The angle formed by the cylindrical ejector pin's reaction force and the horizontal plane.

From the balance equation we obtained:

$$F = F_p \sin\alpha + F_1 \tag{1}$$

$$F_s = F_p \cos\alpha \tag{2}$$

Figure 11 shows the force diagram of the cylindrical top rod.

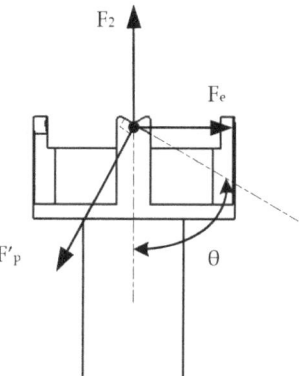

Figure 11. Force diagram of cylindrical top rod.

F_2—The elastic force of the ejector spring,
F'_p—The inclined surface of the cylindrical ejector rod receives the reaction force of the cylindrical push rod,
F_e—Ratchet chute reaction force,
θ—The angle between the inclined plane of the top of the cylindrical top rod and the vertical plane.

From the balance equation we obtained:

$$F_2 = F'_p \sin\theta \tag{3}$$

$$F_e = F'_p \cos\theta \tag{4}$$

Figure 12 shows the inner sleeve's force state.

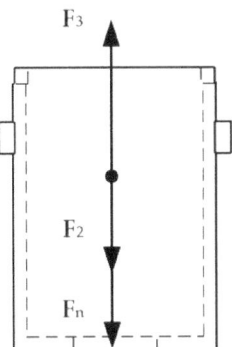

Figure 12. Force diagram of the inner sleeve.

F_2—The elastic force of the ejector spring,
F_3—The elastic force of the supporting spring,
F_n—The reaction force of the ratchet.

From the balance equation we obtained:

$$F_3 = F_2 + F_n \tag{5}$$

The force of the ratchet is shown in Figure 13.

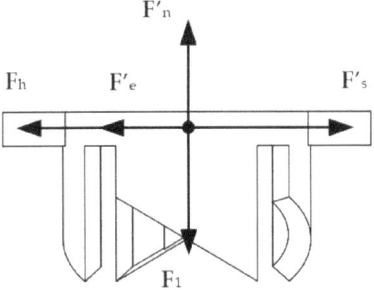

Figure 13. Force diagram of ratchet.

F_1—The restoring force of the return spring,
F'_n—Supporting force of the inner sleeve,
F'_s—Forces acting on the cylindrical push rod,
F'_e—Reaction forces of the cylindrical top rod,
F_h—Supporting forces of the tail shell.

From the balance equation we obtained:

$$F_1 = F'_n \tag{6}$$

$$F_h + F'_e = F'_s \tag{7}$$

In addition:

$$F_n = F'_n \tag{8}$$

$$F_p = F'_p \tag{9}$$

$$F_s = F'_s \tag{10}$$

$$F_e = F'_e \tag{11}$$

$$\alpha = \theta \tag{12}$$

The above equations can be combined to obtain Equation (13).

$$F = F_3 = F_1 + F_2 \tag{13}$$

According to Hooke's law, the following could be deduced:

$$k_3 \cdot \Delta x_3 = k_1 \cdot \Delta x_1 + k_2 \cdot \Delta x_2 \tag{14}$$

where k_1 is the elastic coefficient of the return spring, k_2 is the elastic coefficient of the ejector spring, k_3 is the elastic coefficient of the supporting spring, Δx_1 is the deformation of the return spring in the critical state, Δx_2 is the deformation of the ejector spring in the critical state, and Δx_3 is the deformation of the supporting spring in the critical state. Δx_1 is the distance between the cylindrical push rod and the ratchet wheel, which is determined by the ratchet wheel's size. It is a constant b, and the movement distance of the cylindrical push rod relative to the sleeve is also $\Delta x_2 = b$.

Thus:

$$F = b(k_1 + k_2) \tag{15}$$

3.2. Clamping State

When the temporary fastener is fastened in Figure 14, the cylindrical ejector rod is tight and secured, due to the combined action of the ejector spring, supporting spring, and clamping jaw. The cylindrical push rod, ratchet wheel, and return spring are all free-floating. For simplicity of analysis, the gravity of the parts is ignored. Therefore, only the force analysis of the cylindrical top rod and the inner sleeve is performed here.

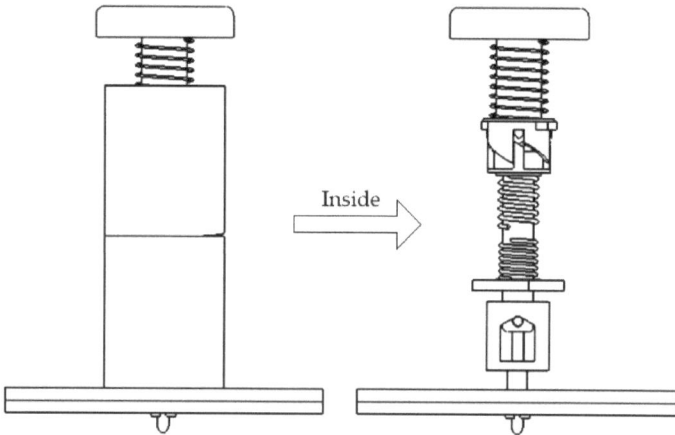

Figure 14. Clamping state of temporary fasteners.

The force of the cylindrical top rod can be seen in Figure 15.

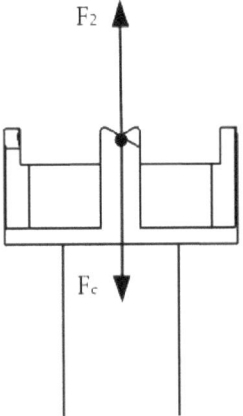

Figure 15. Force relationship of the cylindrical top rod.

F_2—The elastic force of the ejector spring,
F_c—The clamping force of the connecting panels on the clamping jaw.

Thus:
$$F_2 = F_c \tag{16}$$

The force relationship of the inner sleeve is illustrated in Figure 16.

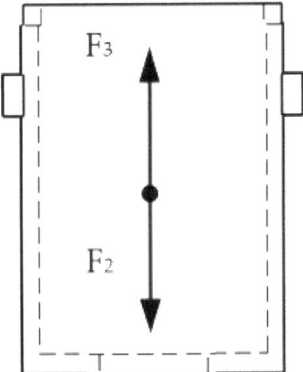

Figure 16. Force relationship of the inner sleeve.

From this diagram we acquired:
$$F_2 = F_3 \tag{17}$$

Simultaneous equations result in:
$$F_c = F_2 = F_3 = k_3 \cdot \Delta x_3 \tag{18}$$

The schematic diagram is shown in Figure 17.

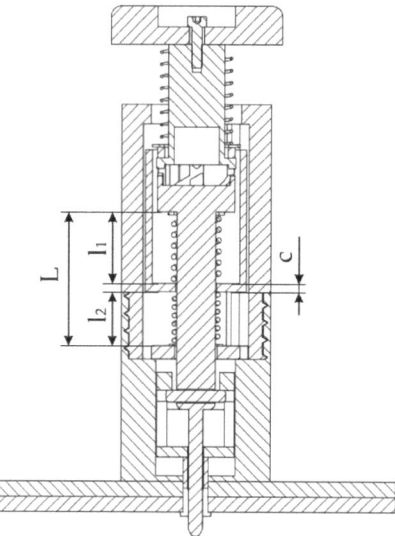

Figure 17. Schematic diagram of the inner sleeve and the cylindrical top rod in the clamping state.

Because $F_2 = F_3$,

$$\begin{cases} k_2 \Delta x_2 = k_3 \Delta x_3 \\ l_1 + l_2 = L - c \\ \Delta x_2 = h_1 - l_1 \\ \Delta x_2 = h_2 - l_2 \end{cases} \quad (19)$$

In the above formula, l_1 is the length of the ejector spring in the clamped state, l_2 is the length of the supporting spring in the clamped state, h_1 is the free height of the ejector spring, h_2 is the free height of the supporting spring, L is the distance from the baffle plate to the bottom surface of the cylindrical top rod in the clamped state, and c is the thickness of the bottom of the inner sleeve.

Combining Formulas (19), we solve

$$\begin{cases} l_1 = L - c - \frac{k_3 h_2 - k_2 h_1 + k_2(L-c)}{k_2 + k_3} \\ l_2 = \frac{k_3 h_2 - k_2 h_1 + k_2(L-c)}{k_2 + k_3} \end{cases} \quad (20)$$

Thus:

$$F_c = \frac{k_2 k_3 (h_1 + h_2 - L + c)}{k_2 + k_3} \quad (21)$$

4. Example Verification

4.1. Experiment Materials and Device

Figure 18a depicts the physical map of the experiment device after manufacture in accordance with the design drawings. The self-locking quick-press temporary fasteners were put on one side of two thin wall parts. These parts were composed of aluminum plate 7075, the same material as airplane plates. The experiment devices included one support frame, two aluminum plates, one pressure sensor, one amplifying conditioner, one 24 V power supply, one pressure gauge, and one quick-press and self-locking temporary fastener.

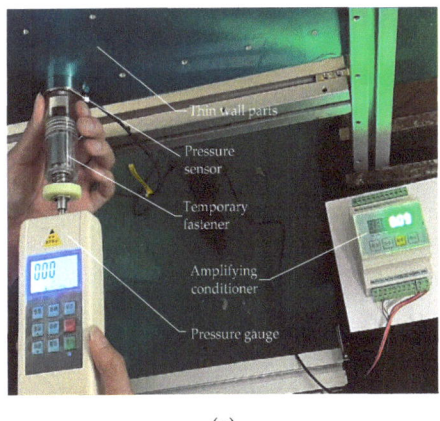 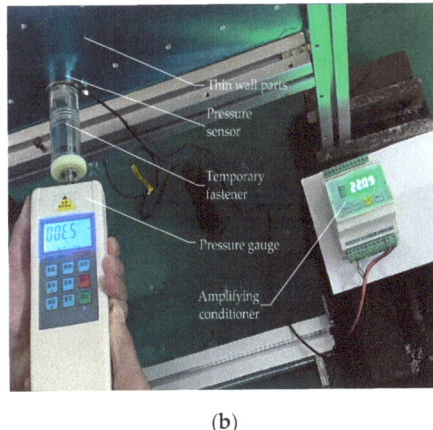

(a) (b)

Figure 18. (**a**) The physical diagram of the experiment device; (**b**) Experimental measured results.

Ensuring the reliability of temporary fastener connections requires the careful selection of materials for component processing, which directly affects the smoothness of movement between parts. This is particularly important for clamping claw components, which require materials with a certain level of flexibility to ensure their ability to expand and contract as well as to prevent fatigue failure and fracture. Some scholars have conducted research on related materials [21–23]. According to a study by Rae et al. [24], the mechanical properties of PEEK 450 G were extensively investigated, including compressive, tensile, and Taylor impact properties, as well as large-strain compression tests and fracture toughness measurements. The study found that the mechanical response of PEEK 450 G is strongly dependent on strain rate and testing temperature. The authors also reported a previously observed darkening phenomenon in Taylor impacted samples, which was attributed to reduced crystallinity resulting from a large compressive strain. Additionally, the study found that reduced crystallinity was also found to decrease Vickers hardness. PEEK 450 G exhibits good toughness and can meet the basic requirements for temporary fastener clamping claw components. Springs are also vulnerable components that can be replaced at regular intervals or with higher-performance materials to effectively increase the service life of the fastener. Table 2 displays the necessary parameters of related parts. They were put together using aluminum profiles to form a support frame. In this experiment, a hole with a diameter of 5 mm was drilled into the thin wall parts, corresponding to the clamping jaw. Considering the influence of tolerance in assembly [25], the accuracy of this test hole is H8, to ensure that the claw part of the clamping claw can pass through the hole smoothly and that the claw can clamp the connecting plates when the claw taper expands.

Table 2. Main parameters of parts.

Main Parts	Material	Related Size				
Thin wall parts	Aluminum alloy 7075	length 800 mm	width 500 mm	thickness 2.5 mm		
Cylindrical top rod	Stainless steel 316 L	length 80 mm	maximum diameter 15.52 mm	minimum diameter 2.85 mm		
Supporting spring	Stainless steel 304	external diameter 12 mm	internal diameter 9.2 mm	Free-height 15 mm	Effective laps 3 laps	
Spring of ejector rod	alloy steel 55CrSi	external diameter 12.5 mm	internal diameter 8.5 mm	Free-height 15 mm	Ultimate pressure 40.2 N	Ultimate compression rate 65%
Return spring	Spring steel	external diameter 16 mm	internal diameter 13.6 mm	Free-height 20 mm	Effective laps 3 laps	
Body of fastener	Resin r4600	maximum length 115.5 mm	minimum length 109.4 mm	diameter 30 mm		
Clamping claw	PEEK-450 G	length 15.5 mm	width 15.5 mm	height 38 mm		

4.2. Experiment Procedure

(1) Put the two aluminum plates to be overlapped into the chute of the support frame so that the round holes of the front and rear aluminum plates correspond one by one.
(2) Install the pressure sensor and the amplifier conditioner according to the circuit diagram and provide the 24 V power supply.
(3) Turn on the power switch and set the value on the amplifier conditioner to zero.
(4) Assemble the quick-pressing self-locking temporary fasteners, set the pressure sensor on the hole surface of the aluminum plates, insert the clamping claw through the circular hole, and concentrically press the pressure gauge and the fastener. The maximum value of the pressure gauge is recorded before the clamping jaw rotates.
(5) Let the temporary fastener's head shell stay tightly attached to the pressure sensor's surface and reach the self-locking stage. Make a note of the values on the pressure gauge and the amplifying conditioner. Perform the above experiment five times to obtain the average value.

4.3. Experiment Results and Analysis

4.3.1. Theoretical Calculation

From the relative parameters of the springs we obtained:

$$k_1 = \frac{Gd}{8nC^3} = \frac{80{,}000 \times 1.2}{8 \times 3 \times \left(\frac{16-1.2}{1.2}\right)^3} \text{ N/mm} = 2.13 \text{ N/mm} \tag{22}$$

$$k_2 = \frac{F_{max}}{65\% h_1} = \frac{40.2}{65\% \times 15} \text{ N/mm} = 4.12 \text{ N/mm} \tag{23}$$

$$k_3 = \frac{Gd}{8nC^3} = \frac{70{,}300 \times 1.4}{8 \times 3 \times \left(\frac{12-1.4}{1.4}\right)^3} \text{ N/mm} = 9.45 \text{ N/mm} \tag{24}$$

From Equation (15) and the actual measurement of $b = 7.8$ mm, the pressure force F can be calculated:

$$F = b(k_1 + k_2) = 7.8 \times (2.13 + 4.12) \text{ N} = 48.75 \text{ N} \tag{25}$$

Therefore, the theoretical pressure force is 48.75 N.

The actual measurements could be $L = 24.2$ mm, $c = 1.55$ mm, so the clamping force F_c can be obtained from (21):

$$F_c = \frac{k_2 k_3 (h_1 + h_2 - L + c)}{k_2 + k_3} = \frac{4.12 \times 9.45 \times (15 + 15 - 24.2 + 1.55)}{4.12 + 9.45} \text{ N} = 21.09 \text{ N} \tag{26}$$

4.3.2. Experimental Data Analysis and Discussion

The measured results of the pressure gauge and pressure sensor are shown in Figure 18b.

After five experiments, the average value was taken to obtain the measured values. The measured values and the theoretical values for this example are illustrated in Table 3.

Table 3. Comparison of results.

Forces	Measured Value/N	Theoretical Value/N	Error Rate
Pressure force F	53.00	48.75	8.01%
Clamping force F_c	22.09	21.09	4.53%

According to the experimental results, the fastener's pressure force and clamping force are slightly different from the theoretical values. Because the theoretical analysis ignored the gravity and friction of the parts, and because there are some inaccuracies in manual measurement, the actual measured values are greater than the theoretical ones.

The experiment also showed that the fastener could achieve quick installation and removal, and a simple operation could achieve unilateral loading and unloading, which is conducive to automatic loading and unloading.

The advantages of the fastener are demonstrated in Table 4.

Table 4. Advantages of fastener.

Reuse	Unilateral Operation	Self-Locking
Adopt a four-petals claw structure with elastic, which can be recycled.	Only need to press one button continuously to realize clamping and uninstalling.	Coordination among the spring, the clamping jaw and shell with buckle, to hold the claw firmly.

5. Conclusions

This article presents a novel, quick-pressing, self-locking temporary fastener designed for pre-joining aircraft wall panels. The working principles of the fastener are comprehensively calculated and explained, and its feasibility is experimentally validated.

(1) This research has proposed a quick-pressing self-locking temporary fastener to address the issues of low work efficiency and the cumbersome installation of traditional bolts for panels. This fastener can not only carry out automatic bonding of thin-walled metal components, but it can also perform unilateral fastening and detaching.

(2) The major components of this temporary fastener are theoretically calculated and statically analyzed. Aiming at the temporary connection of thin-walled plates with a large area, this temporary fastener is meant to achieve single-sided quick assembly and disassembly through the organic combination of a ratchet mechanism, clamping mechanism, and spring. After its analysis and verification, all parts satisfied work requirements under normal settings and proved the device's practicality.

(3) An experiment with a quick-pressing self-locking temporary fastener was performed. According to the results of the experiment, this temporary fastener had a high installation efficiency and could reach the required range of clamping force. Its movement status is essentially compatible with the established movement circumstances. The measured forces and the theoretical calculation values are both within a defined error range, with errors of 8.01% and 4.53%, respectively. The experiment results have shown that the temporary fastener could perform the tightening function, and its effect is close to the theoretical effect. Meanwhile, this fastener can perform unilateral operations, fast loading and unloading, recycling, and improving efficiency, which makes it suitable for large-scale application in automated panel manufacturing.

(4) In addition to the assembly of thin-walled aircraft parts, this fastener can also be employed to assemble thin-walled vehicle parts. For example, after the sheet metal components have been positioned and clamped, fasteners are used to connect two or more sheet metal pieces in order to remove the gaps between or among the sheet metal parts, allowing the sheet metal parts to be welded.

Author Contributions: Conceptualization, W.T. and W.Q.; methodology, W.T.; validation, Y.X.; formal analysis, J.H.; investigation, J.H.; resources, C.L.; data curation, Y.X.; writing—original draft preparation, J.H.; writing—review and editing, W.T.; visualization, J.H.; supervision, J.Y.; project administration, W.T. and W.Q.; funding acquisition, W.T. and H.L. All authors have read and agreed to the published version of the manuscript.

Funding: This research was funded by School-level Scientific Research Project of Shaoguan University (No. SZ2020KJ12), National Natural Science Foundation of China (No. 51775495) and Scientific Research Project of Shaoguan University for Talent Introduction (No. 440-99000620).

Institutional Review Board Statement: Not applicable.

Informed Consent Statement: Not applicable.

Data Availability Statement: Not applicable.

Conflicts of Interest: The authors declare no conflict of interest.

References

1. Jia, Z.; Bhatia, A.; Aronson, R.M.; Bourne, D.; Mason, M.T. A survey of automated threaded fastening. *IEEE Trans. Autom. Sci. Eng.* **2018**, *16*, 298–310. [CrossRef]
2. Ranjan, B.S.C.; Vikranth, H.N.; Ghosal, A. A novel prevailing torque threaded fastener and its analysis. *J. Mech. Des.* **2013**, *135*, 101007. [CrossRef]
3. Gong, H.; Ding, X.; Liu, J.; Feng, H. Review of research on loosening of threaded fasteners. *Friction* **2021**, *10*, 335–359. [CrossRef]
4. Shan, Z.W.; Su, R.K.L. Behavior of shear connectors joined by direct fastening. *Eng. Struct.* **2019**, *196*, 109321. [CrossRef]
5. Mourad, S. *Behaviour of Blind Bolted Moment Connections for Square HSS Columns*; McMaster University: Hamilton, ON, Canada, 1994.
6. Sadri, S.M.; Plunkett, M.R.; Hicks, M.R. High Strength Blind Bolt with Uniform High Clamp over an Extended Grip Range. U.S. Patent US05603592A, 18 February 1997.
7. Gang, L.; Tang, W.; Ke, Y.L.; Chen, Q.L.; Bi, Y.B. Modeling of fast pre-joining processes optimization for skin-stringer panels. *Assem. Autom.* **2014**, *34*, 323–332.
8. Gang, L.; Tang, W.; Ke, Y.L.; Chen, Q.L.; Chen, X.M. Pre-joining process planning model for a batch of skin-stringer panels based on statistical clearances. *Int. J. Adv. Manuf. Technol.* **2015**, *78*, 41–51.
9. Qu, W.W.; Tang, W.; Ke, Y.L. Pre-joining processes optimization method for panel orienting to the clearances suppression of units and the clearances flow among units. *Int. J. Adv. Manuf. Technol.* **2018**, *94*, 1357–1371. [CrossRef]
10. Kim, C.; Bonjoon, G.; Moo, H.S.; Yi, S. Accurate Fastening of Blind Rivet Nuts: A Study. *Trans. Mater. Process.* **2020**, *29*, 331–337.
11. Van de Velde, A.; Debruyne, D.; Maeyens, J.; Wevers, M.; Coppieters, S. Towards best practice in numerical simulation of blind rivet nut installation. *Int. J. Mater. Form.* **2021**, *14*, 1139–1155. [CrossRef]
12. Klasztorny, M.; Nycz, D. Modelling and numerical study of blind rivet nut/bolt joints of composite shell segments. In *Shell Structures: Theory and Application*; CRC Press: Boca Raton, FL, USA, 2013; pp. 409–412.
13. Studziński, R. Experimental investigation of the use of blind rivets in sandwich panels. *J. Sandw. Struct. Mater.* **2021**, *23*, 3669–3684. [CrossRef]
14. Sun, L.; Liu, M.; Liu, Y.; Wang, P.; Zhao, H.; Sun, J.; Shang, Y. Studies on T-shaped one-side bolted connection to hollow section column under bending. *J. Constr. Steel Res.* **2020**, *175*, 106359. [CrossRef]
15. Nikoukalam, M.T.; Mirghaderi, S.R.; Dolatshahi, K.M. Shear slotted bolted connection. *Struct. Des. Tall Spec. Build.* **2017**, *26*, e1313. [CrossRef]
16. Nakajima, K.; Suzuki, H.; Kawabe, Y.; Fujii, K. *Experimental Study on High Strength One-Side Bolted Joints*; Taylor & Francis Group: London, UK, 2012.
17. Vilela, P.M.L.; Carvalho, H.; Baião, O.T. Numerical simulation of bolted connections. *Lat. Am. J. Solids Struct.* **2018**, *15*, e94. [CrossRef]
18. Ungermann, D.; Luebke, S. Innovative fastening of sandwich panels in one face sheet only. *STAHLBAU* **2012**, *81*, 912-U112. [CrossRef]
19. Xu, F.; Cai, Y.; Chan, T.M.; Young, B. Tube wall deformation behaviour of tensile-loaded blind-bolted connections in octagonal hollow section tubes. *Thin-Walled Struct.* **2023**, *184*, 110447. [CrossRef]
20. Tang, W.; Xie, X.; Ye, Y.K.; Qu, W.W. Design of a Fast Temporary Fastener with the Labor-Saving and Reversible Ability. *Coatings* **2021**, *11*, 1101. [CrossRef]
21. Wang, W.; Hua, D.; Zhou, Q.; Li, S.; Eder, S.J.; Shi, J.; Wang, Z.; Wang, H.; Liu, W. Effect of a water film on the material removal behavior of Invar during chemical mechanical polishing. *Appl. Surf. Sci.* **2023**, *616*, 156490. [CrossRef]
22. Ye, W.; Xie, M.; Huang, Z.; Wang, H.; Zhou, Q.; Wang, L.; Chen, B.; Wang, H.; Liu, W. Microstructure and tribological properties of in-situ carbide/CoCrFeNiMn high entropy alloy composites synthesized by flake powder metallurgy. *Tribol. Int.* **2023**, *181*, 108295. [CrossRef]
23. Jia, Q.; He, W.; Hua, D.; Zhou, Q.; Du, Y.; Ren, Y.; Lu, Z.; Wang, H.; Zhou, F.; Wang, J. Effects of structure relaxation and surface oxidation on nanoscopic wear behaviors of metallic glass. *Acta Mater.* **2022**, *232*, 117934. [CrossRef]
24. Rae, P.J.; Brown, E.N.; Orler, E.B. The mechanical properties of poly(ether-ether-ketone) (PEEK) with emphasis on the large compressive strain response. *Polymer* **2007**, *48*, 598–615. [CrossRef]
25. Sadowski, T.; Golewski, P. Effect of Tolerance in the Fitting of Rivets in the Holes of Double Lap Joints Subjected to Uniaxial Tension. In *Key Engineering Materials*; Trans Tech Publications Ltd.: Zurich, Switzerland, 2014; Volume 607, pp. 49–54.

Disclaimer/Publisher's Note: The statements, opinions and data contained in all publications are solely those of the individual author(s) and contributor(s) and not of MDPI and/or the editor(s). MDPI and/or the editor(s) disclaim responsibility for any injury to people or property resulting from any ideas, methods, instructions or products referred to in the content.

Article

Investigation of Spatial Symmetry Error Measurement, Evaluation and Compensation Model for Herringbone Gears

Zhipeng Liang and Huawei Zhou *

School of Civil Engineering, Architecture & Environment, Hubei University of Technology, Wuhan 430068, China; liangzhipeng@hbut.edu.cn
* Correspondence: zhouhuawei@hbut.edu.cn

Abstract: In the machining process for herringbone gears manufactured by numerical control gear-shaping machines, out-of-tolerance problems of symmetry error generally exist. This paper proposed a high-precision control of spatial symmetry error in the one-time forming machining for herringbone gear. To improve the machining symmetry accuracy and quality of herringbone gear, a mathematical model of measurement, evaluation and compensation for spatial symmetry error was established based on the least square method. Meanwhile, a new shaping machining method based on spatial symmetry error detection and compensation was proposed. The test results indicated that the proposed method can maintain symmetry within 0.02 mm. This study provided a novel spatial symmetry error detection and compensation machining method for herringbone gear that has advantages compared to traditional methods in terms of machining accuracy, efficiency, and continuous machining type.

Keywords: herringbone gear; spatial symmetry error; measurement; evaluation and compensation; mathematical model; shaping machining

Citation: Liang, Z.; Zhou, H. Investigation of Spatial Symmetry Error Measurement, Evaluation and Compensation Model for Herringbone Gears. *Appl. Sci.* **2023**, *13*, 8340. https://doi.org/10.3390/app13148340

Academic Editor: Wei Li

Received: 30 June 2023
Revised: 12 July 2023
Accepted: 18 July 2023
Published: 19 July 2023

Copyright: © 2023 by the authors. Licensee MDPI, Basel, Switzerland. This article is an open access article distributed under the terms and conditions of the Creative Commons Attribution (CC BY) license (https://creativecommons.org/licenses/by/4.0/).

1. Introduction

Modern gear transmissions are being developed for higher speeds and heavier loads, which pose higher requirements for the static accuracy and dynamic performance of gears [1–3]. As an important transmission component, herringbone gears are widely used in high-speed, heavy-duty, and high-power transmission systems such as aviation and vessel transmission equipment and other mechanical transmission areas because of their advantages in transmission stability and strong bearing capacity [4–6]. Therefore, high accuracy in the manufacture of herringbone gears is increasingly required [7–10]. Even more, the spatial symmetry of herringbone gears directly affects transmission errors, transmission efficiency and service life, which are significant for transmission systems [11,12]. At present, tooth profile and tooth direction modifications are research priorities that can improve the stability of and reduce vibrations in gear transmission systems [13–17]. Thus far, manufacturers have lacked a high-precision and high-efficiency control processing method for on-line detection and compensation of spatial symmetry errors in herringbone gears [18].

In recent years, many scholars at home and abroad have conducted numerous related studies on herringbone gear machining methods and the principles of processing error influence on transmission characteristics. Meanwhile, advanced machining methods based on online detection and compensation machining technology have great reference value. Okafor et al. [19] proposed the development of kinematic error models accounting for geometric and thermal errors in the vertical machining center, and used the error model to calculate and predict the resultant error vector at the tool–workpiece interface for error compensation. Kramer et al. [20] developed a feature-based inspection and control system to realize completion of whole machining and detection and compensation processes on machine tools. Kang et al. [14] developed a new double-helical test setup for operating a double-helical gear pair under realistic torque and speed ranges. Liu et al. [21] proposed a dynamic model that includes friction and tooth profile error excitation for herringbone gears and used the proposed model in the dynamic analysis of the variable speed process of a herringbone gear transmission system. Guiassa et al. [22] proposed a cutting compliance coefficient model to estimate corrections for the tool path at the finish cut based on a finite number of measured errors at discrete locations for previous cuts, and presented an integrated methodology for compensation errors detected with an on-machine touch probe. Mao et al. [23] studied the influence mechanism of manufacturing error and assembly error on the load sharing characteristics of a transmission system. Zhou et al. [24] investigated the effects of centering error and angular misalignment on crack initiation life in herringbone gears. Mallipeddi et al. [25] compared gear surface characteristics generated by grinding, honing and superfinishing of case-hardened steel. Gao et al. [26] proposed an error compensation machining method that improves complex surface components based on analyzing the error factors influencing the inspection accuracy of on-machine detection systems. Yang et al. [27] established a mathematical model of comprehensive error compensation for complex thin-wall parts and performed machining tests of error compensation. In a word, the above research findings developed on-line detection and compensation machining technology to some degree. However, they had some limitations that could not be effectively applied to real-time spatial symmetry error detection and compensation machining processes for herringbone gears. Further, investigations reporting on the measurement and evaluation of spatial symmetry errors in herringbone gears and machining methods for their compensation have not been reported so far.

In this study, an accurate shaping machining method based on spatial symmetry error detection and compensation (SSEDC) for herringbone gears is proposed. A mathematical model of spatial symmetry error was established based on spatial projection and the least square method (LSM). On the basis of analyzing symmetry out of tolerance as well as methods of measurement and evaluation of spatial symmetry error, a new machining method based on SSEDC is proposed for the first time. The test results indicate that the machining method based on SSEDC can consistently keep symmetry within 0.02 mm.

2. Measurement, Evaluation and Compensation Model for Spatial Symmetry Errors
2.1. Measurement and Evaluation Model for Spatial Symmetry Errors

Spatial symmetry errors in herringbone gears come from deviations in the starting machining position between the upper and lower teeth. If the involute curve of a herringbone gear is enlarged indefinitely, the shape of the herringbone gear will be similar to an oblique gear rack, and the actual spatial symmetry error shown in Figure 1 will be the offset error of the center position for the upper and lower teeth. Thus, the spatial symmetry error of the herringbone gear shown in Figure 2 can be assumed to be a circular angle error. Therefore, in order to identify a herringbone gear's spatial symmetry error, it is important to calculate and acquire the circular angle error of the upper and lower teeth through measurement and calculation using a mathematic model.

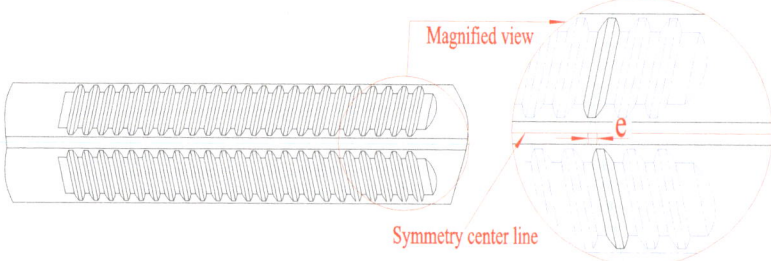

Figure 1. Symmetry error of oblique gear rack.

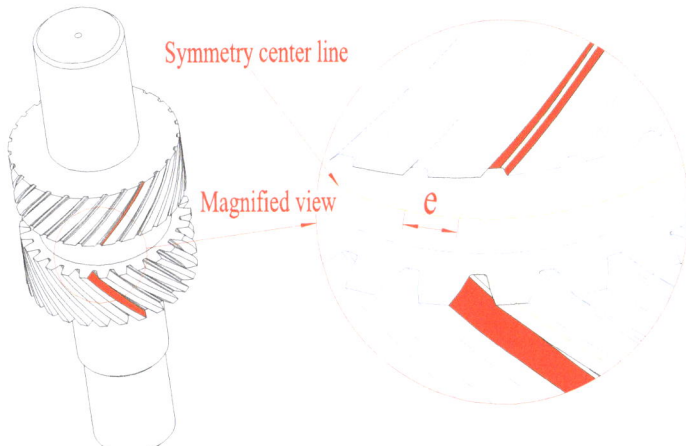

Figure 2. Spatial symmetry error of herringbone gear.

The phase error at the symmetrical position of the upper and lower helical teeth of the herringbone gear is detected by the probe. After many tests, the measurement of the spatial symmetry error value of the herringbone gear is completed.

To realize the detection and compensation of a herringbone gear's spatial symmetry error, the symmetry plane of the left and right revolving gear is defined as the symmetry center plane O. As shown in Figure 3, the position measurements of planes A, B, C and D are completed with the touch probe, and the n random points can be written as $A_1 \sim A_n$, $B_1 \sim B_n$, $C_1 \sim C_n$ and $D_1 \sim D_n$. Further, the position coordinates of midpoints connected with corresponding points of the same height can be expressed as $A_i(X_{Ai}, Y_{Ai}, Z_{Ai})$, $B_i(X_{Bi}, Y_{Bi}, Z_{Bi})$, $C_i(X_{Ci}, Y_{Ci}, Z_{Ci})$ and $D_i(X_{Di}, Y_{Di}, Z_{Di})$, $i \in [1, n]$. Using a plane fitting method, the fitting symmetry plates E and F based on the position coordinates of the midpoints are calculated respectively. Using a spatial projection method, the projection line equations of plane E and F projecting on the plane O are calculated, respectively. As shown in Figure 4, we ensure the two projection lines are parallel through approximate processing of the projection line equations, and then calculate the linear distance e of the two projection lines. In fact, the spatial symmetry error is usually relatively small in the machining process. Thus, the deflection chord length, that is, spatial symmetry error, is infinitely equivalent to the linear distance e.

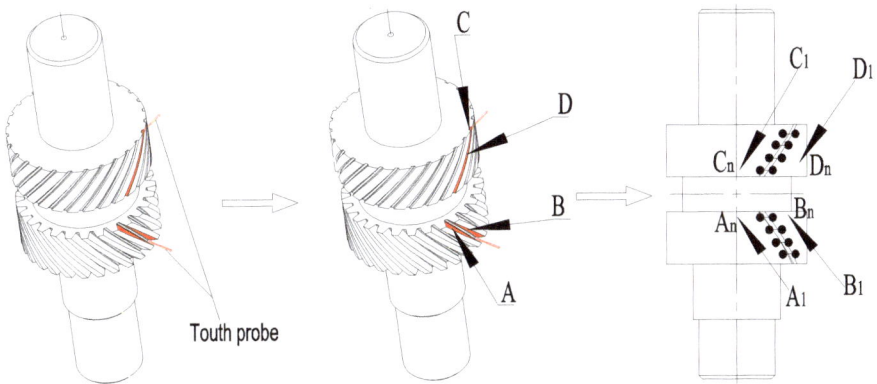

Figure 3. Schematic diagram of detected spatial symmetry error.

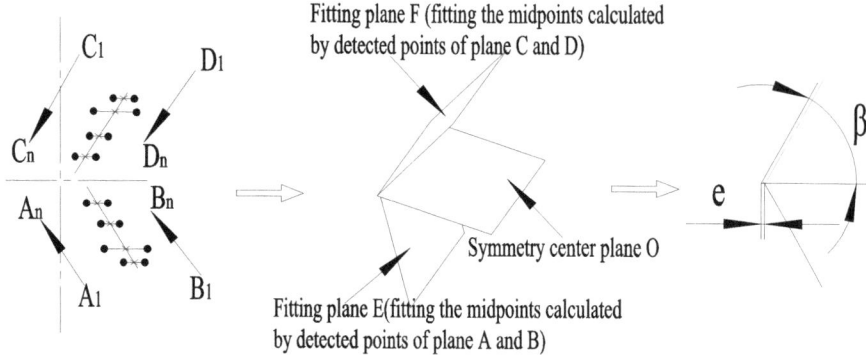

Figure 4. Schematic diagram of evaluated spatial symmetry error.

The sets of position coordinate midpoints connected with plane A and B corresponding to points of the same height can be written as follows:

$$(x_i, y_i, z_i) = \left\{\left(\frac{X_{Ai} + X_{Bi}}{2}, \frac{Y_{Ai} + Y_{Bi}}{2}, \frac{Z_{Ai} + Z_{Bi}}{2}\right)\right\} i \in [1, n] \quad (1)$$

In the same way, the sets of position coordinate midpoints connected with plane C and D corresponding to points of the same height can be written as follows:

$$(x'_i, y'_i, z'_i) = \left\{\left(\frac{X_{Ci} + X_{Di}}{2}, \frac{Y_{Ci} + Y_{Di}}{2}, \frac{Z_{Ci} + Z_{Di}}{2}\right)\right\} i \in [1, n] \quad (2)$$

The fitting symmetry plate E and F can be calculated based on spatial analytic geometry and the calculated midpoint sets. The equations of plane E and F can be formulated as follows:

$$z = a_0 x + a_1 y + a_2 \quad (3)$$

$$z' = a'_0 x + a'_1 y + a'_2 \quad (4)$$

Utilizing LSM to calculate the fitting symmetry planes, the results can be calculated as follows:

$$\begin{bmatrix} a_0 \\ a_1 \\ a_2 \end{bmatrix} = \begin{pmatrix} \sum x_i^2 & \sum x_i y_i & \sum x_i \\ \sum x_i y_i & \sum y_i^2 & \sum y_i \\ \sum x_i & \sum y_i & n \end{pmatrix}^{-1} \begin{pmatrix} \sum x_i z_i \\ \sum y_i z_i \\ \sum z_i \end{pmatrix} \quad (5)$$

$$\begin{bmatrix} a'_0 \\ a'_1 \\ a'_2 \end{bmatrix} = \begin{pmatrix} \sum x'^2_i & \sum x'_i y'_i & \sum x'_i \\ \sum x'_i y'_i & \sum y'^2_i & \sum y'_i \\ \sum x'_i & \sum y'_i & n \end{pmatrix}^{-1} \begin{pmatrix} \sum x'_i z'_i \\ \sum y'_i z'_i \\ \sum z'_i \end{pmatrix} \quad (6)$$

The fitting planes E and F intersect with symmetry center plane O in the spatial, and the intersection line equations can be calculated based on spatial analytic geometry. Further, the two intersection lines should not be completely parallel in theory, but approximate processing should be performed to ensure they are parallel in practice. Thus, the herringbone gear's spatial symmetry error is the X-axis coordinate distance e in XOY coordinate system for the two intersection lines.

2.2. Compensation Model of Spatial Symmetry Error

On the basis of the proposed measurement and evaluation model for a herringbone gear' spatial symmetry error, the spatial symmetry error is translated into displacement deviation e. In fact, the herringbone gear's spatial symmetry error cannot be compensated through rotating the gear or controlling the worktable's rotating axis. To achieve compensation of the spatial symmetry error, the controlled target is translated into the gear shaping cutter according to the generating machining method. Thus, the movements involved in the gear shaping cutter need to be analyzed.

As shown in Figure 5, the movements of the gear shaping cutter mainly include the principal cutting movement (P), circular cutting motion of numerical control (NC) axis C2 (C2), cutter back-off motion (B) and movement of oblique knife (S). Apparently, the angle error compensation of the tangential direction cannot be realized through controlling movement P; moreover, the simplex control of movement C2 can make tangential displacement in the gear machining process, and the motion B only involves the axial direction because the spatial symmetry error is translated into displacement deviation e at the X-axis coordinate. Therefore, the method of controlling movement S is proposed to compensate for the displacement deviation e, and this method is viable to compensate for the tangential displacement through approximation in theory. The compensation model of the herringbone gear's spatial symmetry error is shown in Figure 6. Finally, the whole closed loop system of measurement and compensation machining on the herringbone gear's spatial symmetry error is realized.

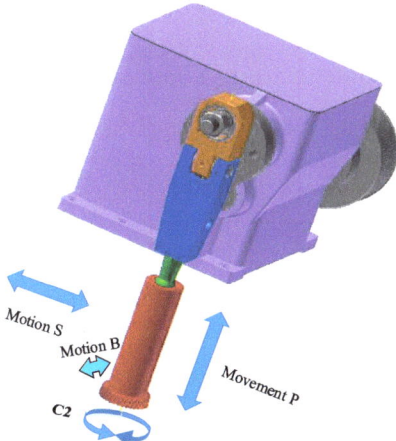

Figure 5. Schematic diagram of movements involved in gear shaping cutter.

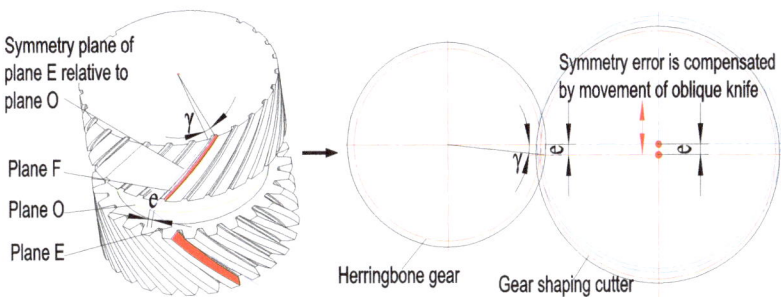

Figure 6. Compensation model of spatial symmetry error.

On the basis of the proposed compensation model for the herringbone gear's spatial symmetry error, the spatial symmetry error is translated into displacement deviation e and can be written as follows. Further, the movement of the oblique knife is adjusted, and then the gear shaping cutter should be adjusted to confirm the mesh after compensating for the spatial symmetry error. The angle α_1 can be written as follows:

$$e \approx mz \frac{\sin \gamma}{\cos \beta} = \frac{d \sin \gamma}{2 \cos \beta} \tag{7}$$

$$\alpha_1 \approx \arcsin \frac{e \cos \beta}{MZ} = \arcsin \frac{2e \cos \beta}{D} \tag{8}$$

where m, z, d, and γ are the herringbone gear's module, tooth number, pitch diameter and angle error, respectively, where M, Z, D and α_1 are the gear shaping cutter's module, tooth number, pitch diameter and angle error, respectively.

Therefore, by setting up the measurement and evaluation and compensation model of the herringbone gear's spatial symmetry error, the machining process for on-line detection and compensation of the herringbone gear's spatial symmetry error can be intuitively displayed, providing theoretical support for instance machining.

3. Herringbone Gear Machining Method Based on SSEDC
3.1. Machining Flow

Herringbone gears are composed of left and right screw surfaces. The left and right screw surface intersection can constitute multiple planes. The plane symmetry to the gear face is usually called the herringbone gear center plane. Because of restriction of the reducer structure and normal meshing transmission requirement, the herringbone gear must set the position when assembling, and positioning error of he plane must be controlled in the allowed range of the assembly adjustment amount, which means that the symmetry of the left- and right-hand gears must be well-maintained, and the position error should be generally controlled within 0.05 mm.

According to the above analysis, a machining flow chart for a herringbone gear based on SSEDC is proposed, combined with the machining process for the gear, as shown in Figure 7. The key point in the machining process is to achieve detection through a measuring device and control it to detect the phase symmetry of the upper right-hand and lower left-hand groove center of the herringbone gear. Then, on the basis of the proposed method, the spatial symmetry error can be calculated and compensated in the machining process.

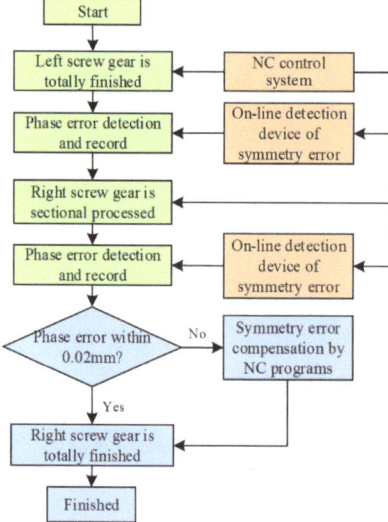

Figure 7. Machining flow chart for herringbone gear based on SSEDC.

Combined with the actual herringbone gear machining process, the basic machining flow chart for the herringbone gear based on SSEDC is shown in Figure 8.

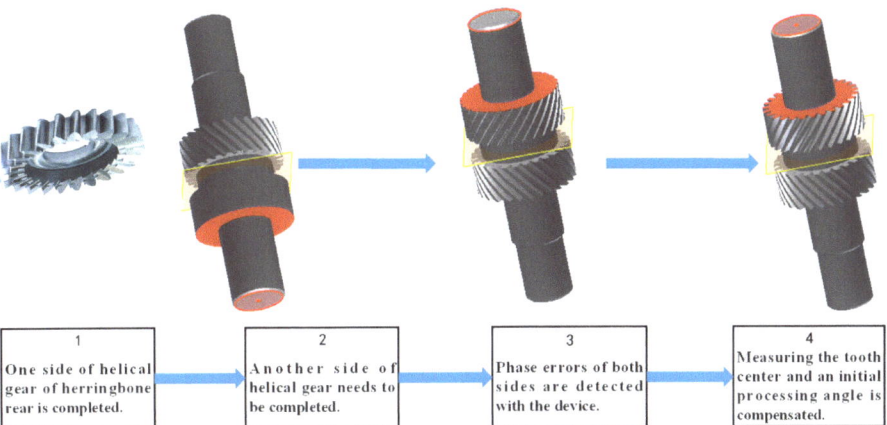

Figure 8. Flow chart of actual herringbone gear machining process based on SSEDC.

3.2. Design of Fixture and On-Line Device for Spatial Symmetry Error Measurement

To clamp the herringbone gear and ensure the accuracy and efficiency of herringbone gear machining, a general fixture for hydraulic drive self-clamping is designed; it is composed of a pull rod, core clamper, spring, collect chuck, positioning sleeve, fixture body, etc., as shown in Figure 9. When the hydraulic cylinder drives the pull rod downward, the pull rod drives the collect chuck to clamp the shaft diameter of the herringbone gear and ensures that the positioning surface of the herringbone gear is attached to the positioning plane of the fixture, in order to facilitate automatic clamping of the herringbone gear. Table 1 lists the basic parameters of the herringbone gear.

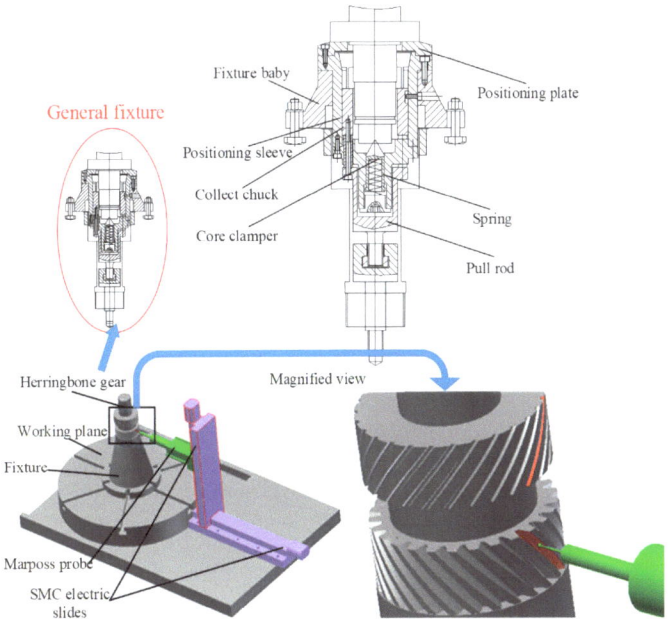

Figure 9. Schematic diagram of designed fixture and OMFSDD.

Table 1. Basic parameters of herringbone gear.

Module-m (mm)	1.65
Tooth-z	28
Pressure angle-α (°)	20
Helix angle-β (°)	15
Pitch diameter-d (mm)	56.172

Meanwhile, an on-line spatial symmetry error measuring device controlled by the program of an NC system is designed to measure points on surfaces of the machining teeth. The symmetry center plane can be calculated based on the proposed method. As shown in Figure 9, the on-line measuring device is composed of a Marposs T25 probe and two electric slides [28]. The horizontal and vertical electric slides allow multi-degree freedom of movement of the Marposs probe. On that basis, measurements of gears of different heights and sizes can be realized.

The detection principle and process of the device are as follows. The NC program controls the electric slides to turn the measuring head into the left-handed slot of the gear (as shown in Figure 9). After measuring the tooth centers of the up and down gears, an initial processing angle will be compensated and corrected according to the center deviation value to meet the requirements of symmetry.

4. Case Study

4.1. Measurement and Compensation of Spatial Symmetry Error

To improve machining efficiency in the detection and compensation process, actually, the quantity of detected points can be reduced to two points for each tooth surface. Because the gear shaping cutter has high accuracy and the processed helix angle is constant, the three-dimensional spatial symmetry error can be reduced to a one-dimensional displacement deviation. Meanwhile, in order to compare and validate the detected data, it is necessary to detect two points for each tooth surface. Hence, in the actual machining process, the spatial symmetry error amount is calculated based on the data for a total of eight detected points on four tooth surfaces.

As shown in Figure 10, the positioning end plane is defined as the reference plane, and a total of four points whose heights are, respectively, h_1, $H - h_1$, h_2 and $H - h_2$ are detected by the on-line measuring device. As shown in Figure 11, corresponding to the heights of h_1, $-h_1$, h_2 and $H - h_2$, points $A_1(X_{A1}, Y_{A1}, Z_{A1})$ and $B_1(X_{B1}, Y_{B1}, Z_{B1})$, $C_1(X_{C1}, Y_{C1}, Z_{C1})$ and $D_1(X_{D1}, Y_{D1}, Z_{D1})$, $A_2(X_{A2}, Y_{A2}, Z_{A2})$ and $B_2(X_{B2}, Y_{B2}, Z_{B2})$, $C_2(X_{C2}, Y_{C2}, Z_{C2})$ and $D_2(X_{D2}, Y_{D2}, Z_{D2})$ are respectively detected. Based on the calculation and compensation methods in the actual machining process, the X-axis coordinates are chosen to calculate the spatial symmetry error. Therefore, the displacement error e_1 and e_2 can be written as follows:

$$e_1 = \frac{X_{B1} - X_{A1}}{2} - \frac{X_{D1} - X_{C1}}{2} \tag{9}$$

$$e_2 = \frac{X_{B2} - X_{A2}}{2} - \frac{X_{D2} - X_{C2}}{2} \tag{10}$$

Then, through comparing the calculated error, the spatial symmetry error e in the actual machining process can be written as follows:

$$e = \frac{e_1 + e_2}{2} \tag{11}$$

The actual detection and compensation process is shown in Figure 12. The diagram of the NC shaping machine drive system is shown in Figure 13.

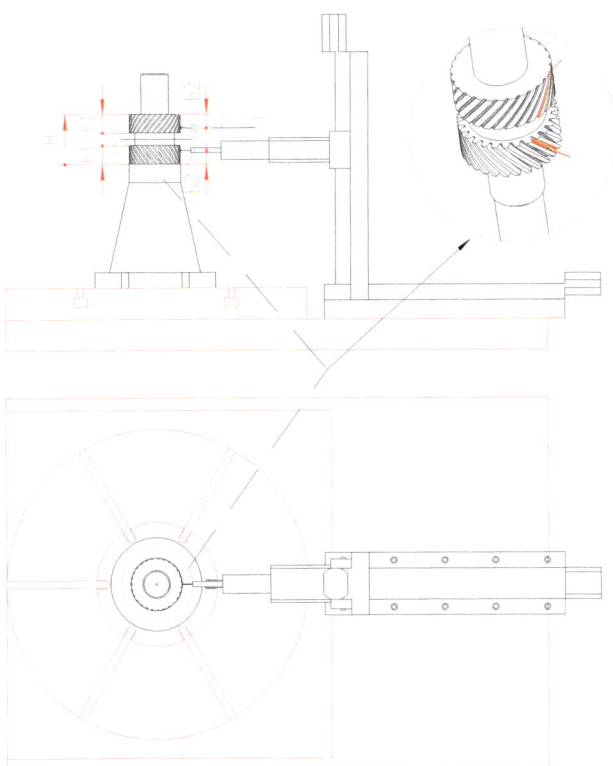

Figure 10. Schematic diagram of requirement for corresponding detected points.

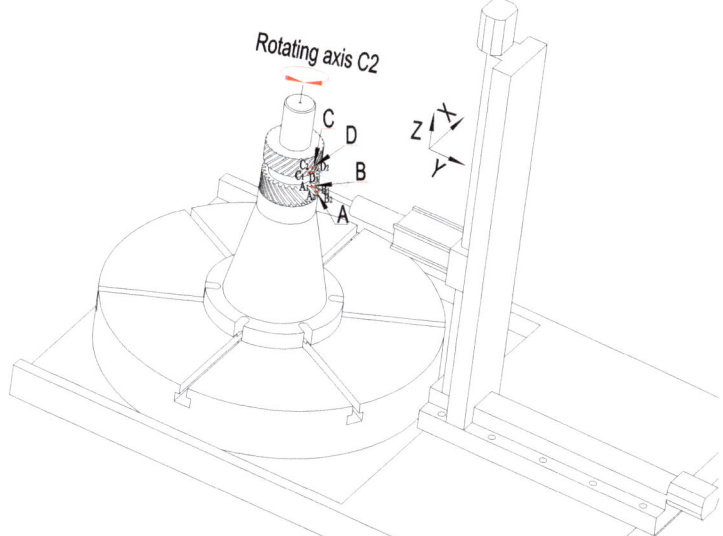

Figure 11. Schematic diagram of actual detection process based on SSEDC.

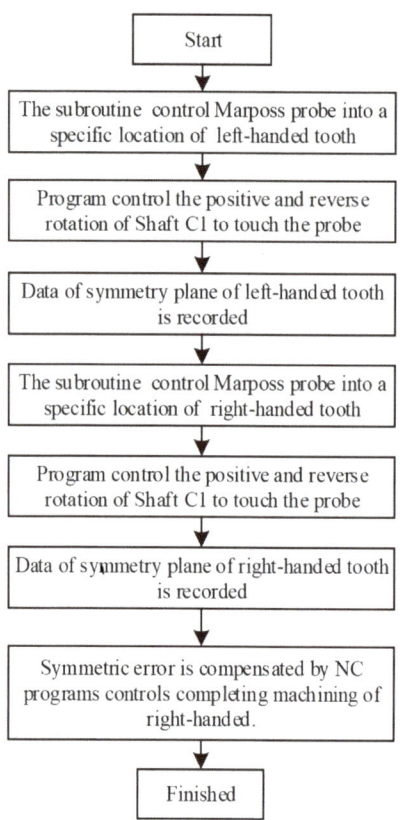

Figure 12. Flow chart of the actual detection and compensation process.

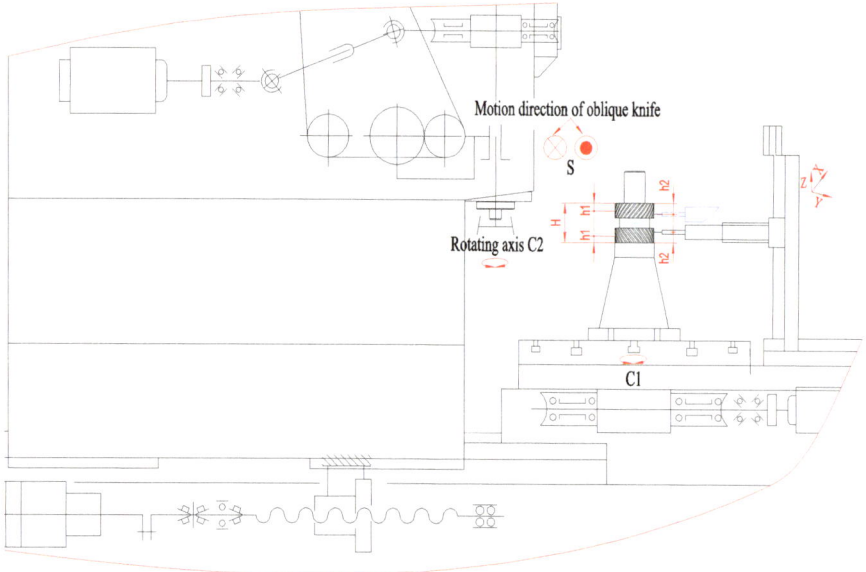

Figure 13. Diagram of the shaping machine drive system and on-line symmetry error detection device.

4.2. Machining and Accuracy

Shown in Figure 14 is a diagram of the herringbone gear machining process for a special gear-shaping machine. Firstly, the NC program should be developed according to the flow chart of the actual detection and compensation process, including the right- and left-hand gear machining programs and symmetry error detection programs. Secondly, the preparation work should be performed before the machining of herringbone gears, including gear clamping, positioning, alignment, program debugging, etc. Then, the numerical control program controls the gear shaper to complete the processing of the right-handed gear and controls the Marposs probe to locate and determine the symmetrical position of the calibration slot.

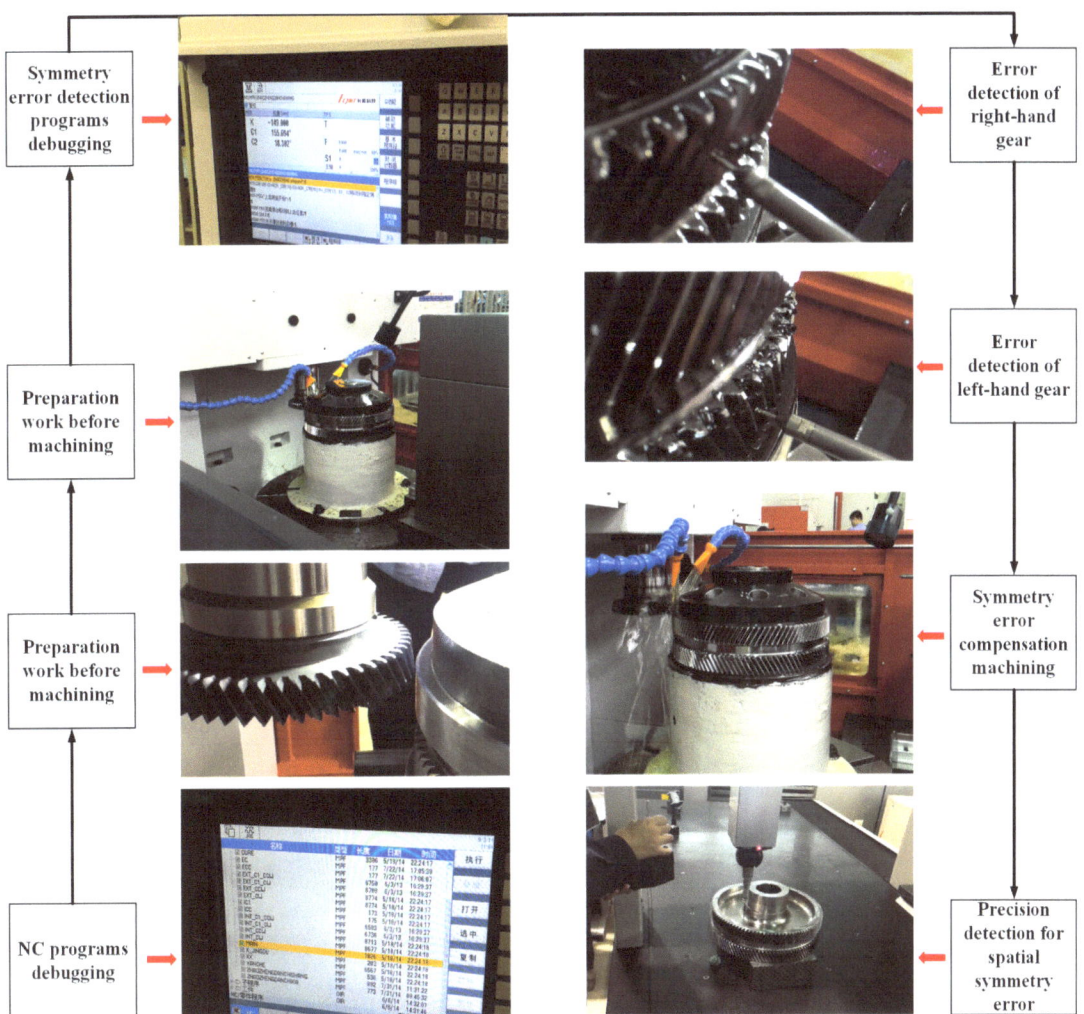

Figure 14. Diagram of machining process for herringbone gear with a special-gear shaping machine.

After that, the herringbone gear is turned over and clamped, and the above steps are repeated to complete the processing of the left-handed gear (without cutting to the tooth depth). The numerical control program controls the Marposs probe to complete the measurement of the left-handed tooth space position corresponding to the position of the right-handed gear calibration slot. Finally, the calculation of the spatial symmetry error is completed, and the phase compensation processing is carried out. Based on the designed special fixture, specific NC machining programs are developed and debugged, and three types of herringbone gears are manufactured on this special NC gear-shaping machine.

The machining process for the measurement and compensation of herringbone gear spatial symmetry error is shown in Figure 14, including NC program debugging, preparation work before machining, without shaping to the tooth depth, symmetry error detection program debugging, detection of right- and left-hand gear errors, symmetry error compensation machining and precision detection of spatial symmetry error.

Based on the proposed machining method, the results of the machining experiments indicated that the symmetry can be reliably controlled within 0.015 mm. As shown in Figure 15a, the machining instances for herringbone gear were extended to other sizes. As shown in Figure 15b, the machining accuracy of symmetry detected by the coordinate measuring machine can be controlled within 0.02 mm with SSEDC. Comparing the traditional and novel machining methods, the contrasting results are shown in Table 2.

 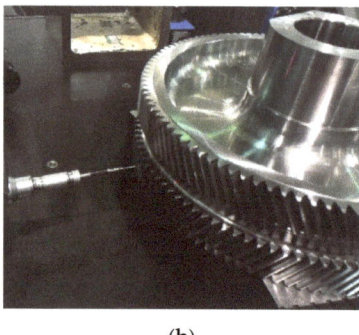 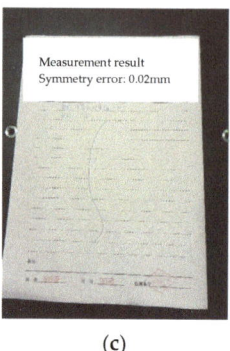

(a) (b) (c)

Figure 15. Diagram of herringbone gear machining and detection with SSEDC. (**a**) Machining process. (**b**) Accuracy measurement. (**c**) Measurement results.

Table 2. Comparison of herringbone gear machining accuracy and efficiency with different machining methods.

Machining Method	Machining Accuracy (mm)	Efficiency (h)	Batch Machining Feature
Traditional method	0.1~0.2	2.5 h/piece	Machining with single piece repeat
Novel method	0.02	0.8 h/piece	Continuous machining

5. Conclusions

We proposed a novel shaping and machining method based on SSEDC for herringbone gears that can realize high-precision control of spatial symmetry error in a one-time forming and machining process. First, a herringbone gear spatial symmetry error measurement and evaluation model was initially established based on spatial projection and LSM. Then, a herringbone gear spatial symmetry error compensation model was further established. Finally, an online detection and compensation machining method for herringbone gear spatial symmetry errors was first created.

Based on the established spatial symmetry error measurement, evolution and compensation mathematical model, a general fixture and an on-line spatial symmetry error detection device were designed for automatic detection and control of spatial symmetry errors. Additionally, to improve machining efficiency in the detection and compensation process, three-dimensional spatial symmetry errors were reasonably reduced to one-dimensional displacement deviations. Further, the specific processes of practical engineering were proposed and applied.

Numerous machining cases were performed based on the proposed SSEDC method and extended to other, different sizes of herringbone gears. The machining cases indicated that the proposed machining method could consistently maintain symmetry within 0.02 mm. Thus, the proposed SSEDC method for solving the out-of-tolerance problem of spatial symmetry error shows reliability and stability.

Author Contributions: Conceptualization, Z.L.; Methodology, H.Z.; Validation, H.Z.; Investigation, Z.L.; Writing—original draft, H.Z.; Writing—review and editing, Z.L.; Project administration, H.Z. All authors have read and agreed to the published version of the manuscript.

Funding: This research work was supported by the Youth Fund project of the National Natural Science Foundation of China (No. 52109157).

Institutional Review Board Statement: Not applicable.

Informed Consent Statement: Not applicable.

Data Availability Statement: Data sharing not applicable.

Acknowledgments: The authors thank the reviewers and editors for useful comments and suggestions that helped to improve the paper.

Conflicts of Interest: The authors declare no conflict of interest.

References

1. Wang, Y.Z.; Lan, Z.; Hou, L.W.; Chu, X.M.; Yin, Y.Y. An efficient honing method for face gear with tooth profile modification. *Int. J. Adv. Manuf. Technol.* **2017**, *90*, 1155–1163. [CrossRef]
2. Su, J.Z.; Li, X.D.; Yin, X.M.; Jia, H.T.; Guo, F. Design and form grinding principle of linear triangular end relief for double helical gears. *J. Mech. Eng.* **2023**, *59*, 121–129.
3. Jia, J.Y.; Shen, Y.B.; Cao, J.F. Influence of symmetry deviation of herringbone gears on the system vibration characteristics. *J. Xi'an Technol. Univ.* **2022**, *42*, 230–237.
4. Dong, J.C.; Wang, S.M.; Lin, H.; Wang, Y. Dynamic modeling of double-helical gear with Timoshenko beam theory and experiment verification. *Adv. Mech. Eng.* **2016**, *8*, 1687814016647230. [CrossRef]
5. Ren, F.; Qin, D.T.; Lim, T.C.; Lyu, S.K. Study on dynamic characteristics and load sharing of a herringbone planetary gear with manufacturing errors. *Int. J. Precis. Eng. Manuf.* **2014**, *15*, 1925–1934. [CrossRef]
6. Wang, F.Z.; Fang, D.; Li, S.J.; Li, J.H.; Jiang, J.K. Analysis optimization and experimental verification of herringbone gear transmission system. *J. Mech. Eng.* **2015**, *51*, 34–42. [CrossRef]
7. Li, Z.B.; Wang, S.M. Study on nonlinear dynamic characteristics of power six-branch herringbone gear transmission system with 3D modification. *Proc. Inst. Mech. Eng.* **2023**, *237*, 193–219. [CrossRef]
8. Wei, K.; Lu, F.X.; Bao, H.Y.; Zhu, R.P. Mechanism and reduction of windage power losses for high speed herringbone gear. *Proc. Inst. Mech. Eng. Part C J. Mech. Eng. Sci.* **2023**, *237*, 2014–2029. [CrossRef]
9. Ma, Y.G.; Zhang, X.J.; Fang, Z.D.; Yin, X.M.; Xu, Y.Q. A new analysis technology of the vibration characteristic of the gearbox case of herringbone gear reducer. *Appl. Acoust.* **2023**, *205*, 109289.
10. Wang, L.; Du, Z.K.; Wang, Y.; Zheng, Z.Z.; Chen, G.D. Temperature measurement and error analysis of the transverse plane of oil-jet-lubrication herringbone gear with infrared pyrometers. *Rev. Sci. Instrum.* **2023**, *94*, 024902. [CrossRef]
11. Wei, J.; Gao, P.; Hu, X.L.; Sun, W.; Zeng, J. Effects of dynamic transmission errors and vibration stability in helical gears. *J. Mech. Sci. Technol.* **2014**, *28*, 2253–2262. [CrossRef]
12. Zhai, H.F.; Zhu, C.C.; Song, C.S.; Liu, H.J.; Li, G.F.; Ma, F. Dynamic modeling and analysis for transmission system of high-power wind turbine gearbox. *J. Mech. Sci. Technol.* **2015**, *29*, 4073–4082. [CrossRef]
13. Wang, Y.; Yang, W.; Tang, X.; Lin, X.; He, Z. Power Flow and Efficiency Analysis of High-Speed Heavy Load Herringbone Planetary Transmission Using a Hypergraph-Based Method. *Appl. Sci.* **2020**, *10*, 5849. [CrossRef]
14. Kang, M.R.; Kahraman, A. An experimental and theoretical study of the dynamic behavior of double-helical gear sets. *J. Sound Vib.* **2015**, *350*, 11–29. [CrossRef]
15. Tesfahunegn, Y.A.; Rosa, F.; Gorla, C. The effects of the shape of tooth profile modifications on the transmission error, bending, and contact stress of spur gears. *Proc. Inst. Mech. Eng. Part C J. Mech. Eng. Sci.* **2010**, *224*, 1749–1758. [CrossRef]
16. Wang, C. Optimization of Tooth Profile Modification Based on Dynamic Characteristics of Helical Gear Pair. *Iran. J. Sci. Technol. Trans. Mech. Eng.* **2019**, *43*, 631–639. [CrossRef]
17. Yang, S.; Di, H.; Tang, J.; Wan, G. Research of the Design of Double Helical Gear Modification based on KISSsoft Software. *J. Mech. Trans.* **2018**, *42*, 1–6.
18. Bauer, R.; Dix, M. Novel method for manufacturing herringbone gears by power skiving. *Procedia CIRP* **2022**, *112*, 310–315. [CrossRef]

19. Okafor, A.C.; Ertekin, Y.M. Derivation of machine tool error models and error compensation procedure for three axes vertical machining center using rigid body kinematics. *Int. J. Mach. Tools Manuf.* **2000**, *40*, 1199–1213. [CrossRef]
20. Kramer, T.R.; Huang, H.; Messina, E.; Proctor, F.M.; Scott, H. A feature-based inspection and machining system. *Comput. Aided Des.* **2001**, *33*, 653–669. [CrossRef]
21. Liu, C.Z.; Qin, D.T.; Liao, Y.H. Dynamic Model of Variable Speed Process for Herringbone Gears Including Friction Calculated by Variable Friction Coefficient. *J. Mech. Des.* **2014**, *4*, 041006. [CrossRef]
22. Guiassa, R.; Mayer, J.R.R.; Balazinski, M.; Engin, S.; Delorme, F.E. Closed door machining error compensation of complex surfaces using the cutting compliance coefficient and on-machine measurement for a milling process. *Int. J. Comput. Integr. Manuf.* **2014**, *27*, 1022–1030. [CrossRef]
23. Mo, S.; Zhang, T.; Zhu, S. Influence mechanism of multi-coupling error on the load sharing characteristics of herringbone gear planetary transmission system. *Proc. Inst. Mech. Eng. Part K J. Multi-Body Dyn.* **2019**, *233*, 792–816. [CrossRef]
24. Zhou, C.; Ning, L.; Wang, H.; Tang, L. Effects of centring error and angular misalignment on crack initiation life in herringbone gears. *Eng. Fail. Anal.* **2021**, *120*, 105082. [CrossRef]
25. Mallipeddi, D.; Norell, M.; Sosa, M.; Nyborg, L. The effect of manufacturing method and running-in load on the surface integrity of efficiency tested ground, honed and superfinished gears. *Tribol. Int.* **2019**, *131*, 277–287. [CrossRef]
26. Gao, J.; Chen, Y.P.; Deng, H.X.; Yang, Z.P.; Chen, X. In-situ Inspection Error Compensation for Machining Accuracy Improvement of Complex Components. *J. Mech. Eng.* **2013**, *49*, 133–143. [CrossRef]
27. Yang, J.H.; Zhang, D.H.; Wu, B.H. A Comprehensive Error Compensation Approach Considering Machining Process for Complex Thin-wall Parts Machining. *Acta Aeronaut. Astronaut. Sin.* **2014**, *35*, 3174–3181.
28. Zhao, C.H.; Liang, Z.P.; Zhou, H.W.; Qin, H.L. Investigation on shaping machining method for deep hole keyway based on on-line symmetry detection and compensation. *J. Mech. Sci. Technol.* **2017**, *31*, 1373–1381. [CrossRef]

Disclaimer/Publisher's Note: The statements, opinions and data contained in all publications are solely those of the individual author(s) and contributor(s) and not of MDPI and/or the editor(s). MDPI and/or the editor(s) disclaim responsibility for any injury to people or property resulting from any ideas, methods, instructions or products referred to in the content.

Article

Flexible Job Shop Scheduling Optimization for Green Manufacturing Based on Improved Multi-Objective Wolf Pack Algorithm

Jian Li [1,2,*], Huankun Li [1], Pengbo He [1], Liping Xu [1,2], Kui He [1,2] and Shanhui Liu [3]

1 School of Mechatronics Engineering, Henan University of Science and Technology, Luoyang 471000, China; lhkkk545@163.com (H.L.); hepengbo666@163.com (P.H.); xlpzz@163.com (L.X.); hekui@haust.edu.cn (K.H.)
2 Collaborative Innovation Center of Machinery Equipment Advanced Manufacturing, Luoyang 471000, China
3 Faculty of Printing, Packaging Engineering and Digital Media Technology, Xi'An University of Technology, Xi'an 710048, China; shanhuiliu@xaut.edu.cn
* Correspondence: li_jian@haust.edu.cn

Abstract: Green manufacturing has become a new production mode for the development and operation of modern and future manufacturing industries. The flexible job shop scheduling problem (FJSP), as one of the key core problems in the field of green manufacturing process planning, has become a hot topic and a difficult issue in manufacturing production research. In this paper, an improved multi-objective wolf pack algorithm (MOWPA) is proposed for solving a multi-objective flexible job shop scheduling problem with transportation constraints. Firstly, a multi-objective flexible job shop scheduling model with transportation constraints is established, which takes the maximum completion time and total energy consumption as the optimization objectives. Secondly, an improved wolf pack algorithm is proposed, which designs individual codes from two levels of process and machine. The precedence operation crossover (POX) operation is used to improve the intelligent behavior of wolves, and the optimal Pareto solution set is obtained by introducing non-dominated congestion ranking. Thirdly, the Pareto solution set is selected using the gray relational decision analysis method and analytic hierarchy process to obtain the optimal scheduling scheme. Finally, the proposed algorithm is compared with other algorithms through a variety of standard examples. The analysis results show that the improved multi-objective wolf pack algorithm is superior to other algorithms in terms of solving speed and convergence performance of the Pareto solution, which shows that the proposed algorithm has advantages when solving FJSPs.

Keywords: flexible job shop scheduling problem; multi-objective wolf pack algorithm; transportation time; maximum completion time; energy consumption

1. Introduction

The manufacturing industry is an important part of the modern economy and an important symbol with which to measure a country's comprehensive national strength. While the manufacturing industry is moving forward, a series of problems such as energy depletion, environmental pollution and global warming have become the focus of attention in the world today, and the manufacturing industry is facing the new challenge of green transformation. Green manufacturing, as a new modern manufacturing model that comprehensively considers environmental impacts and resource consumption, aims to reduce the negative impact of manufacturing on the environment and improve resource utilization. As the most basic production unit in the manufacturing industry, job shops play an irreplaceable role in the manufacturing industry. Reasonable workshop scheduling can make the conversion of products more efficient and maximize the utilization of resources, so as to reduce the cost of enterprises and improve production efficiency. As an extension of the traditional job shop scheduling problem (JSP), the FJSP is one of the core issues in the field of green manufacturing process planning. Since it was proposed, it has become a classic NP hard combinatorial optimization problem in computer science and operations research [1]. In the beginning, FJSP tended to focus on single-objective optimization for minimizing maximum completion time, economic cost, energy consumption, total delay time, and total overrun time [2–4]. With the continuous development of the manufacturing industry and the continuous optimization of product performance, focusing solely on single-objective optimization can no longer meet the development requirements of today's manufacturing industry. Therefore, the research on multi-objective flexible job shop scheduling problems (MOFJSP), which is a deeper step compared to FJSP, has become a hot topic in the industry.

For MOFJSP, many scholars have improved the traditional intelligent algorithms such as Genetic Algorithm (GA), Ant Colony Algorithm (ACO), Particle Swarm Algorithm (PSO) and Artificial Bee Colony Algorithm (ABC). For example, An et al. [5] established a multi-objective mathematical model to minimize the maximum completion time, total delay time, total production cost and total energy consumption, and proposed a hybrid multi-objective evolutionary algorithm based on the Pareto elite storage strategy to solve it. Zheng et al. [6] proposed a fruit fly collaborative multi-objective optimization algorithm to solve green scheduling with the objective of minimizing the maximum completion time and minimum total carbon emissions. Luo et al. [7] used an improved multi-objective Gray Wolf algorithm for optimization, with minimizing the maximum completion time and total energy consumption as the optimization objective. Wu et al. [8] optimized from the aspect of operations management, with minimizing the maximum completion time, energy consumption and machine switching times as the optimization objectives, and adopted an improved Non-Dominated Sorting Genetic Algorithm (NSGA-II) for optimization. Zhao et al. [9] took minimizing the maximum completion time, energy consumption and noise as the optimization objectives of the multi-objective mathematical model, and embedded the improved simulated annealing algorithm into the imperialist competition algorithm to overcome the premature convergence problem of the imperialist competition algorithm. Hasani et al. [10] introduced the NSGA-II to solve the multi-objective mathematical model aiming at production cost and energy consumption. Zhu et al. [11] designed a gray wolf algorithm with a new coding method and job priority repair mechanism for MOFJSP with priority constraints. Caldeira et al. [12] proposed a multi-objective discrete Jaya algorithm to optimize the flexible job shop, with minimizing the maximum completion time, total machine workload and key machine workload as optimization indicators. Chen Kui et al. [13] established a flexible job shop scheduling model considering transportation time, proposed a hybrid discrete particle swarm optimization algorithm for optimization, and introduced a competitive learning mechanism and random restart algorithm to avoid premature algorithms. Huang et al. [14] proposed an improved NSGA-III algorithm, which introduced the reference-based niche selection mechanism to improve the diversity of the algorithm, and was used to solve the MOFJSP with the goal of minimizing the maximum completion time, total machine load, maximum machine load and machine energy consumption. Mehdi et al. [15] used a mixed integer linear programming model to solve the green flowshop scheduling problem with the objective of minimizing the maximum completion time and total carbon emissions. Chen et al. [16] proposed an improved non-dominated sorting genetic algorithm to solve the hybrid process shop scheduling problem under time-of-use and step tariff system with the optimization objective of minimizing the maximum completion time with respect to the total shop energy consumption. Liu et al. [17] established a multi-objective mathematical model of flexible workshop with crane transportation constraints to minimize the maximum completion time and energy consumption, and optimized the model by combining a genetic algorithm with a firefly swarm optimization algorithm. However, with the deepening complexity of the mathematical model of MOFJSP, the traditional intelligent optimization algorithm often has some disadvantages in solving MOFJSP, such as slow running speed and fast algorithm convergence, and is easy to fall into local optimization in the iterative process. With the continuous updating of the new intelligent algorithm, it provides a new idea for solving the MOFJSP problem more efficiently.

The Wolf Pack Algorithm (WPA) is a pack intelligence optimization algorithm that simulates the division of labor and collaboration of wolves in nature to capture prey [18], with strong global search capability and computational robustness, and is used to solve problems such as multi-distribution center vehicle path [19], Traveling Salesman Problem (TSP) [20], and unmanned helicopter route path planning [21]. However, for workshop scheduling problems, there are still fewer WPA-related applications involved. In this paper, an improved Multi-Objective Wolf Pack Algorithm (MOWPA) is designed to solve the Multi-Objective Flexible job shop green scheduling mathematical model with the optimization objectives of minimizing the maximum completion time and minimum energy consumption, and generate the Pareto optimal solution set. The gray relational decision analysis method and Analytic Hierarchy Process (AHP) are introduced to select the Pareto solution set, and a new scheme is proposed to effectively solve the multi-objective flexible job shop problem. The contribution of this article can be summarized in three aspects: (1) In order to be more in line with actual production and processing, FJSP is extended according to the definition of FJSP, and a MOFJSP with transportation constraints is established. (2) An improved multi-objective wolf swarm algorithm is designed. The crossover and mutation operations of the genetic algorithm and pox crossover operations are introduced to improve the three intelligent behaviors of the wolf swarm algorithm. To comply with the multi-objective problem constraints, the WPA update method is designed and combined with non-dominated congestion ranking to solve the optimal Pareto solution set. (3) In order to facilitate the decision-maker to better select a scheduling scheme, this paper introduces the gray relational decision analysis method and analytic hierarchy process to calculate the Pareto solution set, and the decision-maker selects a scheduling scheme that is more consistent with the workshop processing according to the calculation results.

The framework of the rest of the paper is as follows. In Section 2, a brief description of the FJSP definition is given and a mathematical model of MOFJSP with transportation constraints is developed based on the problem definition and constraints. In Section 3, an improved multi-objective wolf pack algorithm is proposed and a detailed description of the algorithm if solving MOFJSP is given. In Section 4, simulation tests and analyses are conducted. A method for selecting the Pareto solution set is introduced in conjunction with an actual job shop. Additionally, a comparison between the MOWPA algorithm and the NSGA-II algorithm is performed to further validate the effectiveness of the proposed method. Finally, Section 5 summarizes the entire text.

2. Problem Description and Modeling

2.1. Problem Description

The FJSP problem can be described as follows: n workpieces are processed on m machines. Each workpiece has multiple processing processes, and each process can be executed on more than one machine. All processes of n workpieces are scheduled on m machines according to a specified processing sequence. The processing time and energy consumption values of the processes vary depending on the selected processing machines [22]. The following assumptions are made to establish the mathematical model:

(1) Each workpiece must be processed in the previous process before it can be processed in the next process;
(2) Each process of each workpiece can only be processed on one machine;
(3) The workpiece will not be interrupted during processing;
(4) At the same time, each machine can only process one workpiece, and each workpiece can only be processed by one machine;
(5) At the initial moment, all workpieces and machines are ready;
(6) For the first process of each workpiece, transportation time and energy consumption are not considered;

(7) The idle start time of each machine is the end time of the last process, and the idle end time is the start time of the first process;
(8) During the transportation of workpieces, problems such as transportation failures are not considered.

To establish the mathematical model for the maximum completion time and total workshop energy consumption, the following symbolic descriptions are provided, as presented in Table 1.

Table 1. Symbol descriptions.

	Symbols	Definitions
Parameters	N	Workpieces
	J	Working sequence
	M	Machines
	$O_{i,j}$	The j-th process of the i-th workpiece
	$T_{i,j,k}$	Processing time of $O_{i,j}$ on machine k
	$T_{i(j-1)jmk}$	Time for transporting N from machine tool M_m to machine tool M_k between operation $O_{i,j-1}$ and $O_{i,j}$ of workpiece N
	$U_{i,j,k}$	Integer variable, takes 0 or 1 if $O_{i,j}$ is processed on machine k, otherwise 0
	P_c^k	Machining power of machine tool k
	P_{idle}^k	Standby power of machine tool k
	$P_{i(j-1)jmk}$	Power for transporting N from machine tool M_m to machine tool M_k between operation $O_{i,j-1}$ and $O_{i,j}$ of workpiece N
Variables	$S_{i,j,k}$	Starting processing time of $O_{i,j}$ at machine k
	$F_{i,j,k}$	$O_{i,j}$ end processing time on machine k
	C_i	Completion time for workpiece i
	T_c^k	Machining time of machine tool k
	T_{idle}^k	Standby time of machine tool k
	E_k	Total energy consumption of machine tool k
	E_c^k	Machining energy consumption of machine tool k
	E_{idle}^k	Standby energy consumption of machine tool k
	E_{trans}	Total transportation energy consumption

2.2. Mathematical Model Building

Workshop energy consumption comprises machine tool energy consumption and transportation energy consumption. In Figure 1, which represents a simplified model of the input power of a machine tool during the machining process [23], the energy consumption of a single piece of equipment can be divided into four states: starting state, processing state, no-load state, and stop state. During equipment start-up and shut-down, there is a significant fluctuation in power, but the duration is short. Frequent start–stop operations can negatively impact the machine's lifespan and processing quality. Typically, a machine performs only one start–stop operation, which is not the primary factor affecting energy consumption. Hence, it is not considered in the model. Consequently, only the processing state and no-load state of a single equipment are taken into account when considering energy consumption.

The machining energy consumption is determined by the machining power and machining time of the machine tool.

$$E_c = \sum_k^m E_c^k = \sum_k^m P_c^k \times T_c^k \quad (1)$$

The no-load energy consumption is generated by the idling state of the machine tool before the workpiece is processed, and is determined by the no-load time and no-load power of the machine tool.

$$E_{idle} = \sum_k^m E_{idle}^k = \sum_k^m P_{idle}^k \times T_{idle}^k \quad (2)$$

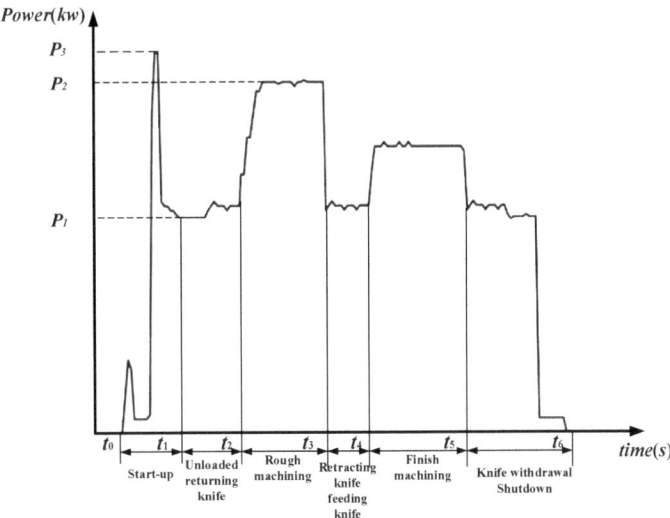

Figure 1. Energy consumption diagram of machine tool processing.

During the entire processing process, workpieces need to be transported from one machine tool to another for processing, necessitating transportation. Assuming a constant transportation power, the transportation time is determined by the distance between the two machine tools. The transportation energy consumption can be calculated as the product of the transportation power and the transportation time.

$$E_{trans} = \sum_{i=1}^{n} \sum_{j=1}^{q} T_{i(j-1)jmk} \times P_{i(j-1)jmk} \quad (3)$$

The total energy consumption of the workshop is thus obtained as:

$$E = E_c + E_{idle} + E_{trans} = \sum_{k}^{m} P_c^k \times T_c^k + \sum_{k}^{m} P_{idle}^k \times T_{idle}^k + \sum_{i=1}^{n} \sum_{j=1}^{q} T_{i(j-1)jmk} \times P_{i(j-1)jmk} \quad (4)$$

A multi-objective mathematical model is established with the maximum completion time f_1 and total energy consumption of the workshop f_2.

$$\min f_1 = C = \max_{1 \leq i \leq n} C_i$$
$$\min f_2 = E \quad (5)$$

The constraints are as follows:

$$S_{i,j} \geq F_{i,j-1} + T_{i(j-1)jmk} \quad (6)$$

$$\sum_{k=1}^{m} U_{i,j,k} = 1, i \in N \quad (7)$$

$$F_{i,k} \leq S_{i\prime,k}, i \in N, i\prime \in N, k \in M \quad (8)$$

$$C_i = F_{i,q} \quad (9)$$

where Equation (6) indicates that the start time of the process of the workpiece is greater than the end time of the previous process plus the transportation time of the workpiece operation; Equation (7) indicates that each process can only be processed on one machine;

Equation (8) indicates that the machine can only start processing the next workpiece after finishing processing one workpiece; Equation (9) indicates that the processing time of the workpiece is the completion time of the last process, q is the final process of the workpiece. The specific operation is shown in Figure 2.

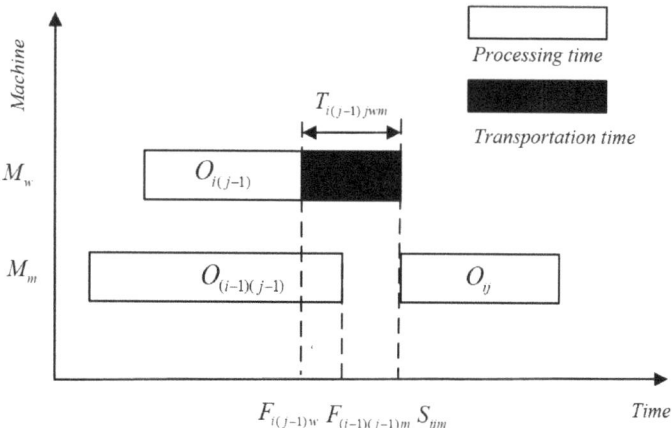

Figure 2. Constraint Description Gantt Chart.

3. Improved Multi-Objective Wolf Pack Algorithm Design

The WPA is an intelligence optimization algorithm inspired by the behavior of wolves preying on their prey. The WPA algorithm abstracts three intelligent behaviors: wandering behavior, calling behavior, and siege behavior. In the algorithm, the head wolf represents the best wolf, and a wolf pack renewal method is employed to retain the best wolves and eliminate the inferior ones [24]. Originally designed for solving continuous function optimization problems, WPA has been found to suffer from the drawbacks of falling into local optima and premature convergence. To address these limitations and leverage the characteristics of the MOFJSP problem, three intelligent algorithms within WPA have been improved to expand the search range and obtain the global optimal Pareto solution set.

3.1. Encoding and Decoding

According to the discrete characteristics of the FJSP problem, a two-level coding method is adopted, that is, the encoded individual vector is composed of two parts: process sequencing vector and machine selection vector. Additionally, the code length of the process layer and the machine layer are equal, so that the process code and the machine code correspond to each other. The coding method is shown in Table 2.

Table 2. Code segment.

Process layer	1	1	2	3	3	1	2	2	3
Machine layer	1	2	2	1	2	2	2	1	3

The first row of the table represents the process order, where the number represents the name of the workpiece and the number of times it appears represents the process of the workpiece. For example, if "1" means workpiece 1, the first occurrence of "1" means the first process of workpiece 1, and the second occurrence of "1" means the second process of workpiece 1, and so on. The second row is the machine selection problem for the machining process. The machines that can be processed by each machining process correspond to a set of machines, and each number indicates the index of the location of its machine set. For example, the processing machine set for process $O_{2,1}$ is $[M_2, M_4]$ (M_2 and M_4 denote machine 2 and machine 4, respectively), and 2 means that its processing machine is the second position in the machine set, which is M_4, indicating that process $O_{2,1}$ is processed on machine 4.

3.2. Population Initialization

The quality of the initial solution directly affects the performance of the algorithm. Random initialization is a widely used method which ensures diversity in the initial population but does not guarantee the quality of the solutions. In the case of MOFJSP optimization, three rules are employed to generate the initial population: the minimization of maximum completion time method, the minimization of energy consumption value method, and the random generation method. The population size for each rule is set at 40%, 40%, and 30%, respectively, aiming to improve the quality of the initial solutions.

3.3. Non-Dominated Crowding Ranking

The non-dominated crowding ranking method is used to calculate the level of individuals, stratify them, and calculate the crowding degree between individuals at the same level. This realizes the preservation of optimal solutions and elimination of inferior solutions for wolf packs, allowing wolf packs to update the position of artificial wolves during the iteration process. The non-dominated sorting is shown in Figure 3.

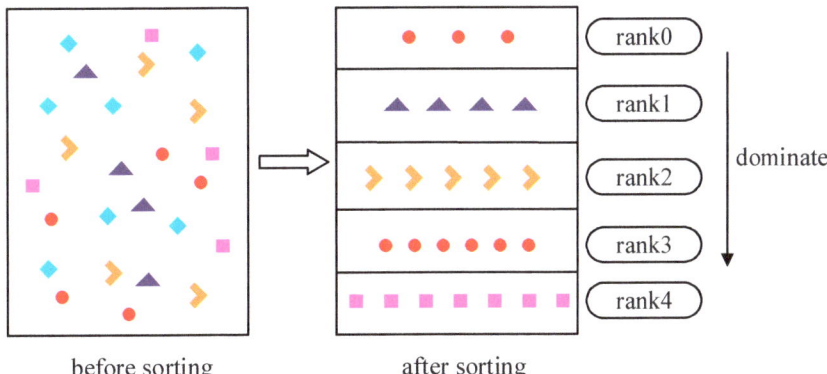

Figure 3. Non-dominated sorting.

After individual stratification, it is necessary to distinguish the individuals of the same layer. The crowding distance is used to distinguish the advantages and disadvantages among individuals. The formula for calculating the crowding distance of individuals is shown in Formula (10). The individuals with larger crowding distance are far away from other individuals. According to the crowding distance, the distribution uniformity of solution set can be judged.

$$P[i]_{dis\tan ce} = \frac{P[i+1]\bullet f_1 - P[i-1]\bullet f_1}{f_1^{\max} - f_1^{\min}} + \frac{P[i+1]\bullet f_2 - P[i-1]\bullet f_2}{f_2^{\max} - f_2^{\min}} \quad (10)$$

where $P[i]_{\text{distance}}$ denotes the crowding distance of an individual: $P[i]\bullet f_1$ and $P[i]\bullet f_2$ represent two objective function values of individual i; $f_1^{\max}$, $f_1^{\min}$ denote the maximum and minimum values of the objective function f_1, respectively; $f_2^{\max}$, $f_2^{\min}$ denote the maximum and minimum values of the objective function f_2, respectively.

3.4. Intelligent Behavior Design

For each of the three intelligent behaviors in WPA, the crossover and variation operators from the genetic algorithm are incorporated to maintain the diversity of feasible solutions and enhance the local search capability of the algorithm. Additionally, the elite retention strategy and non-dominated ranking method are employed to improve the algorithm's ability to seek promising solutions. Considering the encoding method and features of FJSP, efficient crossover and mutation operations have been specifically designed to prevent the generation of illegal solutions and ensure the validity of the solutions after applying intelligent behaviors. The wandering behavior incorporates a double-layer mutation, the summoning behavior utilizes the POX crossover [25], and the besieging behavior incorporates a mutation operator.

Wandering behavior: take the process wandering and machine wandering in two ways. For wandering walking, as shown in Figure 4, first, according to the process code, the walking step length $step_{a1}$ is defined as the number of individual position vectors for the detection wolf to walk, $step_{a1}$ process codes containing different workpieces are randomly extracted, randomly sorted, and then the sorted codes are placed in the spare position of the original process code in order.

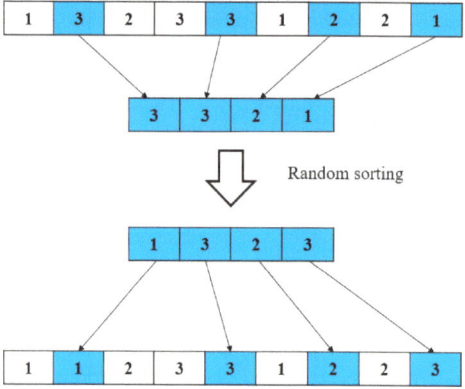

Figure 4. Process wandering behavior.

For machine code wandering operation, assuming machine wandering step $step_{a2}= 1$, the process of any one processing machine set of no less than two machines is randomly selected in its corresponding machine set, as shown in Figure 5.

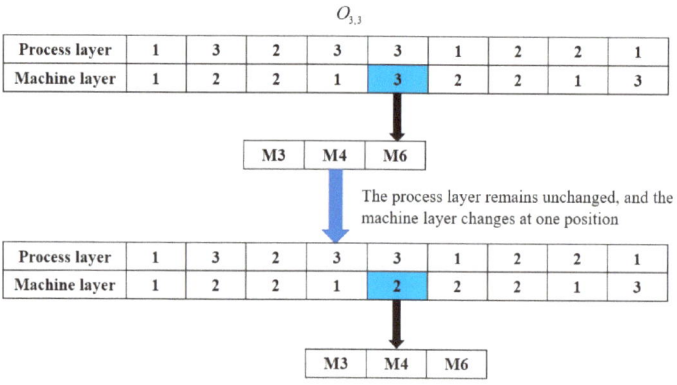

Figure 5. Machine wandering behavior.

(2) Calling behavior. The wolf pack is ranked using the non-dominated crowding degree ranking method, and one of the solution sets is randomly selected from the optimal Pareto solution set as X_{leader}. The POX crossover operation is then performed as follows: the workpiece serial numbers are randomly assigned to two non-empty and complementary sets Q_1 and Q_2, the workpiece serial numbers containing the set Q_1 are selected from the parent X_1, the position of each workpiece serial number is kept unchanged, and copied to

the child X_1'. The set Q_2 workpiece serial numbers are selected from the parent X_{leader}, and these are inserted to the vacant positions of the child X_1' in order. Similarly, the workpiece serial numbers from the parent X_{leader} containing the set Q_1 are selected, while the position of each workpiece serial number is kept unchanged, and then copied to the child X_{leader}'. The set Q_2 workpiece serial numbers from the parent X_1 are selected and inserted into the vacant positions of the child X_{leader}', in order. The POX crossover operation is shown in Figure 6.

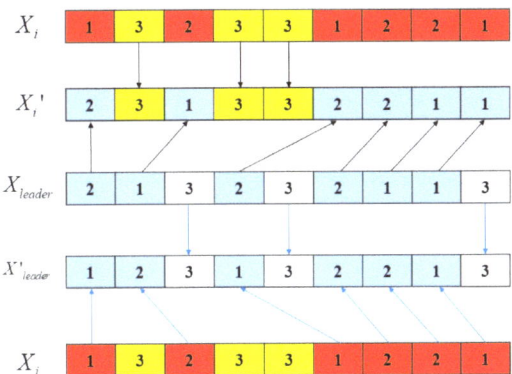

Figure 6. Schematic diagram of POX crossover operation.

The siege behavior is only for the process code, and the machine code can be transformed accordingly. Similar to the improved wandering behavior, the siege step size is set to $step_c$ and defined as an integer. For example, the process code of artificial wolf X_i is [1, 1, 2, 3, 3, 1, 2, 2, 3] and its individual code number is 9. The siege step $step_c$ will be taken as a random number of [0, 9]. Due to the large setting of the siege step size, it is easy for the value to jump out of the optimal solution range. Generally, the step size is set to be 1/3 to 1/2 of the number of individual codes.

The wolf pack update mechanism is achieved by using a non-dominated crowding sorting method after conducting a siege behavior to remove the R artificial wolves with the lowest odor concentration value (i.e., the higher objective function value) and generate R artificial wolves. Generally $R \in [M/(2 \times \beta), M/\beta]$, β is the population update proportion factor, and M is the number of artificial wolves.

3.5. Algorithm Flow

To sum up, the flow chart of the MOWPA algorithm steps is shown in Figure 7, and the details are described as follows:

Step 1: Initialize the algorithm parameters.

Step 2: Set the external file $Q = \varnothing$, calculate the objective function value of each artificial wolf in the initial population, layer the individuals through rapid non-dominated sorting, and update the external files set.

Step 3: Calculate the fitness value, select some of the better artificial wolves to perform the double walk behavior of process coding and machine coding for the detection wolves, update the location of the detection wolves and judge whether the number of walks reaches the maximum number of walks $T_{\max}$; if so, go to step 4.

Step 4: The remaining artificial wolves are selected as the fierce wolves, and the detecting wolves initiate the summoning behavior, and the POX crossover with the fierce wolves is randomly selected among the detection wolves to calculate the prey odor concentration value perceived by each artificial wolf and update the location of the fierce wolves.

Step 5: The detection wolf teams up with the fierce wolf to execute the siege behavior. In this behavior, the artificial wolf position with the best fitness value for each optimized subgoal is randomly selected as the target for the siege. After the siege behavior is completed, each artificial wolf position is updated, the optimized objective function value is calculated and recorded, and the Pareto better solution is obtained. The external profile set is then updated by sorting the individuals.

Step 6: Renewing populations according to the survival of the strongest.

Step 7: Determine whether the algorithm has reached the termination condition. If it has, output a set of optimal solutions from the Pareto optimal solution set. Otherwise, proceed to step 3.

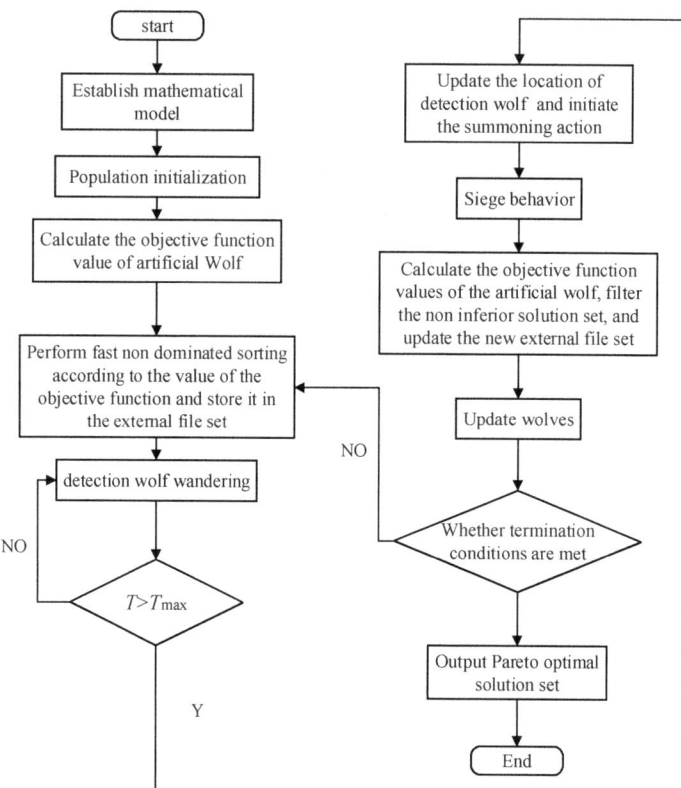

Figure 7. Flow chart of MOWPA algorithm.

4. Simulation Testing and Analysis

4.1. Test Example

In this paper, the Brandimarte example [26] is adopted as a benchmark case. However, since the model in this study incorporates energy consumption as an index, additional data need to be generated and extended accordingly. Random data within a reasonable range were generated, and the corresponding values are presented in Table 3. The table includes transportation energy consumption and transportation time, which have been standardized to a unified dimension.

Table 3. Energy Consumption for Machine Processing.

Machine Power	M_1	M_2	M_3	M_4	M_5	M_6	M_7	M_8	M_9	M_{10}
Processing power	2	1.8	1.6	2.4	2.4	4.1	3.5	4.1	2.8	2.7
standby power	0.5	0.6	0.3	0.4	0.4	0.6	0.8	0.9	0.3	0.4

The transport time of the workpiece in each machine is shown in Table 4. The data in the table express the time required for the workpiece to be transported from machine n to machine M. The transporting time was set as a random integer in the [1,5] interval. The transporting power of the transporting equipment is fixed and its value is $P_{\text{trance}} = 1.89$, which is the unit time power.

Table 4. Transportation time.

Machines	M_1	M_2	M_3	M_4	M_5	M_6	M_7	M_8	M_9	M_{10}
M_1	0	2	1	2	4	3	4	3	2	3
M_2	2	0	2	2	3	2	3	4	4	2
M_3	1	2	0	3	2	4	3	1	5	2
M_4	2	2	3	0	4	4	3	4	3	2
M_5	4	3	2	4	0	1	4	4	3	4
M_6	3	2	4	4	1	0	4	3	2	2
M_7	4	3	3	3	4	4	0	5	1	3
M_8	3	4	1	4	4	3	5	0	4	1
M_9	2	4	5	3	3	2	1	4	0	3
M_{10}	3	2	2	2	4	2	3	1	3	0

The MOWPA algorithm parameters were configured according to Table 5 using MK04 as the test data. By applying the MOWPA algorithm for optimization, the maximum completion time and workshop energy consumption values were obtained, as presented in Table 6. The table displays 11 sets of Pareto solutions generated by the MOWPA algorithm. Each set comprises the maximum completion time and the total energy consumption. The energy consumption values in each set represent the corresponding energy consumption values during the processing stages.

Table 5. Parameter of MOWPA algorithm.

Parameter Name	Numerical Value
Population number	200
Iterations	100
External archive collection size	100
Maximum number of walking	10
Procedure walking step	6
Machine Walking Steps	4
Siege steps	6
Detection wolf scale factor	0.4
Update scale factor	0.3

Table 6. Pareto solution set of MOWPA.

Serial Number	Maximum Completion Time f_1	Total Workshop Energy Consumption f_2	Energy Consumption of Each Part		
			Transportation Energy Consumption	Processing Energy Consumption	Standby Energy Consumption
1	87	1332.60	359.10	856.50	117.00
2	89	1320.76	347.76	854.60	118.40
3	90	1311.08	343.98	836.50	130.60
4	91	1300.91	357.21	836.20	130.50
5	92	1270.43	334.53	828.70	107.20
6	93	1267.99	342.09	826.80	99.10
7	94	1259.91	338.31	824.60	97.00
8	95	1242.32	336.42	805.10	100.80
9	100	1219.09	323.19	765.50	130.40
10	101	1210.43	320.53	763.30	126.60
11	106	1189.47	308.07	743.80	137.60

4.2. Selection of Pareto Optimal Solution Set

For multi-objective problems, there are multiple solutions in the resulting set of Pareto solutions, which makes it difficult for the decision maker to select a better scheduling solution to process the product. Therefore, in order to facilitate the decision maker to better select an optimal scheduling solution from the Pareto solution set, a combination of AHP and gray correlation decision analysis was used to select the Pareto solution set. First, the weight value of each index was obtained through the analytic hierarchy process. After obtaining the weight value of each objective, the gray correlation decision analysis method was used to obtain the optimal solution under the current weight from a group of optimal solutions. The advantage of combining AHP with gray correlation decision analysis is that it not only combines the subjectivity of the decision maker to assign weights to the goal according to the current conditions, but also quantitatively analyses the data obtained from the optimal solution to select the optimal solution.

(1) Calculate the weight value

In order to find the weight value using the hierarchical analysis method, firstly, the judgment matrix is established by the decision makers such as schedulers by comparing the importance of each index and by quantifying the judgment matrix of each index. The weights of the two indices under the maximum completion time and energy consumption are solved according to the nine-level scale method and in combination with production practice. If the order $a_{21} = 2$, then the indices f_2 (total energy consumption) are slightly more important than the indices f_1 (maximum completion time). The resulting judgment matrix and the weights of each indicator are shown in Table 7.

Table 7. Index judgement matrix and weight value.

Indicators	f_1	f_2	Weights ω
f_1	1	1/2	1/3
f_2	2	1	2/3

(2) Data normalization

The purpose of data normalization is to eliminate the difference between variables due to different dimensions and thus eliminate the influence on the results. The normalization method used here is shown in Formula (11).

$$N_{i,j} = \frac{Y_{i,j} - Y_j^{\min}}{Y_j^{\max} - Y_j^{\min}} \tag{11}$$

where $N_{i,j}$ is the matrix after $Y_{i,j}$ normalization and $Y_{i,j}$ is the raw data, representing the j-th objective function value of the group i data, and $Y_j^{\max}$ and $Y_j^{\min}$ are the maximum and minimum values of the j column of the original matrix Y respectively.

(3) Calculation of gray correlation coefficient

The gray correlation coefficient $\gamma_{i,j}$ reflects the degree of association between the j-th indicator of the i-th data set and the ideal value.

$$\gamma_{i,j} = \frac{N_j^{\min} + \rho N_j^{\max}}{N_{i,j} + \rho N_j^{\max}} \tag{12}$$

where $N_j^{\min}$ and $N_j^{\max}$ are, respectively, the minimum and maximum values in the index data group after normalization. ρ is the resolution coefficient, generally taken as 0.5.

(4) Calculation of gray correlation degree

The gray relational degree is the product of the gray relational coefficient and the corresponding weight. The weight value of each indicator has been obtained from the AHP. The calculation method of the gray relational degree is shown in Formula (13).

$$R_i = \sum_{j=1}^{m} \gamma_{i,j} w_j \tag{13}$$

By calculation, the data are shown in Equation (14). Where Y is the raw data, the first and second columns correspond to the maximum completion time and total energy consumption of the workshop, respectively. N is the normalized matrix corresponding to the original data obtained by data normalization, γ is the gray correlation coefficient matrix, ω is the weight matrix of the two objectives obtained by analytic hierarchy process, $\omega = [0.33, 0.67]$, R is the gray correlation matrix.

$$Y = \begin{bmatrix} 87 & 1332.60 \\ 89 & 1320.76 \\ 90 & 1311.08 \\ 91 & 1300.91 \\ 92 & 1370.43 \\ 93 & 1267.99 \\ 94 & 1259.91 \\ 95 & 1242.32 \\ 100 & 1219.09 \\ 101 & 1210.43 \\ 106 & 1189.47 \end{bmatrix}, N = \begin{bmatrix} 0.000 & 1.000 \\ 0.105 & 0.917 \\ 0.158 & 0.850 \\ 0.211 & 0.779 \\ 0.263 & 0.566 \\ 0.316 & 0.549 \\ 0.368 & 0.492 \\ 0.421 & 0.369 \\ 0.684 & 0.207 \\ 0.737 & 0.146 \\ 1.000 & 0.000 \end{bmatrix}, \gamma = \begin{bmatrix} 1.000 & 0.333 \\ 0.826 & 0.353 \\ 0.760 & 0.370 \\ 0.704 & 0.391 \\ 0.655 & 0.469 \\ 0.613 & 0.477 \\ 0.576 & 0.504 \\ 0.543 & 0.575 \\ 0.422 & 0.707 \\ 0.404 & 0.733 \\ 0.333 & 1.000 \end{bmatrix} \tag{14}$$

The weight matrix $\omega = [0.33, 0.67]$ and the data of Equation (14) are substituted into Equation (13) to obtain the correlation matrix R, as shown in Formula (15).

$$R = [0.556\ 0.511\ 0.500\ 0.495\ 0.531\ 0.522\ 0.528\ 0.564\ 0.612\ 0.650\ 0.778]^T \tag{15}$$

The larger the value of R, the better the effect of the corresponding solution under this weight. From the correlation matrix R, it can be seen that the 11th group of data has the largest correlation of 0.778, which corresponds to a maximum completion time of 106 and a total shop floor energy consumption of 1189.47. Therefore, the scheduling solution corresponding to the 11th group of scheduling optimization results is selected for processing, and its scheduling Gantt chart is shown in Figure 8.

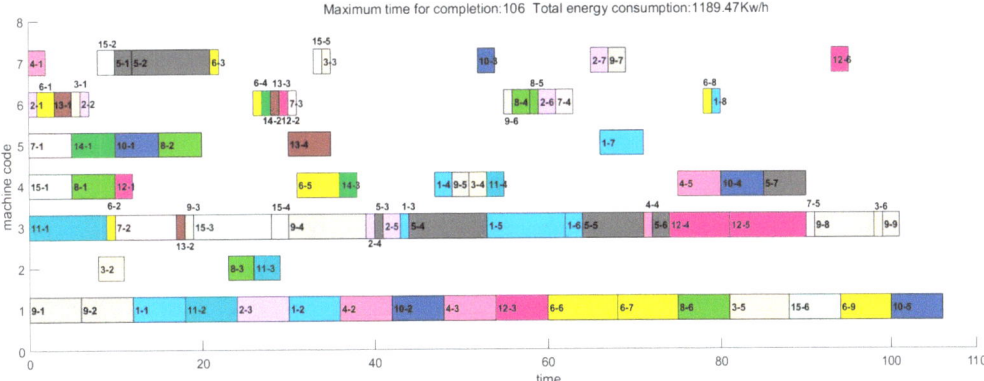

Figure 8. Optimal decision processing Gantt chart.

4.3. Algorithm Performance Evaluation

The parameter settings of the MOWPA algorithm are shown in Table 5. To verify the performance of the algorithm, this article aims to establish a multi-objective mathematical model that considers transportation time and energy consumption to minimize the maximum completion time and minimum energy consumption. MOWPA and NSGA-II are used for solving.

The Pareto optimal solution set obtained through simulation is shown in Table 8. The data format in the Pareto solution set column in the table is $(x; y)$, where x represents the maximum completion time and y represents the total energy consumption of the workshop. From the table, It is evident that the solved range distribution exhibits greater width and uniformity.

Table 8. Pareto solution set table for MOWPA algorithm and NSGA-II algorithm.

Test Data	The Set of Pareto Solutions Obtained by MOWPA	The Set of Pareto Solutions Obtained by NSGA-II
MK01	(46;525.53), (52;516.62), (58;513.43) (47;522.11), (51;518), (45;526.91) (44;530)	(49;546.97), (50;539.37), (51;532.77) (52;524.79), (58;501.11)
MK02	(37;526.91), (38;519.49), (39;514.91) (40;513.09), (41;512.51), (42;512.11) (43;511.47), (44;510.89), (45;509.49)	(38;539.11), (39;534.44), (40;530.68) (43;527.56), (44;522.98)
MK03	(208;3,452.10), (209;3,430.66) (212;3,418.42), (213;3,399.43) (215;3,384.83)	(210;3,462.53), (211;3,439.23) (214;3,410.55), (217;3,398.75) (218;3,375.26)
MK04	(87;1,332.6), (89;1,320.76), (90;1,311.08) (91;1,300.91), (92;1,270.43), (93;1,267.99) (94;1,259.91), (95;1,242.32) (100;1,219.09), (101;1,210.43) (110;1,189.47)	(89;1,357.97), (93;1,337.47), (94;1,313.83) (100;1,289.51), (102;1,276.07), (104;1,259.23) (109;1,251.44)
MK05	(180;1,632.63), (183;1,630.21) (185;1,626.91), (186;1,624.62) (189;1,623.4)	(182;1,669.95), (183;1,652.78) (184;1,644.08), (186;1,625.29)
MK06	(108;1,740.01), (109;1,719.93) (110;1,699.66), (111;1,696.25) (112;1,689.56), (113;1,688.45) (114;1,685.01), (115;1,683.09)	(108;1,799.12), (109;1,750.59) (110;1,740.88), (112;1,730.54) (113;1,720.03), (115;1,690.67)
MK07	(144;1,745.22), (145;1,738.03) (146;1,735.03), (150;1,730.65) (155;1,724.42), (160;1,720.72) (162;1,719.44)	(146;1,766.53), (147;1,754.86) (149;1,750.31), (150;1,743.33)

In order to compare the convergence performance of the two algorithms, this article uses the widely used Coverage (C) [6] and Inverted Generational Distance (IGD) [27] in multi-objective optimization problems as evaluation algorithm indicators. Their meanings and formulas are as follows.

$$C(F_1, F_2) = \frac{|\{sol_2 \in F_2 | \exists sol_1 \in F_1 : sol_1 \succ sol_2\}|}{|F_2|} \quad (16)$$

where F_1 and F_2 are the Pareto fronts by the two algorithms, respectively, and $|F_2|$ is the size of F_2. The larger $C(F_1, F_2)$ is, the better the surface F_1 is. For example, $C(F_1, F_2) = 1$ means that all solutions in F_2 are dominated by F_1, and $C(F_1, F_2) = 0$ means that there is no solution in F_1 that can dominate F_2.

$$IGD(F_1, F*) = \frac{1}{|F*|} \sum_{sol_1 \in F*} \min_{sol_2 \in F_1} d(sol_1, sol_2) \quad (17)$$

where, F^* is the non-dominated solution set of the first frontier, $|F^*|$ is the size of F^*, $d(sol_1, sol_2)$ representing the Euclidean distance between sol_1 and sol_2. The smaller the

$IGD(F_1, F^*)$, the better the F_1. In this paper, the F^* of each example is formed by averaging the non-dominated solution set obtained after each algorithm runs 20 times, respectively. The results are shown in Table 9.

Table 9. Comparison results of calculation examples.

Test Data	C (MOWPA, NSGA-II)	IGD (MOWPA)	IGD (NSGA-II)
MK01	1.00	1.2070	4.8498
MK02	1.00	1.3956	1.2903
MK03	0.60	1.1363	2.3480
MK04	1.00	3.9281	4.5960
MK05	1.00	0.5362	3.0486
MK06	1.00	3.6433	8.4704
MK07	1.00	1.5487	0.8967

Table 9 reveals that in the Brandimarte case, the solutions obtained by the MOWPA algorithm dominate the solutions obtained by the NSGA-II algorithm in the majority of cases. Only in the case of MK03 did there exist individual solutions in NSGA-II that are not dominated. However, considering the overall results, it is evident that the MOWPA algorithm outperforms the NSGA-II algorithm. This implies that the Pareto frontier generated by MOWPA is superior to that of NSGA-II. Additionally, based on the IGD index, it can be observed that the IGD value of MOWPA is consistently smaller than that of NSGA-II in most cases. This indicates that the proposed MOWPA algorithm exhibits better convergence performance compared to the NSGA-II algorithm.

Figure 9 illustrates the population iteration diagram of the maximum completion time and total energy consumption values obtained using the MOWPA algorithm and the NSGA-II algorithm with MK04 data. In Figure 9a, which displays the population iterations for the maximum completion time, the red solid and dashed lines represent the optimal and average values, respectively, obtained by the MOWPA algorithm. Similarly, the blue solid and dashed lines represent the optimal and average values, respectively, obtained by the NSGA-II algorithm. The MOWPA algorithm achieves a stable optimal maximum completion time after approximately 35 generations, while the NSGA-II algorithm achieves this after around 25 generations. Although the MOWPA algorithm has a slower convergence rate compared to the NSGA-II algorithm, it provides better solution accuracy. Figure 9b represents the population iteration diagram for total energy consumption. The red solid line and dotted line correspond to the optimal and average values, respectively, obtained by the MOWPA algorithm. Similarly, the blue solid line and dotted line represent the optimal and average values, respectively, obtained by the NSGA-II algorithm. The MOWPA algorithm maintains a stable optimal solution around 52 generations, whereas the NSGA-II algorithm exhibits more fluctuation. Overall, the MOWPA algorithm demonstrates superior speed and precision compared to the NSGA-II algorithm in terms of both maximum completion time and total energy consumption.

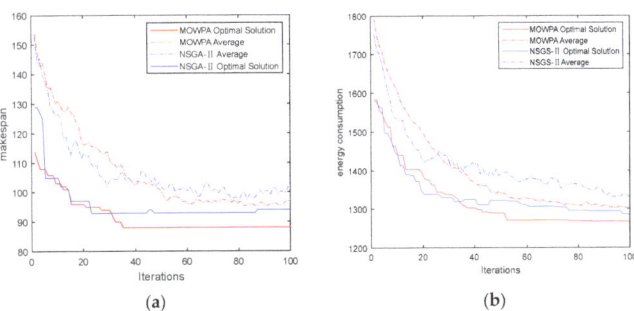

Figure 9. Iterative curves with different objectives; (**a**) Maximum completion time; (**b**) Total energy consumption.

5. Conclusions

This paper explores the multi-objective flexible job shop scheduling problem, taking into account transportation time and energy consumption. We establish a multi-objective mathematical model for a flexible job shop with transportation constraints, where the optimization objectives are maximizing the maximum completion time and minimizing total energy consumption. To address the characteristics of the MOFJSP problem, we propose an enhanced multi-objective wolf pack algorithm as a solution approach. The improvements include designing a coding scheme, introducing a mixed initialization strategy, incorporating crossover and mutation operators, and applying a non-dominated sorting method. Moreover, we extend the traditional algorithm to solve for the optimal Pareto solution set, making it more relevant to real production scenarios. To evaluate the importance of each index, we combine the AHP with the gray relational decision analysis method. This approach allows us to compare the significance of different factors using AHP and quantify their respective weights. Subsequently, we employ gray relational analysis for decision analysis. By combining qualitative and quantitative methods, we can obtain the optimal processing scheme from the Pareto solution set under the current weight settings. This enables enterprises to select the optimal scheduling strategy from a variety of solutions. To verify the algorithm's performance, we compare the proposed algorithm with the non-dominated sorting genetic algorithm. The comparison results demonstrate the superior performance of the proposed algorithm in terms of solving performance and solution distribution. It provides a better decision-making basis for flexible job shop scheduling.

However, this method can only be applied to static flexible job shop scheduling problems. When dealing with dynamic flexible job shop scheduling problems, such as machine failures or changes in workpiece quantities, the data needs to be reprocessed and the calculation process is complicated. Therefore, in the future research, the solution method of the algorithm and the accuracy and efficiency of the algorithm will be further improved, so that it can be more in line with actual production workshop processing.

Author Contributions: Conceptualization, J.L. and H.L.; Data curation, H.L. and P.H.; Funding acquisition, J.L., L.X., K.H. and S.L.; Methodology, J.L.; Writing—original draft, J.L. and H.L.; Writing—review and editing, L.X. All authors have read and agreed to the published version of the manuscript.

Funding: This work was supported by the National Key R&D Program of China [grant number 2018YFB1701205]; and the Technology Innovation Leading Program of Shanxi Province [grant number 2020QFY03-08].

Institutional Review Board Statement: Not applicable.

Informed Consent Statement: Not applicable.

Data Availability Statement: Not applicable.

Conflicts of Interest: The authors declare no conflict of interest.

References

1. Garey, M.R.; Sethi, J.R. The complexity of flow shop and job shop scheduling. *Math. Oper. Res.* **1976**, *1*, 117–129. [CrossRef]
2. Shen, L.; Dauzère, P.; Stéphane; Neufeld, J.S. Solving the flexible job shop scheduling problem with sequence-dependent setup times. *Eur. J. Oper. Res.* **2018**, *265*, 503–516. [CrossRef]
3. Homayouni, S.M.; Fontes, D.; Gonalves, J.F. A multistart biased random key genetic algorithm for the flexible job shop scheduling problem with transportation. *Int. Trans. Oper. Res.* **2020**, *30*, 688–716. [CrossRef]
4. Peng, K.; Pan, Q.K.; Gao, L.; Li, X.; Das, S.; Zhang, B. A multi-start variable neighbourhood descent algorithm for hybrid flow shop rescheduling. *Swarm Evol. Comput.* **2019**, *45*, 92–112. [CrossRef]
5. An, Y.; Chen, X.; Zhang, J.; Li, Y. A hybrid multi-objective evolutionary algorithm to integrate optimization of the production scheduling and imperfect cutting tool maintenance considering total energy consumption. *J. Clean. Prod.* **2020**, *268*, 121540. [CrossRef]
6. Zheng, X.; Wang, L. A Collaborative Multiobjective Fruit Fly Optimization Algorithm for the Resource Constrained Unrelated Parallel Machine Green Scheduling Problem. *IEEE Trans. Syst. Man Cybern. Syst.* **2018**, *48*, 790–800. [CrossRef]
7. Luo, S.; Zhang, L.; Fan, Y. Energy-efficient scheduling for multi-objective flexible job shops with variable processing speeds by grey wolf optimization. *J. Clean. Prod.* **2019**, *234*, 1365–1384. [CrossRef]

8. Wu, X.; Sun, Y. A Green Scheduling Algorithm for Flexible Job Shop with Energy-Saving Measures. *J. Clean. Prod.* **2018**, *172 Pt 3*, 3249–3264. [CrossRef]
9. Peng, Z.; Zhang, H.; Tang, H.; Feng, Y.; Yin, W. Research on flexible job-shop scheduling problem in green sustainable manufacturing based on learning effect. *J. Intell. Manuf.* **2022**, *33*, 1725–1746. [CrossRef]
10. Hasani, A.; Hosseini, S. A bi-objective flexible flow shop scheduling problem with machine-dependent processing stages: Trade-off between production costs and energy consumption. *Appl. Math. Comput.* **2020**, *386*, 125533. [CrossRef]
11. Zhu, Z.; Zhou, X. An efficient evolutionary grey wolf optimizer for multi-objective flexible job shop scheduling problem with hierarchical job precedence constraints. *Comput. Ind. Eng.* **2020**, *140*, 106280. [CrossRef]
12. Caldeira, R.H.; Gnanavelbabu, A. A Pareto based discrete Jaya algorithm for multi-objective flexible job shop scheduling problem. *Expert Syst. Appl.* **2021**, *170*, 114567. [CrossRef]
13. Kui, C.; Li, B. Research on FJSP based on improved particle swarm optimization algorithm considering transportation time. *J. Syst. Simul.* **2021**, *4*, 845–853.
14. Xiabao, H.; Shuling, W. High dimensional multi-objective flexible job shop scheduling considering low carbon. *J. Wuhan Univ. Technol. Inf. Manag. Eng. Ed.* **2019**, *41*, 592–598.
15. Foumani, M.; Smith-miles, K. The impact of various carbon reduction policies on green flowshop scheduling. *Appl. Energy* **2019**, *249*, 300–315. [CrossRef]
16. Chen, W.; Wang, J.; Yu, G.; Hu, Y. Energy-Efficient Hybrid Flow-Shop Scheduling under Time-of-Use and Ladder Electricity Tariffs. *Appl. Sci.* **2022**, *12*, 6456. [CrossRef]
17. Liu, Z.; Guo, S.; Wang, L. Integrated green scheduling optimization of flexible job shop and crane transportation considering comprehensive energy consumption. *J. Clean. Prod.* **2019**, *211*, 765–786. [CrossRef]
18. Chen, X.; Cheng, F.; Liu, C.; Cheng, L.; Mao, Y. An improved Wolf pack algorithm for optimization problems: Design and evaluation. *PLoS ONE* **2021**, *16*, e0254239. [CrossRef]
19. Yong, Y.; Huizhen, Z. Wolf swarm algorithm for vehicle routing problem with multiple distribution centers. *Comput. Appl. Res.* **2017**, *34*, 2590–2593.
20. Shan, G.; Meng, L. Greedy stochastic adaptive gray wolf optimization algorithm for solving TSP problems. *Mod. Electron. Technol.* **2019**, *42*, 50–54.
21. Liwen, W.; Shuyi, S.; Qingxian, W.; Zengliang, H. Unmanned Helicopter Trajectory Planning Based on Improved Wolf Pack Algorithm. Systems Engineering and Electronics Technology 2023.07.22. Available online: http://kns.cnki.net/kcms/detail/11.2422.TN.20221228.1122.005.htm (accessed on 17 June 2023).
22. Shikui, Z. Two-Level Neighborhood Search Hybrid Algorithm for Flexible Workshop Scheduling Problem. *J. Mech. Eng.* **2015**, *51*, 175–184.
23. Jinliang, S.; Fei, L.; Dijian, X.; Guorong, C. Energy-saving Decision-making Model and Practical Method of CNC Machine Tool in No-load Operation. *China Mach. Eng.* **2009**, *20*, 1344–1346.
24. Husheng, W.; Fengming, Z.; Lushan, W. A new swarm intelligence algorithm—The wolf swarm algorithm. *Syst. Eng. Electron. Technol.* **2013**, *35*, 2430–2438.
25. Chaoyong, Z.; Yunqing, R.; Xiangjun, L.; Peigen, L. A Genetic Algorithm Based on POX Intersection for Solving Jobs Shop Scheduling Problem. *China Mech. Eng.* **2004**, *23*, 83–87.
26. Brandimarte, P. Routing and scheduling in a flexible job shop by tabu search. *Ann. Oper. Res.* **1993**, *41*, 157–183. [CrossRef]
27. Czyzzak, P.; Jaszkiewicz, A. Pareto simulated annealing—A metaheuristic technique for multiple-objective combinatorial optimization. *J. Multi-Criteria Decis. Anal.* **1998**, *7*, 34–47. [CrossRef]

Disclaimer/Publisher's Note: The statements, opinions and data contained in all publications are solely those of the individual author(s) and contributor(s) and not of MDPI and/or the editor(s). MDPI and/or the editor(s) disclaim responsibility for any injury to people or property resulting from any ideas, methods, instructions or products referred to in the content.

Article

Research on Visualization Technology of Production Process for Mechanical Manufacturing Workshop

Li Li [1,2], Zhaoyun Wu [2,*] and Liping Lu [1]

1 School of Automobile and Transportation, Henan Polytechnic, Zhengzhou 450046, China
2 School of Mechanical & Electrical Engineering, Henan University of Technology, Zhengzhou 450001, China
* Correspondence: wuzhaoyun@haut.edu.cn

Abstract: The visualization of workshop information can affect production management and efficiency. Information can be presented both graphically and non-graphically (for example, in the form of data lists or tables). Graphical representations are intuitive and clear, but currently, most of them are based on statistical data, which makes it difficult to convey logical linkages between information and cannot help managers make decisions effectively. With the aim of designing the workshop production system with visual processes in small-sized enterprises, the key visualization technologies of the process flow chart, including the visual design of process flow chart, process card management, process flow chart release, process control, and production schedule monitoring, were all addressed in detail. On this basis, the mechanical manufacturing workshop production management system was created using C#.NET as the programming language. The main contribution of the research is that the system designed used the process flow chart as the main line through all functional modules and integrated all process data on the process nodes of the process flow chart to realize the graphical monitoring of workshop production schedule. The visualization technology of the process flow chart makes the system simple to use and easy to understand, which significantly improves information management and work efficiency in the workshop. Additionally, it provides the technical foundation for flow-driven production information transfer in the workshop and can serve as a universal standard for the process module in workshop production management systems.

Keywords: workshop production management; process flow visualization; process flow chart model; production schedule control

Citation: Li, L.; Wu, Z.; Lu, L. Research on Visualization Technology of Production Process for Mechanical Manufacturing Workshop. *Appl. Sci.* **2023**, *13*, 9754. https://doi.org/10.3390/app13179754

Academic Editor: Wei Li

Received: 31 July 2023
Revised: 21 August 2023
Accepted: 26 August 2023
Published: 29 August 2023

Copyright: © 2023 by the authors. Licensee MDPI, Basel, Switzerland. This article is an open access article distributed under the terms and conditions of the Creative Commons Attribution (CC BY) license (https:// creativecommons.org/licenses/by/ 4.0/).

1. Introduction

The informatization management of workshop production has historically been a somewhat weak link in the development of manufacturing informatization [1]. In order to improve the level of workshop information management and aid in promoting overall enterprise competitiveness, various workshop production management systems and MES were developed to address the issue of poor information connection between equipment automation systems and ERP, PDM, and other systems.

Currently, there are many related commercial software available on the market, such as SAP S/4HANA Manufacturing, Beas Manufacturing for SAP Business One, MS Dynamics 365, and many Chinese commercial software with independent copyright (such as Yonyou (Beijing, China), Kingdee (Shenzhen, China), etc.). One of the leading developers of business process management software, SAP, helps companies of all sizes and industries achieve comprehensive enterprise resource management. Now, SAP S/4HANA can process large amounts of data using advanced technologies such as artificial intelligence and machine learning, and its integrated applications can connect all parts of a business into an intelligent suite on a fully digital platform. However, the cost is prohibitive and unsuitable for small- and medium-sized businesses. Beas Manufacturing for SAP Business One is particularly suitable for small- and medium-enterprise manufacturing. It combines the core functions of ERP and the digital core platform of MES and allows users to easily manage and monitor all processes and costs in the manufacturing process. MS Dynamics 365 integrates the functions and processes of CRM and ERP and can be integrated with more Microsoft services to achieve continuous intelligent evolution.

Although the commercial system is very mature and comprehensive, for some small-sized businesses, (1) its corporate structure may not be complete and comprehensive, so an ERP system may not be suitable for small-sized businesses. (2) Small-sized businesses tend to concentrate on producing some particular types of products that are very similar to each other, and their production processes are similar; thus, the requirements for the system are not too complex but can quickly complete the production planning of products. (3) Small-sized businesses must respond quickly to market changes with their products in order to remain competitive; for example, if client order requirements change, the new product must be able to be promptly produced and delivered on schedule. Order-based, small-batch production is not well suited for the standard ERP system, which is frequently created for large-scale items. (4) Small businesses must undergo information and digital transformation in order to keep up with the informatization of enterprise. However, due to financial limitations, small-sized businesses are more concerned with the information and digital transformation of their core industries: the production sector.

The Jiangsu and Zhejiang regions of China have many small enterprises, and they are active in the market economy. In this study, a workshop production management system based on product process was created for a machinery manufacturing company in Ningbo, China. There are over 70 different product types divided into five different categories and specifications in the company. Regardless of the size of the business, in the process of workshop production management, there are a lot of business processes in the various departments of workshop and production processes. The overall business processes between the various departments in the workshop are shown in Figure 1. They are as follows:

(1) The workshop director receives orders;
(2) The workshop director sends out production plan to the craftsman;
(3) The craftsman compiles the production process flow;
(4) The workshop director assigns the production tasks to the team leaders and the quality supervisor;
(5) The team leader assigns the production tasks to the workers;
(6) The quality supervisor assigns the quality inspection (QI) tasks to the quality inspectors;
(7) The worker carries out production tasks in accordance with the production process flow;
(8) The quality inspector inspects the work quality of the workers;
(9) The product is completed and stored.

Process flow, which serves as the vital link between product design and manufacturing, is crucial to the entire manufacturing procedure and has a significant impact on both product quality and manufacturing costs. The actual process flow is usually more complex, as shown in Figure 2. Processes may interact with one another serially or in parallel. There is a strict constraint that the previous procedure must be finished before the subsequent process can be carried out. Traditionally, the production is organized by the workshop after the craftsman manually completes the process flow and process card in accordance with the part drawings. There will be a lot of technical data created during this time, and the management of this technical information depends on how well the relevant managers can remember it and the professional level of the relevant managers.

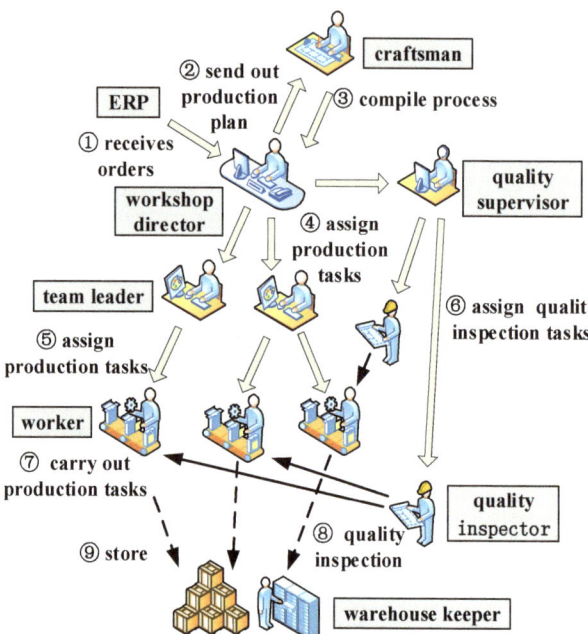

Figure 1. The overall business process in workshop.

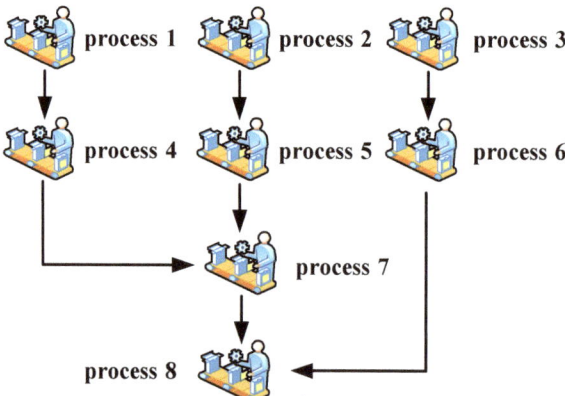

Figure 2. Process flow in workshop.

In addition to process data, a variety of additional production data are also produced in the workshop, including equipment information data, materials data, personnel information, product information, etc. The interaction and presentation of these data may have an impact on how the workshop is managed in real time and how decision makers arrive at their conclusions. The Internet of Things is currently being used by numerous researchers to improve data collection on workshop equipment. Because the data used in workshop production are complicated, it makes sense to present the data visually so that workshop staff may make better use of the information and increase production efficiency. Although domestic and foreign scholars have engaged in extensive research and practice in workshop information management and computer-aided process planning (CAPP) and solved a series of problems such as production scheduling, data collection, process monitoring, logistics scheduling, etc., most workshop production management systems still present complex production processes as data lists or tables lacking an intuitive and visual graphical display. As a result, the overall structure of the process flow and the connections between different process nodes cannot be vividly displayed, which negatively impacts the user experience. Some systems are visual, but their primary focus is not process flow but rather the display of statistical data such as equipment statistics. As a result, the logical linkages between the data are obscured and should be better used to assist managers in making decisions.

The visualization technology of the mechanical manufacturing workshop production process flow was carefully examined in order to find a solution to this issue. The workshop production process flow chart model and the process flow chart storage scheme were proposed, and then, the mechanical manufacturing workshop production management system was developed. The system has the following functions: visual design of process flow charts, process card management, production process control, and production progress monitoring based on process flow charts. The production process management has become more intuitive and visible with the help of the graphical display of production process flows, which significantly improves the readability of key information and greatly improves the friendliness of the system interface. Users can easily and quickly observe the relationships between different process nodes in the process flow, which makes it easier for decision makers to make production decisions.

The remainder of this paper is organized as follows. We review related research in Section 2; then, we present the production process flow chart model in Section 3. In Section 4, we detail key technologies of visualization of production process flow chart. Finally, we provide our conclusions in Section 5.

2. Literature Review

The use of workshop production management can keep resource availability stable and industrial sustainability unaltered, improve workshop production efficiency and information management level, and make production organization more orderly so that the process runs more smoothly, and production cost decreases [2–5]. Approaches to procedure optimization have received increased attention [6]. Several techniques, including lean manufacturing, smart manufacturing, value stream mapping, total productive maintenance, the Internet of Things, fuzzy logic, and artificial intelligence, are now applied in various sectors for process improvement [7]. Lean manufacturing was defined by Womack in the 1990s [8]. Lean manufacturing increases the effectiveness of the operations management system in the workshop, which aids company employees in achieving operational excellence [9]. Under the background of Industry 4.0, multiple strategies are frequently used to improve production management. Lean and smart manufacturing were integrated in a hybrid way by Tripathi et al. [9] to enhance operational excellence in workshop.

The primary production management tool that creates a communication channel between the enterprise planning layer and the workshop control/automation layer is a MES system. The idea of a Manufacturing Execution System (MES) was developed in the mid-1990s [10]. In order to implement real-time management in the workshop, from order reception through finished items, the MES integrates basic production plans with real-time data on operations, materials, and processes from the equipment, controls, and workers in the workshop [11]. The primary functions of the MES include data collection and abstraction, precise operation scheduling, resource allocation and control, production task allocation to people and machines, product quality control, and equipment and tool maintenance [12]. Artificial intelligence (AI) with MES [13], digital twin (DT) [14], and augmented reality (AR) [15] are the three main research frontiers in MES.

Research on CAPP has also been extensively conducted by academics. Neibel [16] first proposed the concept of process plans with computers in 1965, and the first CAPP system was created in 1976 [17]. Since then, CAPP has been the subject of extensive investigation. There are numerous technologies used for CAPP, including agent-based technology, internet-based technology, feature-based technology, knowledge-based system, artificial neural networks, genetic algorithms, ant algorithm, fuzzy theory, and other intelligent algorithms [18]. With the development of optimization algorithms, there will be more effective CAPP technologies. The holistic component manufacturing process planning model based on the integrated approach integrating technological and business considerations was described by Denkena et al. [19]. Borojevic et al. [20] established the platform for integrated CAD/CAPP part design based on the basic machining features and the intelligent setup planning and operation sequencing using the genetic algorithm. Malleswari et al. [21] presented the automated machining feature recognition method by employing the STEP file. For the purpose of determining the machining process sequencing and machine assignment, Deja et al. [22] developed the extended feature taxonomy that corresponds to the requirements of the rational process plan selection for the targeted category of part types.

The informatization of production workshops has been applied in various industries. Ji et al. [23] put forward the digital management technologies and their application in casting enterprises. Wu et al. [24] introduced the production management system used in the furniture industry. With the development of internet technology, some workshop management systems have achieved network transmission of workshop production information based on internet technology, wireless network technology, etc. Luo et al. [25] designed the workshop production management system based on android platform and realized the real-time monitoring and management of workshop status. The web-based workshop production management system was created by Liu et al. [26], with a particular emphasis on the design of the process planning module. Bi [27] developed the wireless terminal-based workshop production information system and completed the mobile internet application of workshop management. Some commercial software such as SAP S/4HANA Manufacturing and MS Dynamics 365 have been able to achieve cloud storage. Under the development requirements of Industry 4.0, it is possible to accomplish intelligent control of workshop equipment by using IoT technology to gather equipment information. Sruthi and Kavitha [28] surveyed various IoT platforms such as Xively, ThingWorx, Thing Square, Sensor Cloud, etc. Zhang [29] discussed the human–computer data gathering system based on RFID that offered a database for tracking and monitoring production. Heidarpour et al. [30] used the data logger device to obtain the data from hydraulic hammers to remote monitoring and adjust process planning. Using OPC technology for data transfer, Wei et al. [31] designed a visual monitoring system that performs tasks like visual production process monitoring and resource management for production lines. Lu et al. [32] used Microsoft's visualization tool PBI as the core of development to handle the production data imported from the existing Excel tables in small- and medium-sized businesses, which presented a visual and explicit interface to realize real-time monitoring and management of production lines. Rosales et al. [33] visualized factory data through augmented reality and mixed-reality-based smart devices. On the main design line of production management system, Zhang et al. [34] developed the production management system with workshop planning and scheduling monitoring as the core. Wu et al. [24] introduced the production management system used in the furniture industry based on customized products. Nicole Oertwig et al. [35] proposed the user-centric process management system for digital transformation in small- and medium-sized businesses in Germany.

Even though there have been several studies on workshop production, most production management systems do not adequately support the production processes, which leads to poor process visualization and information flow between processes. The use of CAPP technology for process optimization is the main focus of research on workshop processes. In this study, the visual technology of the process flow chart was utilized to visualize the information of production processes that small-sized businesses are concerned about and realize the graphical process design and release. Finally, in this way, the production process control based on the process flow chart and the graphical monitoring of the workshop production schedule can be achieved.

3. The Production Process Flow Chart Model

3.1. The Description of Production Process Flow Chart Model

There are typically multiple working processes and many working steps in one working process during the manufacturing of mechanical products. Each process contains a substantial amount of process data, such as process information, step information, operation instructions, inspection standards, and so on. Each process may be serial or parallel. Since the manufacturing process flow chart for mechanical products contains not only process nodes and their relationships but also related process data, it is an amalgamation of heterogeneous as well as complicated data.

This study builds the production process flow model of mechanical products based on typical features of mechanical product manufacturing, as illustrated in Figure 3. The model is made up of two parts: process data and process flow charts, where the latter primarily consists of process nodes and connection links, and process information, step information, step descriptions, and inspection standards are the primary varieties of process data. Their details are as follows:

(1) Process nodes contain process number, process name, coordinate positions, background image, and font setting;
(2) Connection relationships include previous process, follow-up process, arrow pointing, style, line width, and straight/broken line type;
(3) Process information is made up of process ID, process number, process name, product ID, part name, processing equipment, processing material, assigned team, warehousing options, downstream process number, and remarks;
(4) Step information contains step ID, process ID, step number, step content, specific content, piece rate unit price, and reference time;
(5) Step description includes ID, process ID, resource type, resource document, and notes;
(6) Inspection standard is made up of ID, process ID, inspection sequence number, inspection standard, inspection mode, input type, and inspection frequency;
(7) Product information contains product ID, product name, product model, product number, version number, creation time, process flow chart file, and status;
(8) Bad history record includes ID, process ID, resource type, resource document, and notes.

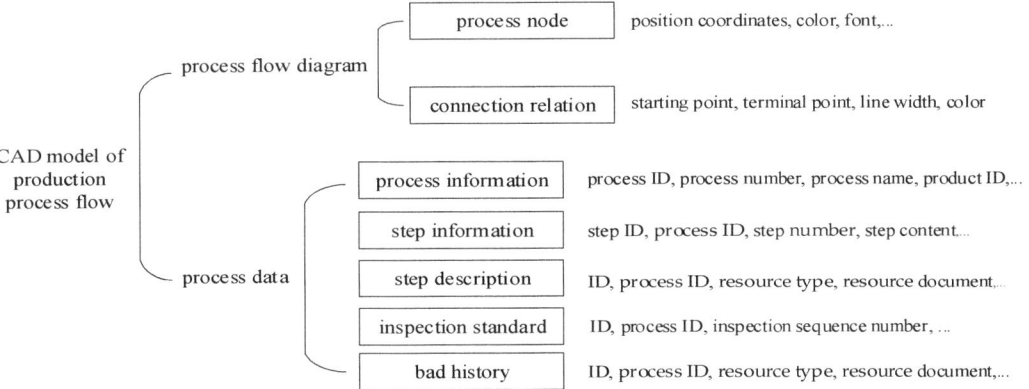

Figure 3. CAD model of production process flow.

3.2. The Storage of Production Process Flow Chart Model

The process flow chart and process data in the CAD model cannot be stored together simply in the workshop production management system due to the high operation response requirements of the process flow chart and the size of the information contained in the process data. This work employs the following strategy to address this issue, as illustrated in Figure 4.

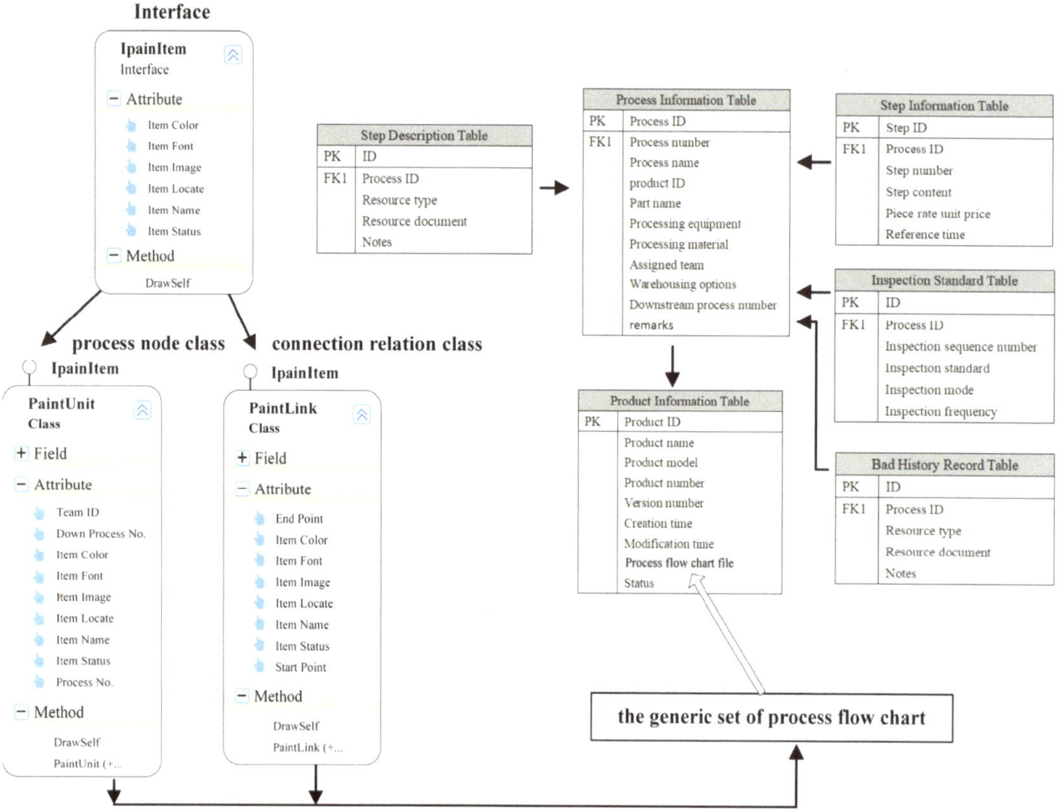

Figure 4. Storage program of CAD model of production process flow.

First, an IPaintItem interface is defined based on the object-oriented design concept in C#.NET [36]. This interface has the attributes of item color, item font, item locate, item name, item status, and DrawSelf method. Next, the PaintUnit class (operation node class) and PaintLink class (connection relation class) are defined, both of which implement the IPaintItem interface. Finally, the process flow diagram can then be expressed in the form of a generic collection list <IPaintItem> and stored by serialization. The product information table, process information table, step information table, step description table, inspection standard table, and bad history record table are built in the relational database SQL Server. The generic set of process flow charts after being serialized is stored in the field of process flow chart file in the product information table. There is a one-to-many mapping between the product information table and the process information table, which are connected by the field of product ID. The process information table also has a one-to-many mapping relationship with the step information table, the step description table, the inspection standard table, and the bad history record table, which are all related by the field of process ID.

Based on the aforementioned process flow chart model storage scheme, the process information flow from product to process flow chart to process to process-related information can be separately saved, associated, and read by accessing the database in the workshop production management system.

4. The Key Technologies of Visualization of Production Process Flow Chart

The mechanical manufacturing workshop production management system was created using SQL Server as the database, VS2019 as the development environment, and C#.NET as the programming language. Figure 5 illustrates the basic interface. The system has a C/S architecture. For data access, a SQL Server database was set up on the server side. The workshop production management system is utilized by the client to carry out the various operations for the production process and associated process data. The system, which is simple to use and has an easy-to-understand interface image, uses the process flow chart as the main line through several functional modules. The process flow diagram is taken as the core thread and the underlying core data of the system. The system's various functional modules, such as process modeling, process card preparation, process control, and production progress monitoring, are all data-driven and displayed through the process flow diagram.

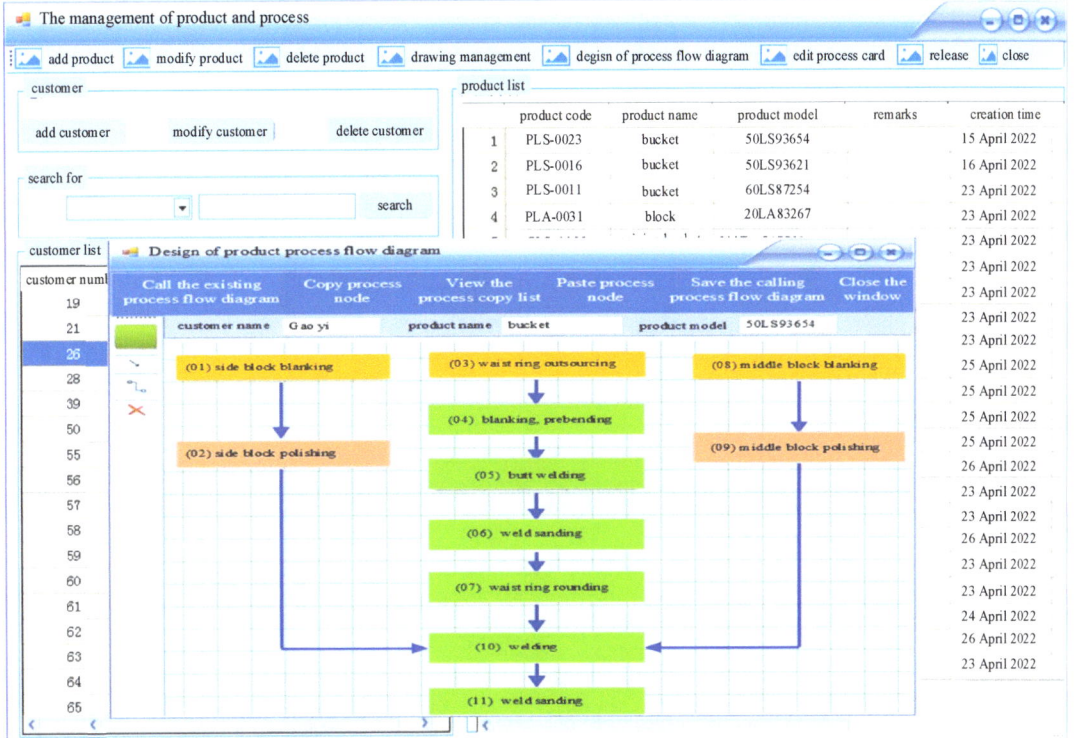

Figure 5. System interface.

4.1. Visual Design of Process Flow Chart

The essential component of the workshop production management system is the visual design of process flow charts, and its interface is shown in Figure 6. At the top of the interface, one can read and present flow charts from databases, copy/paste the process nodes, view the process copy list, save the process flow charts, and close the window. The function menu on the left side of the interface from top to bottom contains the following: drawing process nodes, drawing process lines (straight and broken lines), and delete objects.

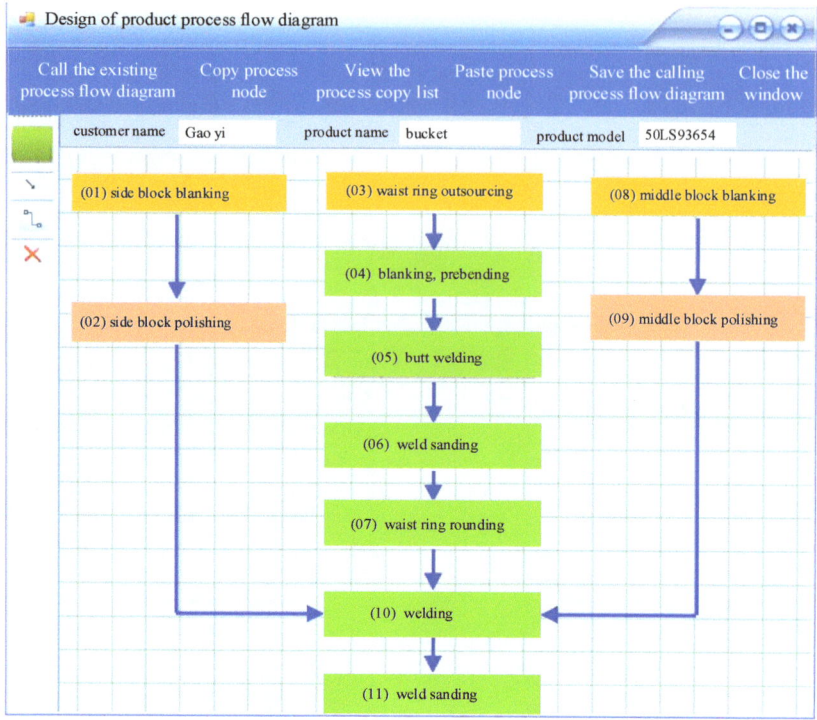

Figure 6. Flow diagram design module.

A product process flow diagram can be created in one of three ways:
(1) Draw completely by hand. Each process node is dragged and dropped individually; then, they are progressively connected in a straight or broken line based on serial and parallel relationships to create a process flow diagram;
(2) Copy or paste some of the current process nodes. One can open the current flow chart, select the process nodes one wants to copy, and then paste them into the desired flow chart if a few of the process nodes in the process flow diagram match those in the existing flow chart. The remaining part is drawn by hand. This technique significantly improves the drawing efficiency;
(3) Alter an existing process flow diagram directly. One can call an existing flow chart and edit it if the process flow chart one wants to create is comparable to one already in existence. This approach can effectively reuse the original process flow chart, which will considerably increase work productivity.

The following is the exact method by which this module function is implemented:
(1) Go through the flow chart. When entering the module interface, one can read the field content of process flow chart file in the product information table through the data access layer and then use the binary serializer to deserialize the data before obtaining the object set of List <IPaintItem>, which includes all of the process nodes and connecting line segments in the flow chart. After that, one traverses the set and calls the DrawSelf method on each object to draw all of them in the form interface;
(2) Draw process nodes. Users can add a process simply by dragging and dropping the process icon from the left toolbar to the appropriate position in the form interface. This function is mainly realized through the DragDrop event of the form. When the user releases the mouse, the node object at the cursor position is established and added to the process flow chart set;

(3) Set up the process basic information. The MouseDoubleClick event triggers a dialog box when the user double-clicks the process node, allowing the user to enter details such as the process number, the process name, and the assigned team. After setting, the process node can display the process number, process name, and associated colors in accordance with the various allocated teams;

(4) Draw connecting line segments between process nodes. The connection relationship is established by drawing a connecting line between process nodes. According to the actual needs, there are two types of connecting lines: straight line and broken line;

(5) Move the process node. The operation node be moved. Users can drag the process node to reposition it when editing the process flow chart. The link between process nodes will automatically and instantly change as the user moves;

(6) Delete the object. The system will determine which object the user has chosen by comparing the click coordinates with the coordinate range of each object. When the delete function is chosen, the specified object is deleted by invoking the Remove method of the set;

(7) Copy/paste process nodes. The ability to copy and paste process nodes is especially useful for process flow chart that contains some same or similar process nodes, which can aid technicians in quickly and effectively drawing the necessary process flow. The realization method is as follows: Initially, the user opens the process flow chart of similar products, selects the process nodes to be copied, and then adds them to the copying list one by one. Next, the user opens the target process flow chart and uses the paste feature to draw the process nodes in the copy list into the flow chart one by one, and at the same time, the associated process data will be automatically copied;

(8) Save the process flow chart. The user verifies the integrity of the flow chart before storing it. The user is asked to complete the process's basic information if it is not already filled out. The flow chart's List <IPaintItem> object set is binary serialized and stored in the database's product information table if the integrity check is successful.

The visual design module of the process flow chart fulfills all functions and can successfully draw, edit, and save the product process flow based on the design of the technical scheme mentioned above. After drawing the process flow chart in the production management system of the workshop, the input and management of all kinds of information for each process can be completed on the flow chart, including the following: craftsman inputs process card information, workshop director setts time limit, team leader assigns operators, etc.

4.2. Process Card Management

Typically, a craftsman will create a process card specifically based on the product's structure and technical specifications. This process card is then issued to the workshop personnel as a technical instruction document. A product corresponds to a complete process flow, which usually includes multiple processes. Each process corresponds to a process card, which includes multiple steps. Due to the high volume of product orders, each process and its steps may correspond to multiple operators.

In the production management system, the machining process card is no longer the traditional paper card but a rich-media form of data integration carrier. The information of each process card can be compiled once the flow chart has been built by the craftsman. The specific procedure is to double-click any process node on the flow chart in order to open the process card interface and navigate to the process card management module. After logging into the process card management module, the user can enter the fundamental details of the process, the step list, the contents of the corresponding description for each step (video, pictures, notes, etc.), the inspection standards of each step, and the bad history of the process. The main interface of this module is shown in Figure 7.

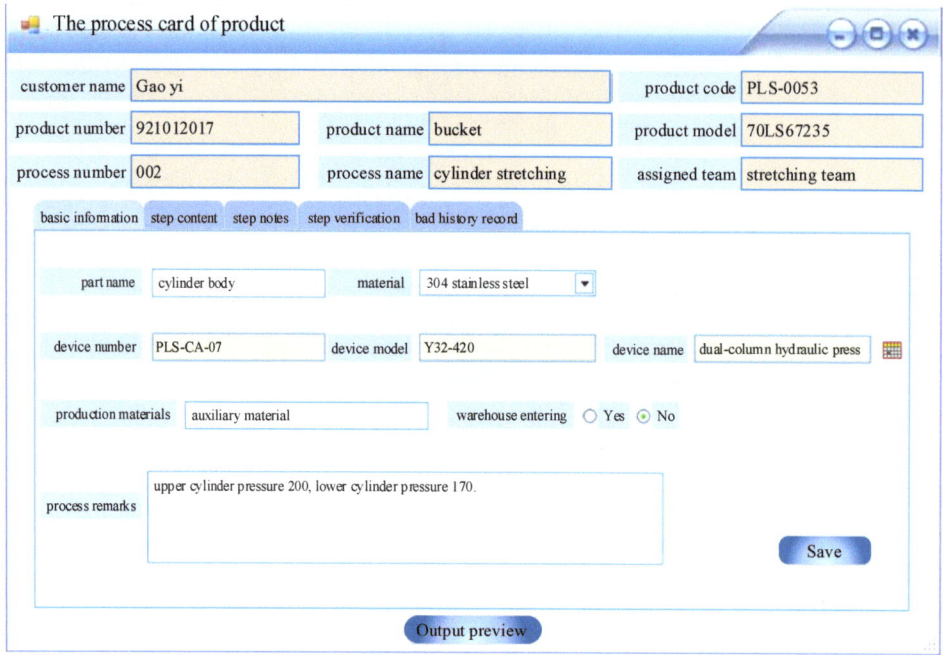

Figure 7. Process card module.

The RDLC report from C#.NET is a powerful, highly adaptable report technology. After designing the interface layout and the data field arrangement for the process card using the RDLC report and binding the data source, the process card in the PDF, Word, Excel, and other document formats can be quickly created.

4.3. Process Flow Chart Release

Products can enter the process release module for official release if they have been compiled with process flow and related information. Process completeness inspection and process version number compilation are two of the module's features. Among them, process completeness inspection is a crucial link that can verify the accuracy and integrity of process data for items that have been released. In Figure 8, the inspection procedure is displayed.

The detailed inspection flow is as follows:

Step 1: Read the process flow diagram;
Step 2: Start to traverse all process nodes in the process flow chart, and let $i = 1$;
Step 3: Start to check the ith process node;
Step 4: For the process node, inspect its fundamental details, its step list, the bad history, the contents of the corresponding description, and the inspection standards of each step sequentially;
Step 5: Have all process nodes been checked? If so, print the check list, as the list describes whether there is some information missed and reminds the user of the lack details; otherwise, let $i = i + 1$, and jump to step 3 for the subsequent node.

After the product process flow is released, the production procedure that uses the process flow will produce a duplicate of the version of the process flow to operate independently. In this way, the production procedure that carries out the initial version of the product process flow can continue to operate after the process flow is adjusted, and a new version is released.

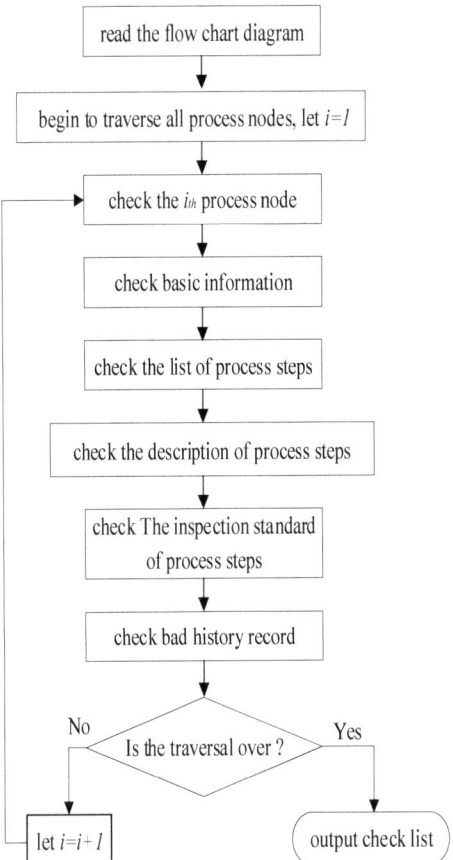

Figure 8. The inspection procedure of process completeness.

4.4. Process Control Based on Process Flow Chart

The operator in the workshop must adhere to the defined process flow to carry out the production in a timely manner, and this process control function can be accomplished with the use of a process flow chart.

In the process flow chart, each process node has three attributes: its own process number, its downstream process number, and its status (not started, in progress, or finished). For process P_i, the process cannot be executed until no previous process or all previous processes have been completed.

The following steps are used to determine if a process with previous processes may be carried out, as shown in Figure 9:

Step 1: Define the execution identity $Flag$, and let $Flag = false$;
Step 2: Start to traverse all the objects in the process flow chart, and let $i = 0$;
Step 3: Find the ith flow chart object $Item(i)$; $Item(i)$ is the process node or connecting line segment in the flow chart;
Step 4: Determine if $Item(i)$ is a process node, and if it is not, let $i = i + 1$, and jump to step 3; otherwise, proceed to step 5;
Step 5: Are the states of the previous processes satisfied? If yes, let $i = i + 1$, and jump to step 3; otherwise, let $Flag = false$, and end the traversal;
Step 6: Is the execution identity $Flag$ false? If it is, the process is allowed; otherwise, it is forbidden.

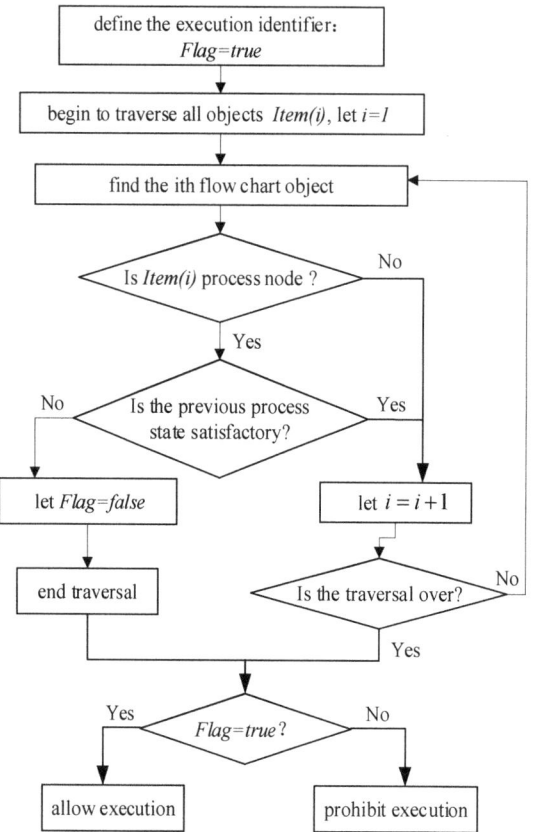

Figure 9. The flow chart for judging process execution status.

4.5. Production Schedule Monitoring Based on Process Flow Chart

The process flow chart can be used to show the execution statuses of the processes in addition to conveying the logical relationships of the process flow, enabling effective monitoring of the production schedule in the workshop. There are three execution statuses of a process: not started, in progress, and finished. Each process node in the flow chart has a different display effect set according to the process's various states. Table 1 lists the rules for setting the display effect of process nodes.

Table 1. The display effect of process nodes.

Execution Status	Display Effect
Not started	Colored background (except gray) (different colors correspond to different teams)
In progress	Flickering background
Finished	Gray background

The implementation procedures of this function are as follows:

Step 1: Traverse each object in the flow chart;

Step 2: Add the process node to the executing node set *PList* if its execution state is in progress; the background will be changed to gray if the process has finished; if the process is not started, leave things alone;

Step 3: Start *Timer* after the traversal is complete, and set the interval to 1 s. In the trigger event, the background image of each node in the set *PList* is alternatively changed to create the flicker effect.

The workshop production schedule monitoring interface is shown in Figure 10.

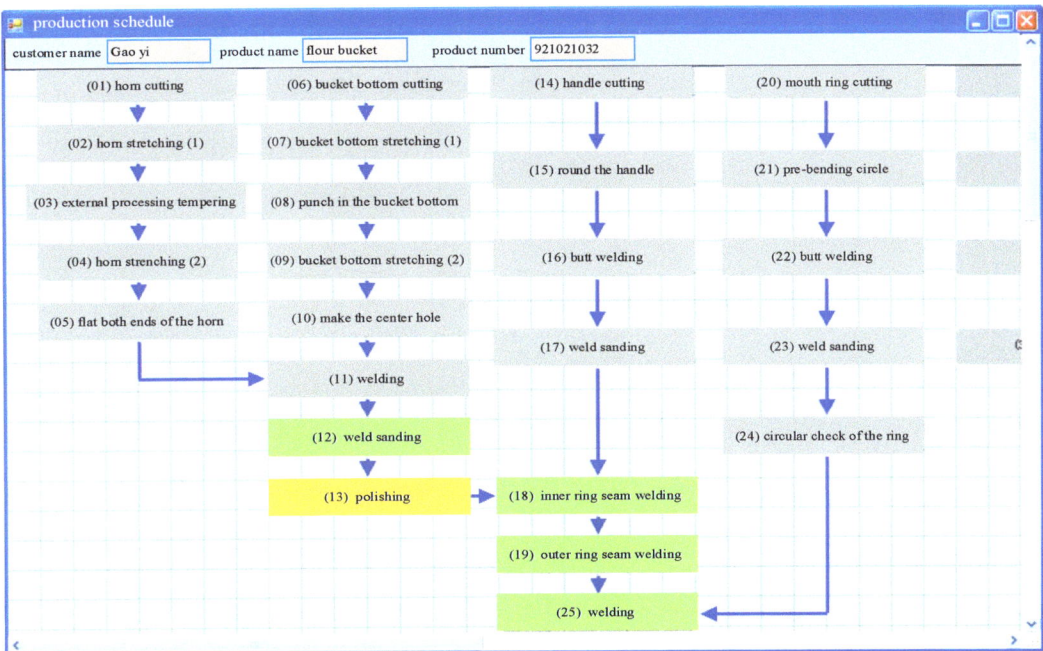

Figure 10. The workshop production schedule monitoring interface.

5. Conclusions

(1) After investigating the visualization technology of the process flow chart in light of the characteristics of the manufacturing process for mechanical products in small-sized businesses, the model of the production process flow chart containing process data and process flow charts was constructed. The database-based process flow chart storage scheme is thus proposed;

(2) The mechanical manufacturing workshop production management system was created using SQL Server as the database, VS2019 as the development environment, and C#.NET as the programming language. The various operations for the production process and associated process data were realized in the system;

(3) The graphical process design, process card data management, and process flow chart release were all finished by the system software created in the study. The judgment method of the process execution status was used to realize the process flow chart process control, and the process execution status display mechanism was applied to visualize the workshop production schedule;

(4) Through the use of the process flow chart visualization technology, the overall structure of the production process and the connection between processes can be graphically displayed, and the system effectively raises the level of information management and work efficiency in the workshop. It also provides the technical foundation for flow-driven production information transfer in the workshop and can serve as a universal standard for the process module in workshop production management systems;

(5) The system developed in the research implements the main functions of workshop production management in small-sized enterprises, but it also has its limitations. First, it is suitable for products with similar production processes. For example, it is currently employed in the machinery manufacturing company in Ningbo, China, which mainly produces various complex structural sheet-metal goods. In terms of product processes, stamping, drawing, welding, polishing, etc., are mostly used. In this way, the process flow chart and corresponding production management of new products can be quickly established by copying and modifying those of the existing products. Second, the system primarily implements production management in small enterprise workshops and lacks other management functions, such as finance and sales. Future research will focus on expanding existing functions or integrating new functions with the enterprise's functional systems. Finally, the system lacks research and application of relevant intelligent methods in the process of production organization, such as the allocation of team members for each process, the intelligent scheduling of workshop production resources, and so on. In the future, we will strengthen the research on intelligent optimization issues related to workshop production management and solve problems such as production task allocation and workshop resource scheduling to further enhance the intelligence level of the workshop production management system.

Author Contributions: Conceptualization, L.L. (Li Li) and L.L. (Liping Lu); methodology, Z.W.; software, L.L. (Li Li) and Z.W.; validation, L.L. (Liping Lu); writing—original draft, L.L. (Li Li); writing—review and editing, L.L. (Li Li) and L.L. (Liping Lu). All authors have read and agreed to the published version of the manuscript.

Funding: This work was supported by the National Natural Science Foundation of China (No. 12072106) and the Science and Technology Project of Henan Province in China (No. 222102220002; 232102221007; 222103810085).

Institutional Review Board Statement: Not applicable.

Informed Consent Statement: Not applicable.

Data Availability Statement: The data presented in this study are available on request from the corresponding author.

Conflicts of Interest: The authors declare no conflict of interest.

References

1. Seeger, P.M.; Yahouni, Z.; Alpan, G. Literature review on using data mining in production planning and scheduling within the context of cyber physical systems. *J. Ind. Inf. Integr.* **2022**, *28*, 100371. [CrossRef]
2. Ramadan, M.; Salah, B.; Othman, M.; Ayubali, A.A. Industry 4.0-based real-time scheduling and dispatching in lean manufacturing systems. *Sustainability* **2020**, *12*, 2272. [CrossRef]
3. Colledani, M.; Tolio, T.; Fischer, A.; Iung, B.; Lanza, G.; Schmitt, R.; Váncza, J. Design and management of manufacturing systems for production quality. *CIRP Ann. Manuf. Technol.* **2014**, *63*, 773–796. [CrossRef]
4. Schuh, G.; Potente, T.; Hauptvogel, A. Methodology for the evaluation of forecast reliability of production planning systems. *Procedia CIRP* **2014**, *17*, 469–474. [CrossRef]
5. İlhami, M.O.; Yaman, B.; Guerrini, G. Designing workshop management system supporting decision making with OODB. *Procedia Technol.* **2012**, *1*, 19–23.
6. Tripathi, V.; Saraswat, S.; Gautam, G.D. A study on implementation of various approaches for shop floor management. *Lect. Notes Electr. Eng.* **2021**, *766*, 371–387.
7. Chang, K.H.; Chiu, A.S.F.; Tan, K.H. Related theories and practical applications of soft computing in the manufacturing process of industry 4.0 2021. *Math. Probl. Eng.* **2022**, *2022*, 9802892. [CrossRef]
8. Womack, J.; Jones, D.; Roos, D. The machine that changed the world: The story of lean production. In *Toyota's Secret Weapon in the Global Car Wars that Is Now Revolutionizing World Industry*; Free Press: New York, NY, USA, 1990.
9. Tripathi, V.; Chattopadhyaya, S.; Mukhopadhyay, A.K.; Sharma, S.; Li, C.; Singh, S.; Hussan, W.U.; Salah, B.; Saleem, W.; Mohamed, A. A sustainable productive method for enhancing operational excellence in shop floor management for industry 4.0 using hybrid integration of lean and smart manufacturing: An ingenious case study. *Sustainability* **2022**, *14*, 7452. [CrossRef]
10. Chen, X.; Voigt, T. Implementation of the manufacturing execution system in the food and beverage industry. *J. Food Eng.* **2020**, *278*, 109932278. [CrossRef]

11. Shojaeinasab, A.; Charter, T.; Jalayer, M.; Khadivi, M.; Ogunfowora, O.; Raiyani, N.; Yaghoubi, M.; Najjaran, H. Intelligent manufacturing execution systems: A systematic review. *J. Manuf. Syst.* **2022**, *6*, 503–522. [CrossRef]
12. Wang, L.; Gao, R.; Váncza, J.; Krüger, J.; Wang, X.V.; Makris, S.; Chryssolouris, G. Symbiotic human-robot collaborative assembly. *CIRP Ann.-Manuf. Technol.* **2019**, *68*, 701–726. [CrossRef]
13. Mumali, F. Artificial neural network-based decision support systems in manufacturing processes: A systematic literature review. *Comput. Ind. Eng.* **2022**, *165*, 107964. [CrossRef]
14. Kritzinger, W.; Karner, M.; Traar, G.; Henjes, J.; Sihn, W. Digital Twin in manufacturing: A categorical literature review and classification. *IFAC-PapersOnline* **2018**, *51*, 1016–1022. [CrossRef]
15. Blaga, A.; Militaru, C.; Mezei, A.D.; Tamas, L. Augmented reality integration into MES for connected workers. *Robot. Comput.-Integr. Manuf.* **2021**, *68*, 102057. [CrossRef]
16. Niebel, B.W. Mechanized process selection for planning new designs. In *ASME 33rd Annual Meeting Collected Papers*; No. 737; ASME: New York NY, USA, 1965; Volume 65.
17. Cay, F.; Chassapis, C. An IT view on perspectives of computer aided process planning research. *Comput. Ind.* **1997**, *34*, 307–337. [CrossRef]
18. Xu, X.; Wang, L.; Newman, S.T. Computer-aided process planning-A critical review of recent developments and future trends. *Int. J. Comput. Integr. Manuf.* **2011**, *24*, 1–31. [CrossRef]
19. Denkena, B.; Shpitalni, M.; Kowalski, P.; Molcho, G.; Zipori, Y. Knowledge Management in Process Planning. *CIRP Ann. Manuf. Technol.* **2007**, *56*, 175–180. [CrossRef]
20. Borojevic, S.; Matic, D.; Dragic, M. An integrated intelligent CAD/CAPP platform: Part II-Operation sequencing based on genetic algorithm. *Teh. Vjesn.* **2022**, *29*, 1686–1695.
21. Malleswari, V.N.; Pragvamsa, P.G. Automatic machining feature recognition from STEP files. *Int. J. Comput. Intergr. Manuf.* **2023**, *36*, 863–880. [CrossRef]
22. Deja, M.; Siemiatkowski, M.S. Machining process sequencing and machine assignment in generative feature-based CAPP for mill-turn parts. *J. Manuf. Syst.* **2018**, *48*, 49–62. [CrossRef]
23. Ji, X.; Ye, H.; Zhou, J.; Deng, W.L. Digital management technology and its application to investment casting enterprises. *China Foundry* **2016**, *13*, 301–309. [CrossRef]
24. Wu, Z.; Zong, F.; Cao, P.; Wang, J.; Zhu, Z.; Guo, X.; Cao, P. Investigation of the customized furniture industry's production management systems. *J. Eng. Res.* **2023**, *in press*. [CrossRef]
25. Luo, Q.; Yu, D.; Hu, Y. Design and implementation of workshop management system based on android mobile terminal. *Modul. Mach. Tool Autom. Manuf. Tech.* **2015**, *10*, 157–160.
26. Liu, J.; Li, Y.; Shi, Y. Workshop production management system based on craft made in manufacture. *Manuf. Autom.* **2011**, *33*, 16–18, 36.
27. Bi, Y. Design of manufacture management system based on wireless terminal. *Mach. Build. Autom.* **2014**, *43*, 128–131.
28. Sruthi, M.; Kavitha, B. A survey on IoT platform. *J. Sci. Res. Mod. Educ.* **2016**, *1*, 468–473.
29. Zhang, L. Research and application of the manufacturing information collection. *Mach. Des. Manuf. Eng.* **2014**, *43*, 40–42.
30. Heidarpour, F.; Ciccolella, A.; Uva, A.E. *Design and Development of an IoT Enabled Device for Remote Monitoring of Hydraulic Hammers*; Springer: Cham, Switzerland, 2023; pp. 390–398.
31. Wei, D.; Wang, H.; Liu, L. Visual monitoring system for small and medium-sized automatic production lines. *China Mech. Eng.* **2020**, *31*, 1351–1359.
32. Lu, L.; Chang, C.; Tung, C.; Lu, C.Y.; Su, T.J.; Lee, L.W. Application of digital visualization in traditional manufacturing transformation. *Sens. Mater.* **2023**, *35*, 2139–2148. [CrossRef]
33. Rosales, J.; Deshpande, S.; Anand, S. IIoT based augmented reality for factory data collection and visualization. *Procedia Manuf.* **2021**, *53*, 618–627. [CrossRef]
34. Zhang, H.; Liang, J.; Li, G. The development and application of production management system based on job shop scheduling and monitoring. *Mach. Des. Manuf.* **2010**, *11*, 239–241.
35. Oertwig, N.; Gering, P.; Knothe, I.T.; Rimmelspacher, S.O. User-centric process management system for digital transformation of production. *Procedia Manuf.* **2019**, *33*, 446–453. [CrossRef]
36. Li, L.; Wu, Z.; Wu, L. Research on information processing technology of title bar for AUTOCAD/ERP integration. *Appl. Mech. Mater.* **2013**, *423*, 2716–2719. [CrossRef]

Disclaimer/Publisher's Note: The statements, opinions and data contained in all publications are solely those of the individual author(s) and contributor(s) and not of MDPI and/or the editor(s). MDPI and/or the editor(s) disclaim responsibility for any injury to people or property resulting from any ideas, methods, instructions or products referred to in the content.

Article

Optimization of Pin Type Single Screw Mixer for Fabrication of Functionally Graded Materials

Shijie Wang [1], Jing Zhou [2] and Guolin Duan [1,*]

[1] School of Mechanical Engineering, Hebei University of Technology, Tianjin 300401, China; leonhebut@163.com
[2] School of Mechanical Engineering, Tianjin University of Science and Technology, Tianjin 300457, China
* Correspondence: glduan@hebut.edu.cn; Tel.: +86-135-0213-0628

Abstract: The direct ink writing (DIW) process, used for creating components with functionally graded materials, holds significant promise for advancement in various advanced fields. However, challenges persist in achieving complex gradient variations in small-sized parts. In this study, we have developed a customized pin shape for an active screw mixer using a combination of quadratic B-Spline, the response surface method, and global optimization. This tailored pin design was implemented in a two-material extrusion-based printing system. The primary objective is to facilitate the transformation of material components with shorter transition distances, overcoming size constraints and enhancing both printing flexibility and resolution. Moreover, we characterized the transition delay time for material component changes and the mixing uniformity of the extruded material by constructing a finite element simulation model based on computational fluid dynamics. Additionally, we employed a particle tracking method to obtain the Lyapunov exponent and Poincaré map of the mixing process. We employed these metrics to represent and compare the degree of chaotic mixing and dispersive mixing ability with two other structurally similar mixers. It was found that the optimized pin-type mixer can reduce the transition delay distance by approximately 30% compared to similar structures. Finally, comparative experiments were carried out to verify the printing performance of the optimized pin-type active mixer and the accuracy of the finite element model.

Keywords: direct ink writing; functionally graded materials; transition delay distance; chaotic mixing; pin type active mixer

1. Introduction

The landscape of industrial applications has evolved to become more diverse and demanding, presenting challenges for the effectiveness of single-material parts in complex scenarios [1,2]. Therefore, a novel type of composite material, termed functionally graded materials (FGMs), which comprise two or more materials, has emerged and is drawing significant academic interest. FGMs are characterized by their material compositions varying spatially through customized gradients, leading to exceptionally satisfactory histocompatibility. This strategic composition mitigates the issue of abrupt interfaces between materials, thus enabling the full exploitation of the inherent potential of each material [3–5]. Specifically, ceramic-based FGMs, when integrated with flexibility-oriented additive manufacturing processes, are becoming increasingly crucial in a variety of critical fields, including military [6–8], bioengineering [9–12], energy [13,14], and aerospace [15–18].

During the last two decades, the field of additive manufacturing (AM) technology has made significant advancements. Layer-based AM processes for the preparation of FGM parts primarily emphasize flexibility and customization. This approach enables the incorporation of both geometric gradients and varying material compositions. For most ceramic-based FGMs, the raw material exists primarily in a liquid phase. Direct ink writing (DIW), as a distinctive form of Directed Energy Deposition (DED), proves to be

Citation: Wang, S.; Zhou, J.; Duan, G. Optimization of Pin Type Single Screw Mixer for Fabrication of Functionally Graded Materials. *Appl. Sci.* **2024**, *14*, 1308.
https://doi.org/10.3390/app14031308

Academic Editor: Arkadiusz Gola

Received: 15 January 2024
Revised: 1 February 2024
Accepted: 3 February 2024
Published: 5 February 2024

Copyright: © 2024 by the authors. Licensee MDPI, Basel, Switzerland. This article is an open access article distributed under the terms and conditions of the Creative Commons Attribution (CC BY) license (https://creativecommons.org/licenses/by/4.0/).

a potent method for preparing liquid-phase FGMs [19]. In addition, DIW demonstrates high applicability across a wide range of liquid-phase materials and offers economic efficiency. Therefore, DIW has been widely adopted in the field of ceramic-based FGM manufacturing [20–22].

The workflow of DIW involves raw material preparation, real-time mixing, and extrusion of mixed materials. Among these steps, rapidly achieving uniform mixing of multi-pastes is crucial when producing composite materials with gradients. Ceramic pastes possess highly viscous properties, which makes mixing challenging. The mixing of highly viscous fluids primarily occurs in a laminar flow in the mixing mechanism, which significantly impedes mixing efficiency. Simultaneously, in the context of the continuous extrusion DIW process, the time required for various proportions of multi-materials to achieve homogeneous mixing in the mixing chamber results in a delay in the transition of printed material composites. This directly impacts the printing resolution [23]. Therefore, it is imperative to optimize the efficiency of the mixing process, minimize the transition delay distance, and enhance print resolution to achieve intricate gradient variations in compact components. It is worth noting that some researchers have successfully prepared ceramic-based FGM parts using static mixers [24,25] or dynamic mixers [26]. Additionally, Computational Fluid Dynamics (CFD) methods have been employed to analyze the fluid dynamics in the mixing chamber. Despite the increased control demands associated with active mixers, they demonstrate superior mixing capabilities in comparison to static mixers. This results in enhanced print resolution and a more streamlined printing system.

The screw mixer represents an active mixing mechanism known for its exceptional back-mixing and transportation capabilities. It has found widespread utilization in multi-material mixing and extrusion processes due to its simple design and low-maintenance advantages [27,28]. A typical screw serves to prolong the material's residence time in the mixing chamber through back-mixing, thereby enhancing the homogeneity of mixed multi-materials. Nevertheless, when preparing FGMs using the DIW process and needing to change material components to improve print resolution while ensuring homogeneous mixing, it becomes crucial to reduce the required mixing time. Therefore, standard screw mixers are unsuitable for processing FGM parts.

Chaotic mixing proves to be the most effective method for enhancing the mixing efficiency of high-viscosity fluids [29]. The emergence of chaotic mixing effects enhances the radial mixing capacity of the screw while reducing axial mixing along the extrusion direction, facilitating the swift completion of material composite transformation [30–32]. Uncomplicated screw mixers excel in axial mixing abilities but are insufficient in generating chaotic mixing effects, which are essential in FGM preparation. In response to this constraint, some researchers have employed more complex differential twin-screw or tri-screw structures to induce chaotic mixing and thereby enhance mixing efficiency [33–39]. Nevertheless, the resulting complexity in the mixing mechanism poses challenges in the accurate control of printed material components and leads to increased assembly requirements and an unwieldy printing system [40]. In an effort to induce chaotic mixing in a simple single-screw structure, Kim and Wiggins et al. developed a novel single-screw mixer with rectangular pins. The existence of chaotic mixing effects induced by this pin-type single screw was confirmed through experiments and numerical analysis [41–44]. Nonetheless, the optimal pin profiling remains an area of exploration, and there is untapped potential in both the regular rectangular pins and structural parameters of the single-screw to further enhance the chaotic mixing effect, thus improving print resolution.

The Response Surface Method (RSM) represents a valuable statistical method ideally suited to address complex multivariate issues. In this context, the Central Composite Design (CCD) approach proves highly effective in analyzing complex factor interactions, thereby facilitating the derivation of a comprehensive and efficient response function. For instance, Park utilized CFD in the framework of the RSM method to optimize screw parameters, enhancing both drying efficiency and self-cleaning capabilities [45]. Likewise, in the domain of food engineering, optimization of relevant screw parameters resulted in improved extrusion efficiency [46]. Additionally, the CCD method was utilized to construct a significant response function for fundamental screw parameters, with the primary objective of evaluating the uniformity of grass seed mixing [47]. These instances highlight the remarkable applicability of the RSM method in addressing the optimization challenges presented by multiple factors in the structural parameters of tailored screw mixers.

In response to these challenges, the primary objective of the present work is to design a specialized pin-type single-screw mixer tailored for use in DIW processes. This mixer aims to reduce the transition delay distance in material composites' transformation and enhance print resolution. Contemporary computer-based optimization design methods offer an alternative to the traditional trial-and-error approach, which heavily relies on designer experience and is time-intensive. Hence, this research employs a combination of data-driven and simulation approaches to develop an efficient pin pattern. Initially, an active mixing chamber's digital model, based on CFD in ANSYS FLUENT, is created. This model simulates the mixing time of an active online flow of FGMs. The transition time for gradient changes is assessed by monitoring the volume fraction change of the mixed fluid at the outlet of the mixing chamber, thus obtaining the gradient material's transition regularity at various ratios during the DIW process. Thereafter, the pin's shape is parametrically defined using a quadratic B-spline, and the optimal pin morphology is determined by integrating RSM with a genetic algorithm (GA), with the aim of achieving the shortest transition time. Additionally, the degree of chaotic mixing in the customized pin-type screw can be assessed in the digital model by tracking particle traces and calculating the Lyapunov exponent [48]. The final stage of this study involves experimental validation using a self-developed FGM-printing prototype equipped with dual extruders operating at different feed rates. Two pastes are extruded at distinct feed rates into the dynamic mixing chamber, where they are continuously blended by the customized pin-type screw mixer and subsequently delivered to the extrusion needle. This process is supported by a movable platform to create FGM samples. The effectiveness of the optimized pinned mixer is confirmed through digital image processing methods, demonstrating that the tailored pin-type single-screw mixer can achieve shorter transition distances in the printed samples.

2. Materials and Methods

In this section, the modeling of the mixing chamber was detailed using ANSYS FLUENT Vision 2020R2 (fluid simulation software) as the initial step. Thereafter, the volume fraction of the mixed material at the outlet and the uniformity of mixing under a specific feed rate ratio for two input materials were monitored to assess the screw mixing performance. Following this, the response function corresponding to the transition delay time was derived with the RSM in conjunction with the feasible position of the screw pin control point. Finally, to determine the optimal pin pattern, the response function was optimized through a genetic algorithm. The effectiveness of this optimized pattern was then verified by comparing the results with simulation data, with a particular focus on identifying discrepancies.

2.1. Governing Equations

In kinetic analysis, a fluid can be regarded as a continuous medium, and its motion adheres to the principles of conservation of mass, momentum, and energy. Among these principles, the conservation of energy is commonly employed for calculations in systems involving heat exchange flows. For the mixing and extrusion processes conducted at room temperature in this study, the mixing pastes were considered incompressible, and heat transfer in the mixing chamber was considered negligible. In addition, the two pastes utilized in this study are classified as non-Newtonian fluids due to their high viscosity. Thus, it was assumed that heat transfer could be disregarded under isothermal conditions, while the influence of gravity was taken into account. The flow of incompressible multicomponent viscous slurries was described using the simplified Navier–Stokes equations [49]. Finally, the continuity equation and momentum conservation equation governing fluid motion are depicted in Equations (1) and (2), respectively.

$$\nabla \cdot (\rho v) = 0 \tag{1}$$

$$\rho \frac{\partial v}{\partial t} + \rho v \cdot \nabla v = -\nabla p + \nabla \cdot \tau + G \tag{2}$$

where ρ represents the fluid density with unit of kg/m^3, v is fluid velocity. p stands for static pressure on the fluid, and t is time. τ indicates the stress tensor, and G is the gravity.

2.2. Finite Element Model

As illustrated in Figure 1a, a dual-extruder system was employed to combine varying feed volume flow rates, using a motor-driven active mixer, to realize the DIW process for printing FGM parts. The primary component in the mixing chamber, the pin-type screw mixer, plays a pivotal role in this process. It possesses specific dimensions, including a length of 60 mm, a minor screw diameter of 6 mm, a pitch of 8 mm, and a flight width of 1 mm. To ensure effective mixing, a shallow screw groove with a depth of 1 mm was incorporated [50]. The customized pin shape was derived using a quadratic B-spline curve featuring three control points. These control points were defined based on their respective coordinates in the local map shown in Figure 1a. To prevent the co-linearity of the three control points, the coordinates of the first control point were established in relation to the third control point. The ranges of these three control points are detailed in Table 1. It is crucial to emphasize that, to guarantee the uniqueness of the quadratic B-spline generated from these three control points, this research utilized an interpolator in the Unigraphics NX 12.0 software, incorporating neither slope nor curvature constraints. Therefore, the sequence of control point insertion ensured the uniqueness of the generated spline curve. The pin height was set at 1 mm, matching the screw flight height. In addition, we evenly distributed thirty pins around the screw to enhance mixing quality [51].

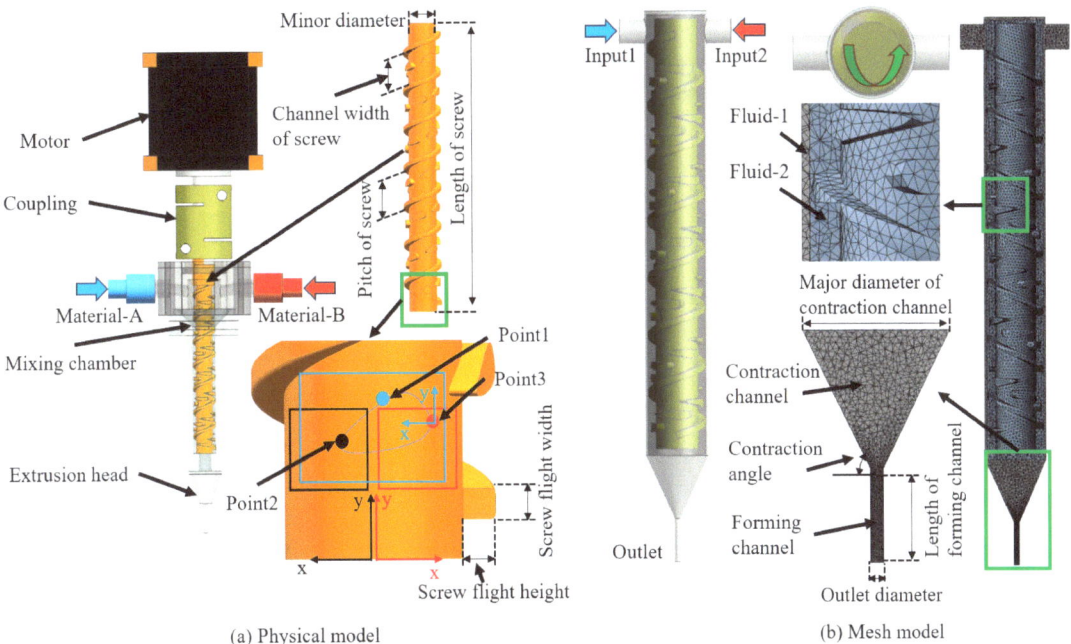

Figure 1. Illustration of: (**a**) physical model and (**b**) mesh model of mixing chamber.

Table 1. Range of coordinate values for the three control points.

	x-Axis	y-Axis
Point 1	0.5~2 mm	0.1~1 mm
Point 2	0.5~2.5 mm	3~5 mm
Point 3	0.5~2.5 mm	3~5 mm

As illustrated in Figure 1b, we depicted the numerical simulation model for the mixing component in a mixing chamber equipped with a custom pin-type single screw structure. The screw is configured to rotate clockwise, with a counterclockwise direction of operation. In addition, two parameters are defined in the model to simulate varying material ratios, while a single outlet is designated to emulate the extruded mixing fluid. Details regarding the structural parameters of the finite element model for the mixing chamber can be found in Table 2.

Table 2. Structural parameter of mixing chamber mesh model.

Name	Value [Unit]
Length of screw	60 mm
Minor diameter of screw	6 mm
Pitch of screw	8 mm
Screw flight width	1 mm
Channel width of screw	7 mm
Screw flight height	1 mm
Pin height	1 mm
Input diameter	2.5 mm
Outlet diameter	1 mm
Contraction angle	65°
Major diameter of contraction channel	9 mm
Length of forming channel	6 mm

During the meshing process, the screw mixer structure is treated as a solid medium, and the remaining portion of the mixing chamber structure is designated as a fluid domain. Notably, the flow of the medium is significantly more vigorous in this region compared to other sections of the mixing chamber, owing to the narrow gap between the chosen screw structure and the inner wall. An unstructured tetrahedral mesh tailored to the irregular spatial characteristics is employed for meshing the fluid domain of the mixing chamber to enhance the accuracy of the calculations. Specifically, the boundary layer mesh is optimized, with local densification observed at the inputs, the boundaries of the rotational domain, and the contraction channel. Finally, a mesh size of 0.2 mm is applied to the rotational domain, while the rest of the region employs a mesh size of 0.3 mm. This results in approximately 1.753 million elements and 0.372 million nodes. It should be noted that the number of elements and nodes may slightly vary due to the different pin control points defined.

2.3. Simulation Settings and Paste Properties

To obtain a definitive solution for the flow field, it is necessary to establish the initial boundary conditions in the simulation domain. When preparing FGM parts with extrusion technology, a pressure-based solver was chosen to analyze the low-velocity, incompressible flow field. The boundary conditions were set separately for the velocity inlet and pressure outlet. The combined feed rate for the two inputs was held constant at 0.5 mm/s. Therefore, the total volumetric flow rate could be determined by calculating the cross-sectional area of the inlet, resulting in a value of 2.4 mm³/s. To simulate the rotating flow field in the mixing zone of the pin-type screw, the transient simulation employed the Rotating Reference Frame (RRF) method. This involved designating Fluid-1 and Fluid-2 (as depicted in Figure 1b) as static and dynamically rotational domains, respectively, with both domains being connected through an interface. In addition, the screw wall was assigned a no-slip boundary condition and was configured as a moving wall to simulate the adjustable operating speed of the screw, ranging from 10 to 50 rpm.

In this research, we employed two readily available types of calcium carbonate-based toothpaste, designated as Material A (white color) and Material B (green color), with similar non-Newtonian rheological properties to simulate the mixing extrusion process. The densities of Materials A and B were determined to be 1120 kg/m³ and 1285 kg/m³, respectively, using the specific gravity method. Both pastes exhibit shear-thinning rheological characteristics. Therefore, the study employed the power-law function, as shown in Equation (3), which is a commonly utilized tool in non-Newtonian fluid modeling, to describe their rheological properties. The rheological parameters for both pastes were assessed using a rotational rheometer (MCR 302, Anton Paar, Graz, Austria) at room temperature. The test results are depicted in Figure 2, and the corresponding rheological parameters were derived through the power-law function, as presented in Table 3. Finally, in the confines of a narrow mixing channel, in conjunction with the aforementioned pin-type screw speed, the viscous behavior of the mixing paste was characterized as laminar flow.

$$\tau = K(\dot{y})^n \tag{3}$$

where is the shear stress with unit of pa, K represents the flow index with a unit of pa·s^n, and n symbolizes the dimensionless flow behavior index, which is less than 1 for shear thinning paste. $\dot{y}$ is the shear rate with a unit of s^{-1}.

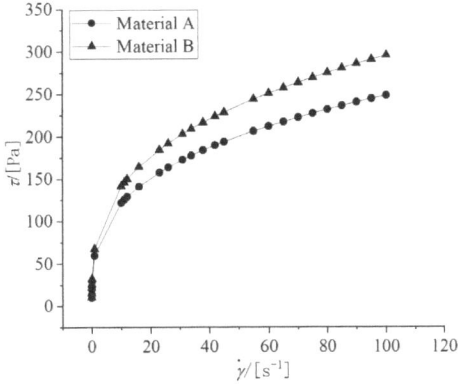

Figure 2. Rheological property curves of two pastes.

Table 3. Rheological parameters of two pastes.

	K	n
Material A	59.59	0.31
Material B	67.68	0.32

2.4. Response Surface Method and Optimization

We employed a second-order RSM design with rotational center composites to achieve significant and highly fitting and accurate statistical results with a limited number of experiments. This design aimed to establish the response function of six coordination variables concerning transition delay time. Thereafter, global optimization was conducted using a genetic algorithm in conjunction with a robust predictive model to identify the optimal pinning pattern. The optimization process is illustrated in Figure 3. Considering the feasible range of the three control points on the surface of the screw minor diameter, their variable boundaries were determined based on star points. Therefore, following the methodology of the rotatable CCD, a six-factor half-quantity experiment was conducted to calculate the normalized distance α from the design centroid to the boundary points of the design space, as described in Equation (4). Table 4 provides information on the range of coordination variable levels for the three control points.

$$\alpha = (2^{F-1})^{\frac{1}{4}} \quad (4)$$

where F is the number of factors.

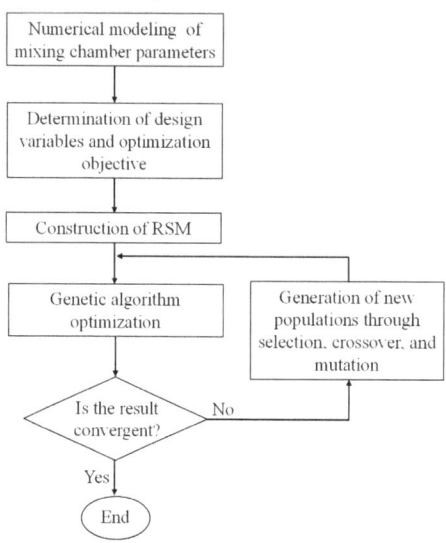

Figure 3. Optimization flowchart based on the RSM and genetic algorithm.

Table 4. Five-level rotatable central composite design.

		Coded Levels				
		−2.378	−1	0	+1	+2.378
Point 1	x-axis	0.5	0.93	1.25	1.57	2
	y-axis	0.1	0.36	0.55	0.74	1
Point 2	x-axis	0.5	1.08	1.5	1.92	2.5
	y-axis	3	3.58	4	4.42	5
Point 3	x-axis	0.5	1.08	1.5	1.92	2.5
	y-axis	3	3.58	4	4.42	5

he response variable for the design experiment was set as the delay time corresponding to scenarios with the most challenging material ratio changes, with the aim of investigating the beneficial impact of varying pin patterns on reducing transition delay time [24]. This scenario represents the highest print resolution achievable. Initially, the material ratio in the mixer chamber was defined as 9:1 for material A to material B, with input feed ratios set at 1:9 while maintaining a total feed rate of 0.5 mm/s. The simulation process maintained a constant screw speed of 25 rpm, consistent with the subsequent experimental phase. The volume fraction of material A at the outlet was continuously monitored and recorded. The tolerance for the component transformation spanned ±5%. In other words, the time interval corresponding to a change in the material A component from 0.86 to 0.14 represented the transition delay time. Figure 4 presents a simulation result for the Nr.35 experimental design condition, illustrating the transition delay time for material mixing transformations and the evolving mixing conditions in the chamber at different time points. In addition, the software Design-Expert 13.0 generated a total of 52 conditional values for the six-factor half-quantity design points, including eight center points. These values were established based on the aforementioned simulation setup to obtain the response values, specifically the transition delay time. The design experiment points and response results are detailed in Table 5.

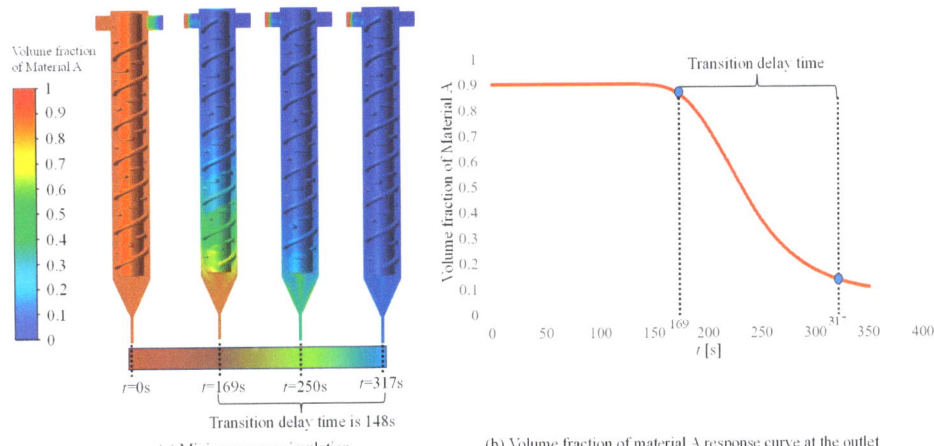

Figure 4. A simulation result of volume fraction change curve of material A (Simulation condition value correspond to Nr.35 experimental design, i.e., the coordinate values for points 1, 2, and 3 are (1.57, 0.74), (1.08, 4.42), and (1.92, 3.58). Response value is 148 s).

Table 5. Coordination values of three points and responses.

Nr.	Point 1	Point 2	Point 3	Delay Time
1	(0.93, 0.36)	(1.92, 3.58)	(1.92, 3.58)	141
2	(1.57, 0.36)	(1.92, 4.42)	(1.92, 3.58)	143
3	(1.25, 0.55)	(1.5, 3)	(1.5, 4)	173
4	(1.57, 0.36)	(1.92, 3.58)	(1.92, 4.42)	175
5	(1.57, 0.74)	(1.08, 3.58)	(1.08, 3.58)	169
6	(1.25, 0.55)	(1.5, 4)	(1.5, 4)	154
7	(0.93, 0.36)	(1.92, 3.58)	(1.08, 4.42)	174
8	(0.5, 0.55)	(1.5, 4)	(1.5, 4)	155
9	(0.93, 0.36)	(1.92, 4.42)	(1.08, 3.58)	151
10	(0.93, 0.74)	(1.08, 4.42)	(1.92, 4.42)	161
11	(1.57, 0.36)	(1.08, 4.42)	(1.08, 3.58)	152
12	(1.57, 0.74)	(1.08, 3.58)	(1.92, 4.42)	174
13	(1.25, 0.55)	(1.5, 4)	(1.5, 5)	187
14	(1.25, 1)	(1.5, 4)	(1.5, 4)	169
15	(0.93, 0.36)	(1.08, 4.42)	(1.08, 4.42)	173
16	(1.25, 0.55)	(1.5, 4)	(1.5, 4)	154
17	(1.57, 0.74)	(1.92, 4.42)	(1.92, 4.42)	156

Table 5. *Cont.*

Nr.	Point 1	Point 2	Point 3	Delay Time
18	(0.93, 0.36)	(1.92, 4.42)	(1.92, 4.42)	163
19	(0.93, 0.74)	(1.92, 3.58)	(1.08, 3.58)	146
20	(1.57, 0.36)	(1.08, 4.42)	(1.92, 4.42)	161
21	(1.25, 0.55)	(1.5, 4)	(1.5, 4)	154
22	(1.25, 0.55)	(2.5, 4)	(1.5, 4)	150
23	(1.25, 0.55)	(1.5, 4)	(2.5, 4)	148
24	(0.93, 0.36)	(1.08, 3.58)	(1.92, 4.42)	173
25	(1.25, 0.55)	(1.5, 4)	(1.5, 4)	154
26	(1.57, 0.74)	(1.92, 4.42)	(1.08, 3.58)	148
27	(1.25, 0.55)	(1.5, 4)	(1.5, 4)	154
28	(1.57, 0.36)	(1.08, 3.58)	(1.92, 3.58)	158
29	(2, 0.55)	(1.5, 4)	(1.5, 4)	158
30	(1.25, 0.55)	(1.5, 4)	(1.5, 4)	154
31	(1.25, 0.55)	(1.5, 4)	(1.5, 3)	149
32	(0.93, 0.36)	(1.08, 3.58)	(1.08, 3.58)	150
33	(0.93, 0.74)	(1.92, 3.58)	(1.92, 4.42)	171
34	(0.93, 0.74)	(1.08, 3.58)	(1.92, 3.58)	150
35 *	(1.57, 0.74)	(1.08, 4.42)	(1.92, 3.58)	148
36	(0.93, 0.36)	(1.08, 4.42)	(1.92, 3.58)	142
37	(0.93, 0.74)	(1.92, 4.42)	(1.92, 3.58)	142
38	(1.25, 0.55)	(1.5, 4)	(1.5, 4)	154
39	(1.57, 0.74)	(1.92, 3.58)	(1.08, 4.42)	175
40	(1.57, 0.74)	(1.92, 3.58)	(1.92, 3.58)	152
41	(1.57, 0.36)	(1.08, 3.58)	(1.079, 4.42)	179
42	(1.25, 0.55)	(1.5, 4)	(0.5, 4)	160
43	(1.25, 0.55)	(1.5, 5)	(1.5, 4)	148
44	(1.25, 0.1)	(1.5, 4)	(1.5, 4)	170
45	(0.93, 0.74)	(1.08, 3.58)	(1.08, 4.42)	181
46	(1.57, 0.36)	(1.92, 4.42)	(1.08, 4.42)	170
47	(0.93, 0.74)	(1.08, 4.42)	(1.08, 3.58)	149
48	(1.57, 0.74)	(1.08, 4.42)	(1.08, 4.42)	162
49	(1.25, 0.55)	(1.5, 4)	(1.5, 4)	154
50	(0.93, 0.74)	(1.92, 4.42)	(1.08, 4.42)	172
51	(1.57, 0.36)	(1.92, 3.58)	(1.08, 3.58)	160
52	(1.25, 0.55)	(0.5, 4)	(1.5, 4)	157

Nr.35 * simulation results are demonstrated in Figure 4.

The significant modified quadratic response regression model was derived through polynomial regression analysis of the experimental data provided in Table 5, yielding the response function for transition delay time as shown in Equation (5).

$$t_d = 269.39 + 74.38 \times x_1 - 82.55 \times y_1 - 3.28 \times x_2 - 34.88 \times y_2 - 7.11 \times x_3 - 39.62 \times y_3 \\ - 17.68 \times x_1 y_3 - 5.83 \times y_2 y_3 + 73.79 \times y_1^2 + 5.94 \times y_2^2 + 13.44 \times y_3^2 \quad (5)$$

where t_d is transition delay time with a unit of s. The x and y correspond to the coordinate values, respectively, and the foot index represents the serial numbers of the control points.

As seen in Equation (5), it involves all of the first terms of the six factors, along with several interaction and squared terms. Finally, the resulting RSM model fit effect had a coefficient of determination R^2 of 93.35%, an adjusted coefficient of determination R^2_{adj} of 91.52%, and a predicted determination coefficient R^2_{pre} of 87.5%. This indicates that the model exhibits decent fitting results, and its predictive capability is considered satisfactory. Figures 5 and 6 depict the response surfaces. The remaining four factors were set to intermediate values to generate the response surfaces. In Figure 5a, the x- and y-values represent relative coordinates concerning the third control point. It is evident that changes in the y-value have a more pronounced impact on the response results, with the middle y-values corresponding to a shorter transition delay time. Figure 5b illustrates the response surface for the x- and y-values of the second control point in relation to the transition delay time. Increasing both the x- and y-values results in a lower response value. Figure 5c displays the influence of the x- and y-axis coordinate values of the third control point on the transition delay time. As the x-value increases and the y-value decreases, the response value decreases accordingly. Additionally, Figure 6 represents the effect of changing the two relative coordinates of the first control point with respect to the third point on the transition delay time. It is evident that changes in the y-value exert a more significant impact on the response value compared to changes in the x-value. The minimum response value occurs when the y-value of the third point is at its minimum, and the y-value at the first point is at its middle value. These response surfaces provide valuable insights into the influence of factor variations on response values. Therefore, it is necessary to employ a global optimization approach for the obtained response function to attain specific optimization results.

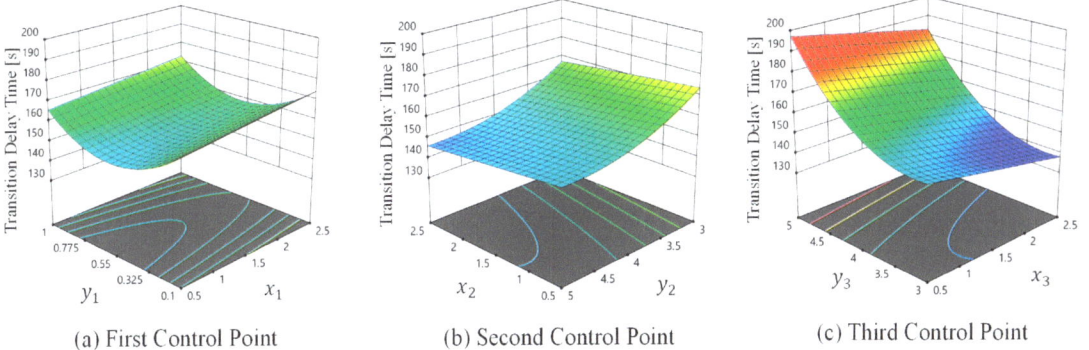

Figure 5. Response surfaces of three control points to transition delay time.

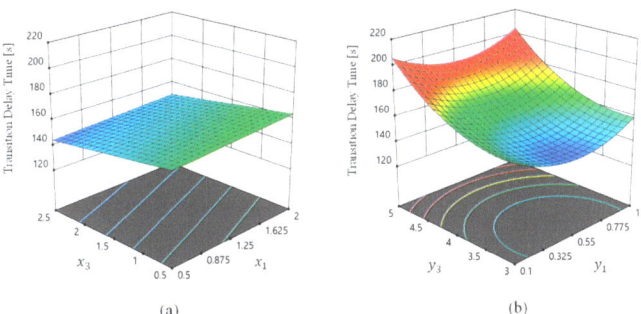

Figure 6. Response surfaces of the first control point with respect to the third control point relative coordinate values to transition delay time. (**a**) corresponds to the coordinates of x-axis, and (**b**) is coordinates of y-axis (x_1 and x_3 correspond to the x-coordinate value of the first point and the x-coordinate value of the third point, respectively. y_1 and y_3 correspond to the y-coordinate value of the first point and the y-coordinate value of the third point, respectively).

A genetic algorithm (GA) is a powerful heuristic algorithm used for global search, especially in tackling multivariate and nonlinear optimization problems. A GA emulates the concept of population evolution, employing continuous iterative processes such as selection, crossover, and mutation to gradually transform individuals until the global optimal solution of the problem is achieved.

In this section, Equation (5) is utilized as the response function and optimized using a GA to determine the coordinates of the three control points, aiming to minimize transition delay time. Firstly, the six factors are encoded in binary with a length of 20 bits, establishing the connection between coordinate parameters and the chromosome bit strings' structure in the genetic algorithm. The GA continuously selects and retains individuals with high fitness values for evolutionary processes until convergence is reached. The fitness value is defined based on Equation (5)'s minimum value. We employed a roulette wheel approach to prevent getting trapped in local optimal solutions during the global search. This approach takes into account that individuals with higher fitness values have a greater probability of being selected for further evolution. Additionally, the population size is set to 30, with a maximum of 200 generations. The crossover rate is set to 0.7, and the mutation operator rate is 0.007, ensuring a robust search range and improved convergence speed. The GA execution process is depicted in Figure 7. The results indicate a minimum transition delay time of 117.69 s. The coordinates of the three control points corresponding to this solution are (0.5, 0.56), (2.5, 4.4), and (2.5, 3), while the single pin pattern area is 4.42 mm^2. Figure 8 displays the optimized pin type screw mixer. Following the optimization results, a simulation of the optimized pin type screw mixer is conducted using the previously defined setup, resulting in a transition delay time of 113 s, which exhibits an acceptable level of error. A detailed numerical verification is presented in the subsequent section.

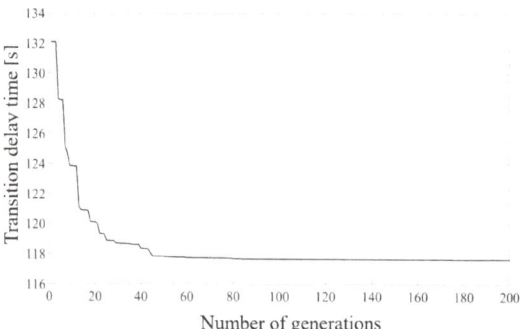

Figure 7. Iteration of objective function.

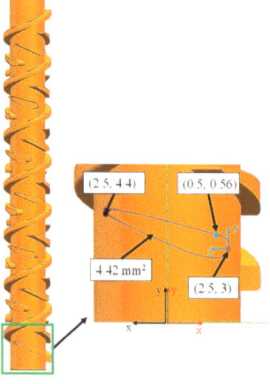

Figure 8. Optimized pin type screw mixer.

3. Results and Discussion
3.1. Numerical Validation

Three different screw configurations were compared to further verify the efficacy of the optimized pinned screw mixer in reducing transition delay time. In addition, the mixing performance of these three screw setups was assessed based on the uniformity of the extruded material and the Lyapunov index. The first screw, illustrated in Table 2 and Figure 9a, represents the original screw without any pins, with its structural parameters, including screw length, pitch, minor screw diameter, and screw flight height, remaining unchanged. Figure 9b showcases the second screw, utilized to demonstrate that the volume in the mixing chamber does not play a decisive role in transition delay times. Custom pins were transformed into cylinders, maintaining the same cross-sectional area and height as the optimized pin-type screw mixer, with a diameter of 2.4 mm and a height of 1 mm. The center of the circle was positioned at the midpoint of the y-axis at an applicable height of (0, 4). The third configuration was the pin-type screw optimized with RSM, as depicted in Figure 8.

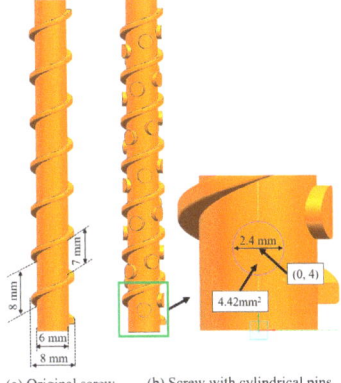

(a) Original screw   (b) Screw with cylindrical pins

Figure 9. Comparison of screw mixers.

This study then compared the transition delay times of three screw mixers based on the simulation setup detailed in the preceding section. The total flow time was set at 400 s for this analysis. In Figure 10a, we have marked the initial moments when the material A component at the outlet shifted to 0.86 and the termination moments when it reached 0.14. This time interval is defined as the transition delay time. The results reveal that the transition delay time for the optimized pin-type mixer, cylindrical pinned mixer, and pinless mixer stands at 113 s, 158 s, and 169 s, respectively. Notably, compared to the pinless screw mixer, the transition delay time reduced by approximately 33.1%. Moreover, it is evident that, when comparing mixers with the same volume, optimizing the pin shape still reduces the transition delay time by 28.5%. Figure 10b illustrates the probability density curve of the residence time distribution, exhibiting the rate of change of material A's volume fraction at the outlet. The results indicate that the maximum rate of change for the optimized pin-shaped screw mixer reaches 2%/s. In contrast, the corresponding maximum rates of change for the cylindrical pin and the pinless screw are only 1.5%/s and 1.3%/s, respectively. In order to ensure the homogeneity of the printed material, the assessment and monitoring of mixing uniformity at the outlet play a crucial role. The uniformity at the outlet was assessed using the coefficient of variance (COV), defining the extruded mixing material as homogeneous when its value exceeded 95% [51]. As depicted in Figure 11, all three mixers were able to meet the criteria for mixing uniformity at the ratio conversion where mixing difficulty is greatest. However, it is worth noting that the change in uniformity during extrusion was more pronounced for the cylindrical pinned screw and the pinless screw.

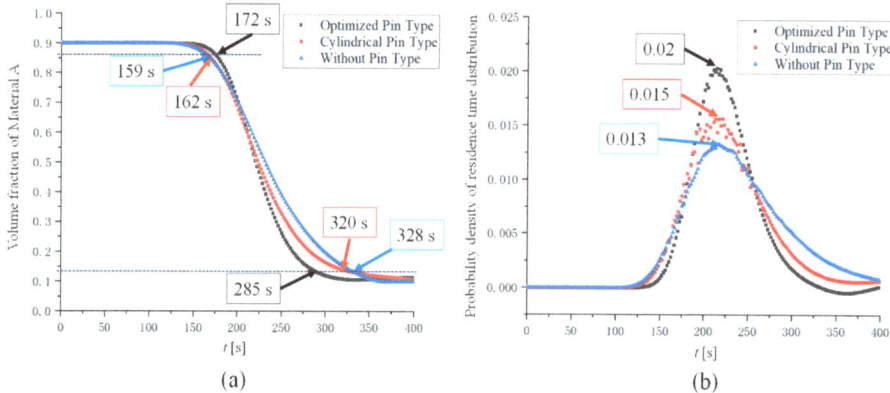

Figure 10. Response curve of three types screw mixer for changes in material A at the outlet. (**a**) is the curve of change in volume fraction of material A at the outlet, and (**b**) is the probability density function of residence time distribution.

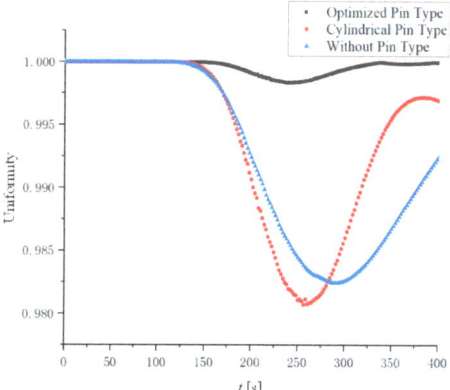

Figure 11. Uniformity curve at the outlet.

Five randomly selected particles' trajectories were tracked from the two inlet points of the three screw types using ANSYS FLUENT Vision 2020R2 (fluid simulation software) to evaluate and compare the efficacy of the optimized pin shape in enhancing the chaotic mixing of the two paste-like substances in the chamber. This tracking yielded the spatial coordinates of the particles as they evolved over time. Analysis of the particle trajectories, as depicted in Figure 12, reveals a higher degree of chaos associated with the optimized pin-type mixer. Moreover, the level of chaotic mixing was quantified using Equation (6)'s Lyapunov exponent.

$$\lambda = \lim_{\substack{t \to \infty \\ \Delta x \to 0}} \frac{1}{t} \ln \frac{|\Delta x(t)|}{|\Delta x(0)|} \tag{6}$$

where $\Delta x(0)$ is the separation of the two particles at the initial time and $\Delta x(t)$ represents the separation at time t.

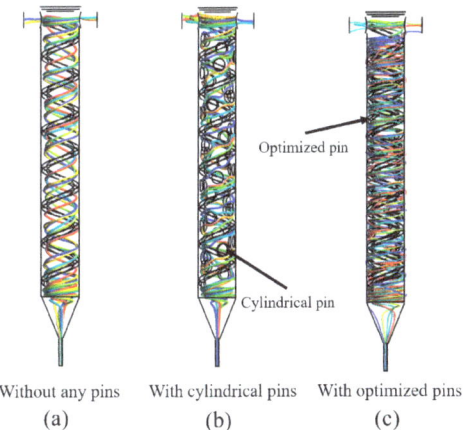

Figure 12. Path line of five random particles in the mixing chamber.

Moreover, the degree of chaotic mixing was quantified through the utilization of Equation (6), which calculates the Lyapunov exponent. A larger positive Lyapunov exponent signifies a more pronounced level of chaotic mixing. During the Lyapunov exponent calculation process, particles with close initial distances were selected as clusters, utilizing the spatial coordinates of the five randomly tracked particles over time, as previously described. The sampling frequency was set at 1 Hz, with a mixing period of 100 s. Each screw type yielded five sets of Lyapunov exponents, which were averaged to characterize the final degree of chaotic mixing, as presented in Table 6. The results clearly demonstrate that the optimized mixer generates over three times the level of chaotic mixing compared to the other two screw types.

Table 6. Lyapunov exponents of each screw mixer.

	Screw without Pins	Screw with Cylindrical Pins	Screw with Optimized Pins
Lyapunov exponents	0.007833	0.00965	0.03402

Figure 13 illustrates the Poincaré map representing the behavior of two isolated particles influenced by the presence of three screws over flow durations of 100 s and 200 s. The x and y coordinates on the Poincaré map represent the specific positions of these particles. The findings demonstrate that a screw devoid of pins and a screw equipped with symmetrically shaped pins yield similar cross-sectional flow trajectories for the two separated particles. This similarity has a detrimental effect on radial mixing. A comparison between Figure 13c,f shows that the optimized pin shape mixer allows the two separated particles more uniformly distributed in the radial direction of the mixing chamber after 100 s of mixing. Moreover, it is observed that the trajectories of these particles exhibit increased chaotic behavior in the cross-section of the optimized pinned screw. This results in a higher number of cross-foldings and, thus, enhances homogeneity in the extrusion process. Thus, it is verified that the optimization-induced asymmetry in the pin shape allows the mixing fluid to continuously overlap and merge after passing through the upper and lower surfaces of the pin. This phenomenon enhances chaotic convection in the mixing chamber, thereby enhancing radial mixing and reducing axial mixing. Finally, this leads to a reduction in the transition delay time.

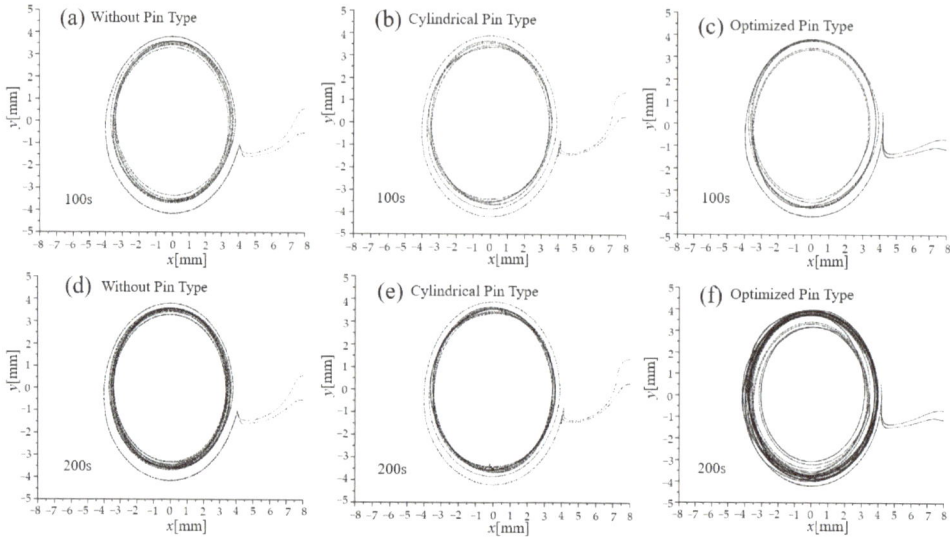

Figure 13. Poincaré map of three screw mixers at different flow times.

3.2. Printing System

Figure 14 illustrates a custom-built printing prototype designed for the preparation of FGM parts. This prototype comprises two primary modules: the data processing module and the spatial motion module. The data processing module serves the function of receiving and analyzing G-codes containing printing information, following the slicing process, facilitated by the upper computer. Thereafter, it translates these G-codes into pulse signals compatible with each motor of the printer. This conversion enables accurate execution of the printing procedure. The spatial motion module, on the other hand, is composed of two principal components, with one being a triaxial gantry structure. A layer-based manufacturing approach is employed to ensure the geometric accuracy of the FGMs parts. The 42-stepping motor can provide a maximum torque of 0.5 Nm. Equipped with a ball screw shaft with lead of 10 mm, a single 42 stepper motor can provide a force of 35 N (seen in Equation (7)).

$$F = \frac{2T}{0.9L\pi} \tag{7}$$

where T is the maximum torque of motor, and L is the lead of ball screw shaft.

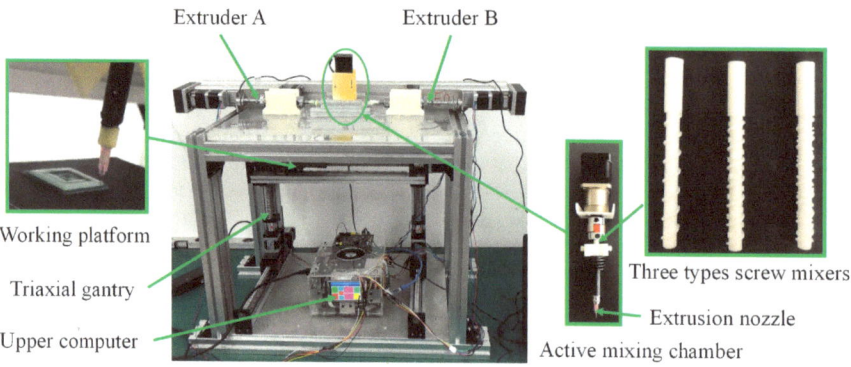

Figure 14. Printing prototype for fabrication of FGM parts.

Therefore, we used double 42-stepping motors into the y-axis and z-axis to ensure sufficient torque, while the x-axis is driven by a single 42-stepping motor. Moreover, this module features a unique component to facilitate variations in material composition, comprising two extruders and an active mixing chamber. Extruder A and extruder B are each equipped with separate 42-stepping motors, enabling the manipulation of material gradients through different feed rates. In the feeding system, in addition to the 42-stepping motors fitted with 10 mm lead ball screws, a 10:1 reducer is also equipped, allowing a maximum thrust of 350 N to be provided by a single motor. Measured via a pressure sensor during the printing process, the required thrust force is about 200 N when feeding at the maximum feed rate of 0.5 mm/s. The screw mixer housed in the active mixing chamber is connected via a coupling to a 42-step motor, and the motor is equipped with a gearbox with a transmission ratio of 10:1 in order to provide sufficient torque for mixing. During the printing experiment, we set the screw to rotate at 25 rpm to match the simulation settings. Figure 14 also presents three screw mixers, which were produced using 3D printing in combination with high strength resins based on the parameters outlined in the previous section. These mixers are intended for use in subsequent practical printing experiments to assess print quality.

3.3. Verification Experiment

With the aforementioned internally developed printing system equipped with three types of mixers, the response was the printing of a 70×70 mm^2 extruded filament displaying gradient variations from 90% of material A (white color) to 10% of material B (green color), and vice versa, as illustrated in Figure 15. Prior to the experiment, the two extruders were supplied in accordance with the initial paste ratio (9:1), and the screw speed was adjusted to 25 rpm for purging the mixing chamber. Thereafter, the dual extruders were supplied at the desired ratio (1:9) until the filament was produced. The printing path followed a zigzag pattern with 5 mm intervals, with the starting point indicated by the arrow in Figure 15. The total length of the extruded filament amounted to 1120 mm. The experimental printing parameters were configured to match the simulation settings. The extrusion head diameter remained at 1 mm, the combined feed rate was 0.5 mm/s, and the extruded flow rate from the nozzle could be estimated at approximately 2.4 mm^3/s. Therefore, to ensure the absence of noticeable overstacking and understacking defects in the printing process, the movement speed of the printing platform was set to approximately 3 mm/s, following the principles of flow conservation. Therefore, the total printing time for the extruded filaments was 373 s. Hence, the transitional delay distance can be computed based on the platform's movement speed combined with the transition delay time.

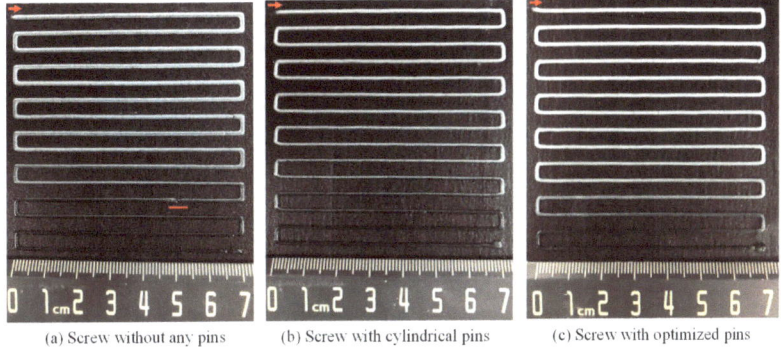

(a) Screw without any pins   (b) Screw with cylindrical pins   (c) Screw with optimized pins

Figure 15. Three mixers extruded filaments with gradient variations.

As depicted in Figure 15, all three mixers are capable of inducing gradient changes in the extruded filaments while maintaining satisfactory geometric print quality. Notably, as highlighted in Figure 15a, filament breakage is evident, primarily attributed to the introduction of air bubbles during the loading of paste-like material into the extruder. Mixers lacking pins exhibit suboptimal dispersal and mixing capabilities, with minimal change in the size of the entrapped bubbles. The occurrence of these bubbles during material loading proves challenging to circumvent, and their dimensions directly impact filament breakage. Therefore, increased volumes of bubbles result in geometric inaccuracies during the printing process and exert a negative effect on the mechanical characteristics of the FGM parts. Conversely, when air bubbles infiltrate screw configurations equipped with pins, the larger bubbles can be dispersed into smaller units through the multiple shearing actions of the pins. This, in turn, translates into enhanced geometric quality, as illustrated in Figure 15b,c.

3.4. Comparison of Transition Delay Distances

It is evident that utilizing image processing methods offers a cost-effective approach for detecting gradient variations in extrusion filament. Firstly, the printed output displayed in Figure 15 was processed through the MATLAB platform and transformed into a grayscale representation to obtain the grayscale value for each individual pixel. Secondly, pixel coordinates were determined based on the locations of sampling points in the grayscale map presented in Figure 16, and the normalized values were characterized as the composition ratio at each of these sampling points. A total of 113 sampling points were acquired, employing a uniform sampling strategy aligned with the length of the extruded filaments, which resulted in a cumulative printing duration of 373 s. Finally, a comparative analysis was conducted between the experimental results and the CFD results, as illustrated in the coordinate system of Figure 16. Additionally, the commencement and conclusion points of the transition delay time for three mixers, as determined using the CFD results, are denoted in Figure 16.

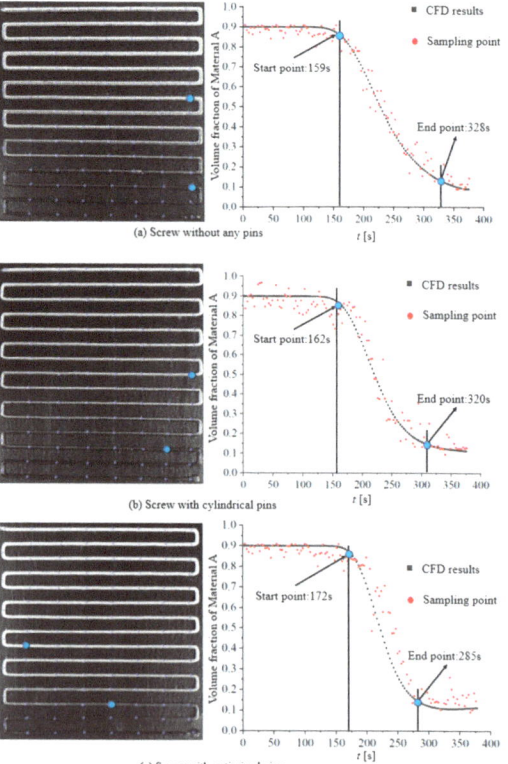

Figure 16. Digital image processing of three print filaments.

From the findings presented in Figure 16, it is evident that all three mixers have the capability to change the gradient of material components in an extruded filament spanning 1120 mm, ranging from a ratio of 9:1 to 1:9. The complete transformation of material components is readily observable through digital image processing methods. Moreover, when comparing the experimental results with those derived from CFD simulations, it is apparent that the simulation results exhibit acceptable deviations, thereby establishing the validity and reasonable accuracy of the FEM model in the context of the mixing process.

In Figure 16a, the analysis results depict the extruded filaments produced by the screw mixer devoid of any pins. The grey values of the sampled points in the transition delay interval are evenly distributed on either side of the CFD results, signifying a considerable delay in the transition process. In Figure 16b, a comparison with the CFD results reveals that the presence of pins in actual printing only marginally enhances the effects of chaotic mixing convection, resulting in a tendency to delay the transformation of material components during practical use. In Figure 16c, the grey scale values of the sampled points from the experiment surpass the CFD results, indicating that in practice, the screw with the optimized pin shape significantly promotes chaotic mixing, leading to shorter transition distances for material gradient changes. This smooth transition of material components in functional gradient materials can substantially reduce interlayer stresses induced by abrupt shifts in material properties, thus enhancing the overall structural integrity and durability of the component. The reduced transition distance allows for more complex and accurate material gradient adjustments between layers in confined dimensions, thereby enhancing printing flexibility and enabling the design of FGM parts that transcend dimensional limitations. This not only maximizes the unique advantages of individual component materials but also offers a wider range of performance combinations.

3.5. Functionally Graded Materials Part Print Specimen

We printed a $35 \times 35 \times 3.2$ mm^3 cube with a gradient variation to verify the printing performance of the optimized pin screw mixer, as illustrated in Figure 17. Each layer was set to a height of 0.8 mm, and a consistent gradient change was maintained in each layer. The printing path followed an offset printing sequence, progressing from the outermost to the innermost regions, and was accompanied by a 100% fill rate. Figure 17a illustrates the gradient variation of the pre-designed printed sample, where the region denoted as 6:4 measures 2 mm in width, the 9:1 region spans 3 mm in width, and the central region accounts for a component ratio of 1.5:8.5. To account for the delay in material component transformation once the printing system receives the G-Code, the mixing chamber was initially purged with a mixture of pastes in a 6:4 ratio before commencing printing. Printing commenced with G-Code specifying a material ratio of 9:1 and continued until the next ratio change point, i.e., (30, 5). From that point onward, the ratio was adjusted to 1.5:8.5 until the completion of the layer. Figure 17b displays the specimen that was printed following the predefined G-Codes and the associated process parameters from the aforementioned experiment. The print results indicate that the specimen exhibits satisfactory surface quality.

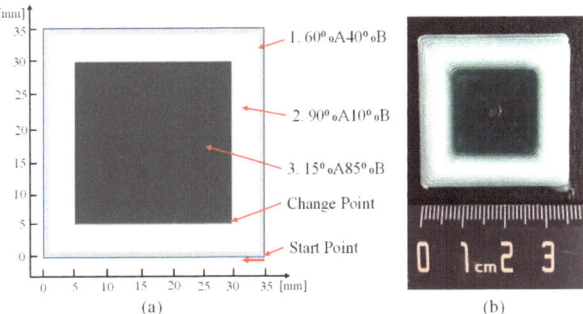

Figure 17. Illustration of: (**a**) pre-designed gradient change, and (**b**) print specimen.

Similarly, digital image processing was employed to analyze the gradient variations of the printed sample in a targeted manner. Sampling components along the designated arrow paths in the greyscale diagram presented in Figure 18 and subsequently comparing them with the expected gradient changes revealed that the transitional region between the ratios of 6:4 and 9:1 spanned approximately 2 mm. In addition, the width of this transition region measured approximately 5 mm after the material feed transition point, set at a ratio of 1.5:8.5. In summary, the optimized pin screw mixer demonstrates a significant capability to achieve the distribution of components as pre-designed.

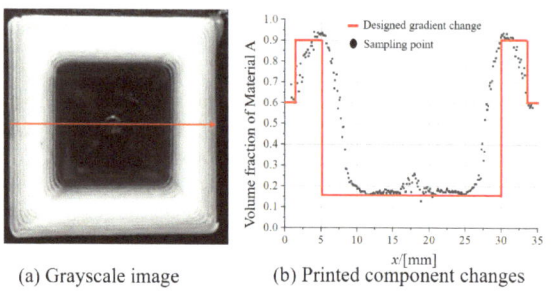

(a) Grayscale image (b) Printed component changes

Figure 18. Digital image processing of print specimen.

Direct ink writing, a sophisticated additive manufacturing method, offers remarkable flexibility and adaptability. This method excels in accurately depositing materials at predetermined locations to create complex geometries and complex structures. However, a significant challenge encountered when preparing FGMs parts with the DIW process is the unavoidable formation of transition delay regions. While these regions may not be functionally critical, they can exert a significant effect on the overall performance of the manufactured parts. Further research should focus on the development of more efficient path planning strategies, along with accurate characterization of the transition delay distances between varying gradient variations. By strategically placing these transition delay regions in non-core functional areas of the part, it is possible to enhance overall part performance and quality without compromising critical functionality.

In this study, we have successfully determined a pin shape for single-screw mixer by virtue of chaotic mixing, combined with several digital optimization techniques. Experimental validation shows that the optimized active screw mixer can effectively shorten the transition delay distance, as well as achieve sufficient distribution mixing capacity, when the material components are transformed. Finally, we successfully prepared printed samples with gradient changes with the optimized screw, which will help the application development in the field of functional gradient materials.

4. Conclusions

The pin-type active screw mixer, developed utilizing RSM in conjunction with a global optimization approach, has proven its efficacy in substantially reducing the distance required for the transition of material components. When compared to two other similar screw types, the optimized pin-type screw mixer reduced the transition distance by approximately 28.5% and 33.1%, respectively, in scenarios where the ratio of material component changes ranged from 9:1 to 1:9. In addition, CFD models with a high degree of accuracy have been generated in this study. These models are unquestionably capable of efficiently and economically characterizing the transition delay time for material component changes and the uniformity of mixing in extruded materials. In conjunction with the simulation results, the response function of the three control points to the transition delay time was eventually determined through the half-composite center design. In the simulation model, the particle tracking method was employed to compute the Lyapunov exponent, which serves to assess the degree of chaotic mixing in the chamber. Additionally, this method evaluates the radial dispersive mixing capability of the mixer through the Poincaré map. Numerical validation results indicate that the Lyapunov exponent of the optimized pin-type screw mixer is 4.3 times higher than that of the mixer lacking pins and 3.5 times higher than that of the cylindrical pinned mixer. The Poincaré map further confirms that the optimized pin-type screw offers superior radial dispersion mixing capabilities. These findings provide evidence that the optimized pin-type screw mixer enhances the chaotic mixing effect by increasing radial mixing while decreasing axial mixing. Through experimental research, the double-extruder printing system, combined with the optimized screw mixer, has successfully prepared FGM parts with smooth variations. Moreover, the gradient change process can be effectively characterized through digital image processing.

In this work, the researchers extensively studied a singular instance of transition delay distance associated with a change in material components. In addition, the CFD model can be employed to explore additional transition delay distances arising from various changes in material components. To streamline the experimental data, this study utilized a quadratic B-spline to characterize the pin's geometry. Subsequent research may involve the utilization of higher-degree B-splines to extend the scope of design possibilities. It is worth noting that nearly all paste-like materials are amenable to the DIW process. This presents exciting opportunities for further exploration into the regulation of printing parameters for pastes exhibiting diverse rheological properties, such as ceramics, polymers, and other non-Newtonian fluids. This exploration holds the potential to unlock a wider array of performance of FGM parts. Regarding the study of print path strategies, future research directions may consist of the consideration of the spatial deployment of the transition region. The objective would be to achieve a transition while minimizing any negative effects on material properties.

Author Contributions: All authors contributed to the study conception and design; The draft of the manuscript was written by S.W.; All authors were involved in analysing the data. J.Z. reviewed this paper; G.D. provided the management for the work. All authors have read and agreed to the published version of the manuscript.

Funding: This project was supported by the Central Guidance for Local Science and Technology Development Fund Project, Hebei Provincial Department of Science and Technology, China (Grant No. 216Z1804G).

Institutional Review Board Statement: Not applicable.

Informed Consent Statement: Not applicable.

Data Availability Statement: Data are contained within the article.

Conflicts of Interest: The authors declare no conflicts of interest.

References

1. Jojith, R.; Sam, M.; Radhika, N. Recent advances in tribological behavior of functionally graded composites: A review. *Eng. Sci. Technol. Int. J.* **2022**, *25*, 100999. [CrossRef]
2. Kumar, J.; Singh, D.; Kalsi, N.S.; Sharma, S.; Pruncu, C.I.; Pimenov, D.Y.; Rao, K.V.; Kapłonek, W. Comparative study on the mechanical, tribological, morphological and structural properties of vortex casting processed, Al–SiC–Cr hybrid metal matrix composites for high strength wear-resistant applications: Fabrication and characterizations. *J. Mater. Res. Technol.* **2020**, *9*, 13607–13615. [CrossRef]
3. Dmitrievskiy, A.A.; Zhigacheva, D.G.; Grigoriev, G.V. Ca-ATZ/Ca-ATZ+SiO$_2$ functionally graded ceramic. *Adv. Appl. Ceram.* **2023**, *122*, 31–35. [CrossRef]
4. Osman, S.; Ahmed, K.; Ahmed, M. Performance of Two-Dimensional Functionally Graded Anode Supported Solid-Oxide Fuel Cells. *J. Energy Resour. Technol.* **2022**, *144*, 070911. [CrossRef]
5. Verma, R.K.; Chopkar, M.K. Dry Sliding Wear Investigation of Centrifugally Casted AA6061–B4C Functionally Graded Metal Matrix Composite Material by Response Surface Methodology (RSM). *Arab. J. Sci. Eng.* **2023**, *48*, 4095–4107. [CrossRef]
6. Huang, C.; Chen, Y. Effect of varied alumina/zirconia content on ballistic performance of a functionally graded material. *Int. J. Refract. Met. Hard Mater.* **2017**, *67*, 129–140. [CrossRef]
7. Huang, C.-Y.; Chen, Y.-L. Design and impact resistant analysis of functionally graded Al$_2$O$_3$–ZrO$_2$ ceramic composite. *Mater. Des.* **2016**, *91*, 294–305. [CrossRef]

8. Huang, C.-Y.; Chen, Y.-L. Effect of mechanical properties on the ballistic resistance capability of Al_2O_3-ZrO_2 functionally graded materials. *Ceram. Int.* 2016, *42*, 12946–12955. [CrossRef]
9. Coffigniez, M.; Grémillard, L.; Boulnat, X. Sinter-Based Additive Manufacturing of Graded Porous Titanium Scaffolds by Multi-Inks 3D Extrusion. *Adv. Eng. Mater.* 2022, *25*, 2201159. [CrossRef]
10. George, S.M.; Nayak, C.; Singh, I.; Balani, K. Multifunctional Hydroxyapatite Composites for Orthopedic Applications: A Review. *ACS Biomater. Sci. Eng.* 2022, *8*, 3162–3186. [CrossRef]
11. Zhang, Y.B.; Yang, H.L.; Lei, S.Q.; Zhu, S.J.; Wang, J.F.; Sun, Y.F.; Guan, S.K. Preparation of Biodegradable Mg/β-TCP Biofunctional Gradient Materials by Friction Stir Processing and Pulse Reverse Current Electrodeposition. *Acta Metall. Sin. (Engl. Lett.)* 2020, *33*, 103–114. [CrossRef]
12. Wang, Y.; Liu, Q.; Lan, Z.-F.; Zhang, B.; Zhang, H.-Q.; Liu, J.-W.; Ye, F. Strong and tough bioinspired nacre-like B4C/Al functionally graded materials with eliminated abrupt interfaces. *Compos. Commun.* 2021, *25*, 100741. [CrossRef]
13. Caño, P.; Hinojosa, M.; Nguyen, H.; Morgan, A.; Fuertes Marrón, D.; García, I.; Johnson, A.; Rey-Stolle, I. Hybrid III-V/SiGe solar cells grown on Si substrates through reverse graded buffers. *Sol. Energy Mater. Sol. Cells* 2020, *205*, 110246. [CrossRef]
14. Du, J.; Zhou, Z.J.; Song, S.X.; Zhong, Z.H.; Ge, C.C. Research on Mo/Cu functionally graded materials by resistance sintering under ultra-high pressure. *AIP Conf. Proc.* 2008, *973*, 862–867. [CrossRef]
15. Hurdoganoglu, D.; Safaei, B.; Sahmani, S.; Onyibo, E.C.; Qin, Z. State-of-the-Art Review of Computational Static and Dynamic Behaviors of Small-Scaled Functionally Graded Multilayer Shallow Arch Structures from Design to Analysis. *Arch. Comput. Methods Eng.* 2023, *31*, 389–453. [CrossRef]
16. Srividhya, S.; Raghu, P.; Rajagopal, A.; Reddy, J.N. Nonlocal nonlinear analysis of functionally graded plates using third-order shear deformation theory. *Int. J. Eng. Sci.* 2018, *125*, 1–22. [CrossRef]
17. Jeshrun Shalem, M.; Devaraju, A.; Karthik, K. Synthesis and Characterization of Functionally Graded Ceramic Material for Aerospace Applications. In *Intelligent Manufacturing and Energy Sustainability*; Springer: Singapore, 2020; pp. 483–488. [CrossRef]
18. Kumar, S.; Reddy, K.V.V.S.M.; Kumar, A.; Devi, G.R. Development and characterization of polymer-ceramic continuous fiber reinforced functionally graded composites for aerospace application. *Aerosp. Sci. Technol.* 2013, *26*, 185–191. [CrossRef]
19. Ramesh, M.; Karthik, A.; Jafrey Daniel James, D.; Karthik Pandiyan, G. Functionally graded materials: Review on manufacturing by Liquid and gas based techniques. *Mater. Res. Express* 2023, *10*, 085305. [CrossRef]
20. Ren, L.; Song, Z.; Liu, H.; Han, Q.; Zhao, C.; Derby, B.; Liu, Q.; Ren, L. 3D printing of materials with spatially non-linearly varying properties. *Mater. Des.* 2018, *156*, 470–479. [CrossRef]
21. Yang, L.; Miyanaji, H.; Janaki Ram, D.; Zandinejad, A.; Zhang, S. Functionally Graded Ceramic Based Materials Using Additive Manufacturing: Review and Progress. *Addit. Manuf. Strateg. Technol. Adv. Ceram.* 2016, *258*, 43–55. [CrossRef]
22. Erisken, C.; Kalyon, D.M.; Wang, H. Functionally graded electrospun polycaprolactone and β-tricalcium phosphate nanocomposites for tissue engineering applications. *Biomaterials* 2008, *29*, 4065–4073. [CrossRef] [PubMed]
23. Brackett, J.; Yan, Y.; Cauthen, D.; Kishore, V.; Lindahl, J.; Smith, T.; Sudbury, Z.; Ning, H.; Kunc, V.; Duty, C. Characterizing material transitions in large-scale Additive Manufacturing. *Addit. Manuf.* 2021, *38*, 101750. [CrossRef]
24. Guo, W.; Jiang, Z.; Zhang, C.; Zhao, L.; Jiang, Z.; Li, X.; Chen, G. Fabrication process of smooth functionally graded materials through a real-time inline control of the component ratio. *J. Eur. Ceram. Soc.* 2021, *41*, 256–265. [CrossRef]
25. Tang, D.; Hao, L.; Li, Y.; Li, Z.; Dadbakhsh, S. Dual gradient direct ink writing for formation of kaolinite ceramic functionally graded materials. *J. Alloys Compd.* 2020, *814*, 152275. [CrossRef]
26. Li, W.; Armani, A.; Martin, A.; Kroehler, B.; Henderson, A.; Huang, T.; Watts, J.; Hilmas, G.; Leu, M. Extrusion-based additive manufacturing of functionally graded ceramics. *J. Eur. Ceram. Soc.* 2021, *41*, 2049–2057. [CrossRef]
27. Netto, J.M.J.; Idogava, H.T.; Santos, L.E.F.; Silveira, Z.D.; Romio, P.; Alves, J.L. Screw-assisted 3D printing with granulated materials: A systematic review. *Int. J. Adv. Manuf. Tech.* 2021, *115*, 2711–2727. [CrossRef] [PubMed]
28. Valkenaers, H.; Vogeler, F.; Ferraris, E.; Voet, A.; Kruth, J.P. A novel approach to additive manufacturing: Screw extrusion 3D-printing. In Proceedings of the International Conference on Multi-Material Micro Manufacture, San Sebastián, Spain, 8–10 October 2013.
29. Cartwright, J.H.E.; Feingold, M.; Piro, O. An Introduction to Chaotic Advection. In *Mixing: Chaos and Turbulence*; Chaté, H., Villermaux, E., Chomaz, J.M., Eds.; Springer: Boston, MA, USA, 1999; pp. 307–342.
30. Castelain, C.; Mokrani, A.; Legentilhomme, P.; Peerhossaini, H. Residence time distribution in twisted pipe flows: Helically coiled system and chaotic system. *Exp. Fluids* 1997, *22*, 359–368. [CrossRef]
31. Aref, H. Stirring by chaotic advection. *J. Fluid Mech.* 1984, *143*, 1–21. [CrossRef]
32. Sundararajan, P.; Stroock, A. Transport Phenomena in Chaotic Laminar Flows. *Annu. Rev. Chem. Biomol. Eng.* 2012, *3*, 473–496. [CrossRef]
33. Xu, B.; Liu, Y.; Yu, H.; Turng, L.; Liu, C. A Numerical Simulation of Enhanced Mixing of a Non-Newtonian Fluid in a Cavity with Asymmetric Non-Twin Rotors. *Macromol. Theory Simul.* 2018, *27*, 1800021. [CrossRef]
34. Xu, B.; Liu, Y.; He, L.; Turng, L.; Liu, C. Effect of centerline distance on mixing of a Non-Newtonian fluid in a cavity with asymmetric rotors. *Phys. Fluids* 2018, *31*, 021205. [CrossRef]
35. Wei, J.J.; Liang, X.L.; Chen, D.; Yang, Y.; Zhou, D.M. Evaluation of the mixing performance for one novel twin screw kneader with particle tracking. *Polym. Eng. Sci.* 2014, *54*, 2407–2419. [CrossRef]

36. Wei, J.; Sun, Q.; Sun, X.; Sun, W. A study on rotor profiles design for a novel twin-screw kneader. *Int. J. Precis. Eng. Manuf.* **2013**, *14*, 451–459. [CrossRef]
37. Zhu, X.Z.; He, Y.D.; Wang, G. Effect of Dynamic Center Region on the Flow and Mixing Efficiency in a New Tri-Screw Extruder Using 3D Finite Element Modeling. *Int. J. Rotating Mach.* **2013**, *2013*, 258197. [CrossRef]
38. Bauer, H.; Matić, J.; Khinast, J. Characteristic parameters and process maps for fully-filled twin-screw extruder elements. *Chem. Eng. Sci.* **2021**, *230*, 116202. [CrossRef]
39. Bhattacharyya, A.; Janarthanan, G.; Tran, H.N.; Ham, H.J.; Yoon, J.; Noh, I. Bioink homogeneity control during 3D bioprinting of multicomponent micro/nanocomposite hydrogel for even tissue regeneration using novel twin screw extrusion system. *Chem. Eng. J.* **2021**, *415*, 128971. [CrossRef]
40. Kohlgrüber, K. 4—Applications of Co-Rotating Twin-Screw Extruders. In *Co-Rotating Twin-Screw Extruders: Applications*; Kohlgrüber, K., Ed.; Hanser: Pawleys Island, SC, USA, 2021; pp. 217–339.
41. Kim, S.J.; Kwon, T.H. Enhancement of mixing performance of single-screw extrusion processes via chaotic flows: Part I. Basic concepts and experimental study. *Adv. Polym. Technol.* **1996**, *15*, 41–54. [CrossRef]
42. Kim, S.J.; Kwon, T.H. Enhancement of mixing performance of single-screw extrusion processes via chaotic flows: Part II. Numerical study. *Adv. Polym. Technol.* **1996**, *15*, 55–69. [CrossRef]
43. Hwang, W.R.; Kwon, T.H. Dynamical modeling of chaos single-screw extruder and its three-dimensional numerical analysis. *Polym. Eng. Sci.* **2000**, *40*, 702–714. [CrossRef]
44. Wiggins, S.; Ottino, J. Foundation of chaotic mixing. *Philos. Transactions. Ser. A Math. Phys. Eng. Sci.* **2004**, *362*, 937–970. [CrossRef]
45. Park, G.; Eom, T.; Kwak, H.; Kim, C. Optimization of Screw Mixer to Improve Drying Performance of Livestock Manure Dryer Using CFD Analysis. *Appl. Sci.* **2022**, *12*, 2872. [CrossRef]
46. Shankar, T.J.; Sokhansanj, S.; Bandyopadhyay, S.; Bawa, A.S. A Case Study on Optimization of Biomass Flow During Single-Screw Extrusion Cooking Using Genetic Algorithm (GA) and Response Surface Method (RSM). *Food Bioprocess Technol.* **2010**, *3*, 498–510. [CrossRef]
47. Liu, T.; Wang, J.; Li, Y.; Liu, Z.; Sun, J.; Liu, D. Design and Experiment of Substrate Grass Seed Blanket Extrusion Device. *Sustainability* **2022**, *14*, 11046. [CrossRef]
48. Phelan Jr, F.; Hughes, N.; Pathak, J. Chaotic Mixing in Microfluidic Devices Driven by Oscillatory Cross Flow. *Phys. Fluids* **2008**, *20*, 023101. [CrossRef]
49. Orisaleye, J.; Adefuye, O.; Ogundare, A.; Fadipe, O. Parametric analysis and design of a screw extruder for slightly non-Newtonian (pseudoplastic) materials. *Eng. Sci. Technol. Int. J.* **2018**, *21*, 229–237. [CrossRef]
50. Rauwendaal, C. (Ed.) 7—Functional Process Analysis. In *Polymer Extrusion*, 5th ed.; Hanser: Pawleys Island, SC, USA, 2014; pp. 255–508.
51. Hosseini, S.M.; Razzaghi, K.; Shahraki, F. Design and characterization of a Low-pressure-drop static mixer. *AIChE J.* **2019**, *65*, 1126–1133. [CrossRef]

Disclaimer/Publisher's Note: The statements, opinions and data contained in all publications are solely those of the individual author(s) and contributor(s) and not of MDPI and/or the editor(s). MDPI and/or the editor(s) disclaim responsibility for any injury to people or property resulting from any ideas, methods, instructions or products referred to in the content.

Article

Stability Analysis of the Rapid Heating Multilayer Structure Mold by the Contact Error and Thickness of Layers

Hyeonmin Lee [1], Youngbae Ko [2,*] and Woochun Choi [1,*]

[1] Department of Mechanical Engineering, Korea University, Seoul 02841, Republic of Korea; ctood09@korea.ac.kr

[2] Clean Energy Transition R&D Department, Korea Institute of Industrial Technology, Jeju 63243, Republic of Korea

* Correspondence: kaiser74@kitech.re.kr (Y.K.); wcchoi@korea.ac.kr (W.C.)

Abstract: Rapid heating of the mold surface is necessary for the high-gloss, high-productivity injection molding process. A rapid heating mold system that uses a carbon nanotube (CNT) as a heating element was investigated because of its structure. For CNT web film to be utilized in the injection molding process, heating must be applied inside the mold. That can cause poor contact at the contact area between the mold and the CNT heating element, leading to local temperature deviation and resistance changes that reduce the heating stability of the CNT surface element. Additionally, the multilayer structure of the CNT web film can cause heat-transfer performance variations due to the different layer thicknesses. To address these issues, an adjustable flush was constructed at the contact area between the electrode inside the mold and the insulator to analyze the heating behavior of the CNT heating element as a function of dimensional deviation. The thermal durability of the CNT web film was also evaluated by analyzing the Raman spectra and measuring resistance changes caused by local overheating. The film can withstand high temperatures, with a flush limit value of 0.3 mm. An optimization analysis was conducted to determine the ideal thicknesses of the multilayer CNT web film, insulator, and electrical insulator. Optimal layer thicknesses were found to be 10 µm, 5 mm, and 0.5 mm, respectively. The main variables of the rapid heating mold required for application to the injection process were identified and reflected in the mold design to suggest directions for commercialization.

Keywords: RHCM; carbon nanotube; heat transfer; optimization; injection molding

Citation: Lee, H.; Ko, Y.; Choi, W. Stability Analysis of the Rapid Heating Multilayer Structure Mold by the Contact Error and Thickness of Layers. *Appl. Sci.* **2024**, *14*, 2813. https://doi.org/10.3390/app14072813

Academic Editor: Kambiz Vafai

Received: 29 February 2024
Revised: 14 March 2024
Accepted: 26 March 2024
Published: 27 March 2024

Copyright: © 2024 by the authors. Licensee MDPI, Basel, Switzerland. This article is an open access article distributed under the terms and conditions of the Creative Commons Attribution (CC BY) license (https://creativecommons.org/licenses/by/4.0/).

1. Introduction

Rapid heating cycle molding (RHCM) has gained attention recently as it can significantly enhance the quality of molded parts. RHCM is especially useful regarding surface quality and gloss, as it eliminates the need for additional processes, such as sanding and painting, which are required for conventional injection molding (CIM) [1,2]. Moreover, RHCM can reduce production costs by shortening the product cycle time. However, if cooling is excessive in CIM, defects may occur in the molded product due to low mold surface temperature. These defects can reduce the surface quality of the product and require additional processing. RHCM may also be applied in the field of microinjection molding [3]. If the cavity surface of the mold is rapidly heated during the resin injection time and maintained above the glass transition temperature of the polymer or the melting point of the semi-crystalline polymer, friction and flow resistance are reduced during resin injection [4–6]. That enables high-quality injection, even for delicate shapes. RHCM is being explored as a production method for precise error control when injecting camera lenses and light guide plates used in smartphones and autonomous vehicles.

The main difference between CIM and RHCM is how the mold temperature is controlled [7]. In the CIM process, the mold temperature is maintained at a constant temperature by circulating coolant. The temperature of the mold is kept constant at the desired level during the entire molding cycle. In the CIM process, the mold temperature is maintained at a much lower level than the resin's glass transition temperature or melting point, making the production cycle efficient. The low-temperature cavity of the CIM process causes the resin to solidify during the resin injection process and form a frozen layer between the hot polymer melt and the cold cavity surface. That leads to defects, such as weld lines, flow marks, swirl marks, low gloss, and cooling to low reproducibility, in the final molded product [8]. However, in the RHCM process, the cavity surface temperature of the mold is brought to a certain level above the glass transition temperature or melting point of the resin used in the process, and the temperature is maintained as the resin is injected. Once the injection is complete, the heating process ends, and the resin filling the cavity is solidified by rapid cooling. The RHCM process has the advantage of increasing the production cycle's efficiency through rapid heating and cooling. It overcomes the limitations of the CIM process, making it possible to produce high-quality molded products in a short time.

In order to implement the RHCM process, which has many advantages in injection molding, methods for rapidly heating and cooling the mold are being actively explored. Rapid mold heating is a critical technology for RHCM. Various heating methods such as infrared heating [9–11], induction heating [12], high-frequency proximity heating [13], gas heating [14], resistance heating [15–17], and steam heating [18] have been studied. Among them, resistance heating with cartridge heaters and steam heaters is widely used in the industry. The RHCM process applied in this way is widely used to replace the CIM process in specific industries that require high-gloss, weld line-free products. It is typically used for TV panels, automotive parts, and other exterior parts.

Cartridge heating and steam heating methods are widely used but have some limitations. These methods involve heating the entire mold by applying a pipe and cartridge heater inside the mold. Because the heat capacity of the mold is large, it is difficult to immediately and accurately control the temperature of the cavity surface using this heating method. Because of this, there is a time delay in heating the cavity surface, and because the structure of the channel where the pipeline and cartridge heater are applied is heated linearly, the temperature distribution is not uniform. Because of these issues, these methods are mainly used for injection molding large parts such as TV panels and automobile parts. They are unsuitable for producing sophisticated parts containing nano or micro units. Steam heating requires a high-pressure steam generator and boiler as additional equipment and many additional facilities, such as steam supply pipes. In addition, once used, steam has the disadvantage of being difficult to recover, resulting in significant energy waste [2].

Surface heating elements complementing the heating method applied through channels are also being investigated. A mold heating method has been developed using a surface heating element. A thin metal film is employed as a heating layer [19]. Recently, a new rapid surface heater has been generated by CVD coating graphene on a silicon wafer [20]. These surface heating elements attract attention as alternatives to linear heating elements because they provide uniform and stable temperature distribution in the application range. However, in the case of thin metal films, the resistance when applying actual power is so low that a large current is easily applied, which reduces electrical stability and is unsuitable for application to molded products of complex shapes. Surface heating elements using graphene coating are easily produced by coating various shapes. However, it is challenging to ensure electrical safety during the process because the area where power is applied and heated is exposed, and impurities in the surrounding environment easily cause discharge, reducing safety.

A multilayer structure mold has been designed to ensure electrical safety using CNT web film as a surface heating element. Reflection of errors occurring in the design of the multilayer structure mold and optimization design was performed to secure good heat-transfer performance.

2. Experiment and Methods

2.1. Fabrication of CNT Web Film Heater

The CNT web film, which serves as a rapid heating source, is produced through the direct spinning method [21]. This film is made by injecting a CNT precursor solution mixed with acetone (94 wt.%), thiophene (4.8 wt.%), ferrocene (1.2 wt.%), and hydrogen gas into a high-temperature furnace. The manufacturing process involves setting the temperature of the high-temperature furnace to 1200 °C, the injection rate to 35 mL/h, and the hydrogen flow rate to 2200 sccm. After the process, the CNT fiber is wound through a cylindrical roll to form a web film, as shown in Figure 1. To stabilize the CNT web film and ensure heat generation uniformity, the CNTs were densified by immersion in isopropyl alcohol (IPA) solution and then underwent a 2-roll pressing process in the post-process [22].

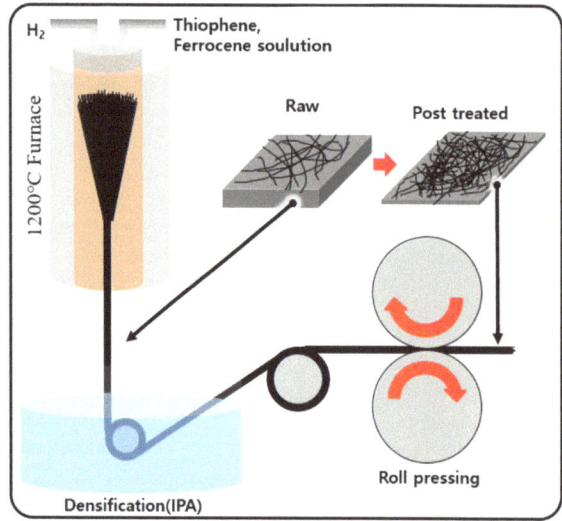

Figure 1. Fabrication of CNT web film.

2.2. Multilayer Structure Mold

A multilayer structure mold was designed to apply CNT web film as a heater in the RHCM process, and rapid heating experiments were conducted. A computer-controlled DC supplier applies electricity (60 V) to the CNT web film and heats the mold cavity surface. The DC controller and infrared (IR) camera transmit the resistance change and temperature data to the computer, respectively (see Figure 2). As a heating source used in this rapid heating mold, the CNT web film generates Joule heat through direct electricity flows. Since electricity is directly applied to the CNT web film, the mold part in contact with the CNT web film is insulated. Therefore, the multilayer structure mold used in this heat-transfer experiment was electrically insulated and was stacked in the following order: mold metal, insulator, CNT web film, insulator, and mold metal, as shown in the cross-sectional view in Figure 3c. The mold was designed as a flat plate, and the CNT web film was also applied to the shape of the flat plate (see Figure 3d). A CNT web film layer exists along with the busbar, which is an electrode, to apply electricity to the CNT web film inside the multilayer structure mold. However, a flush can occur between the busbar and insulator during assembly and parts processing due to tolerances. Because of this flush, the CNT web film inside the multilayer mold cannot fully contact the insulator, resulting in non-contact areas. Hence, when heating is applied with electricity, the CNT web film is oxidized and damaged in non-contact areas, causing a short circuit and making stable heating difficult. To address this problem, an experimental mold set flush differences of 0 mm, 0.1 mm, and 0.3 mm between the busbar and insulator inside the multilayer mold. The damage to the CNT web film based on flush size was measured through Raman spectroscopy. The size of the mold made for the experiment was approximately 200 × 100 × 50 mm, and the main physical properties are listed in Table 1. The multilayer structure mold uses materials such as C1100 and Nak80, which have high thermal conductivity. CNT web film's thermal conductivity is relatively lower than that of these materials. However, the physical property provided in Table 1 is the out-of-plane direction (vertical) thermal conductivity. The in-plane direction thermal conductivity exceeds 600 W/m·K, surpassing that of C1100. By this, when the Joule heat was generated by CNT web film with electricity, the entire film and the mold cavity surface were both heated uniformly.

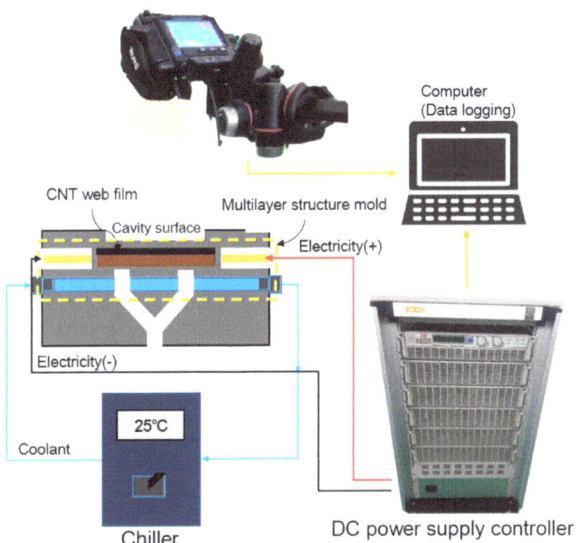

Figure 2. Schematic view of RHCM experiment.

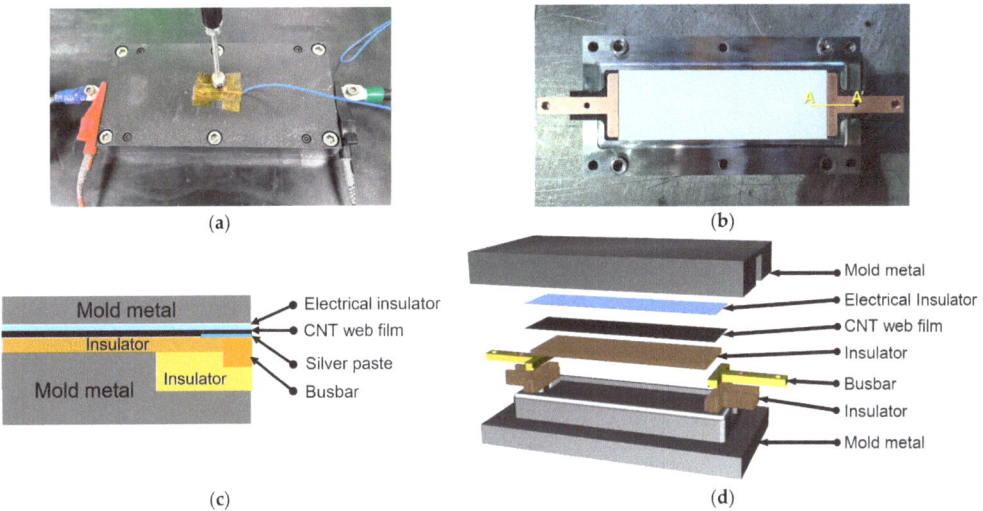

Figure 3. RHCM multilayer structure mold: (**a**) test mold, (**b**) inside of the test mold, (**c**) cross-sectional view of A-A', (**d**) each layer of the multilayer structure mold.

Table 1. Properties of the materials for the multilayer test mold.

Material	Component	Density (g/cm³)	Conductivity (W/m·K)	Specific Heat (J/g·K)	Resistivity (Ohm·cm)
NAK80	Core plate	7.8	41.33	0.481	2.63×10^{-5}
CNT web film	Heater	0.41	(In-plane) 14.65 (Out-of-plane) 600	0.716	2.49×10^{-3}
C1100	Bus bar	8.89	390.79	0.385	1.7×10^{-8}
Glass fiber fabric	Electrical insulator	1.26	1.5	0.65	1×10^{25}
ISOL600	Insulator	1.63	0.33	0.88	-

2.3. Optimization of Multilayer Structure Mold

A multilayer structure mold is a type of structure that involves stacking materials with different physical properties. It requires an optimized design that considers the heat transfer from CNT web film (heat source) to the cavity surface that needs to be heated. The multilayer structure consists of mold metal, an electrical insulator, CNT web film, an insulator, and mold metal, and the thickness of the cavity surface is fixed at 5 mm to withstand an injection pressure of about 100 MPa. To perform optimization analysis on a multilayer structure mold, the thickness of the electrical insulator varied between 0.25 mm, 0.5 mm, 1 mm, 2 mm, and 4 mm, while the thickness of the CNT web film varied between 5 μm, 10 μm, 23 μm, and 37 μm. Also, the thickness of the insulator varied between 0.5 mm, 1 mm, 2 mm, 4 mm, and 10 mm. Multilayer structures were combined for each material thickness, and heat-transfer analysis was performed. The CNT web film has a specific resistance of about 0.00027 Ω·cm, and a constant power density of 57 W/cm² was applied during the test.

2.4. Numerical Simulation for Multilayer Structure Mold

To evaluate the heating performance of the multilayer structure mold, numerical simulation was performed by effectively coupled electrical and thermal finite element analyses. CNT web film, which serves as a heat source, generates Joule heat when electricity flows through it. Joule heat is calculated as Equation (1).

$$\dot{Q} = \sigma \cdot J^2 \tag{1}$$

$$\dot{Q} + \nabla \cdot [k(T)\nabla T] = \rho C(T)\frac{dT}{dt} \tag{2}$$

J is current density, and σ is electrical resistivity. The temperature change of CNT web film is calculated by the transient heat conduction equation as shown in Equation (2). $\rho, k,$ and C refer to the material's density, thermal conductivity, and specific heat. In the multilayer structure mold, each mold layer is tightly attached to the other layers. Hence, the thermal contact conductance of each layer was fixed (Table 2).

Table 2. Thermal contact conductance of multilayer structure mold.

Materials		Thermal Contact Conductance (W/m²·K)
Nak80	Electric insulator	2900
Electric insulator	CNT web film	30,000
CNT web film	Insulator	1000

3. Results

3.1. Flush Mold Heating Test

When 2.5 kW was applied to a single-phase mold without a flush, the temperature of the mold steel was heated to 150 °C. As the temperature increased, resistance increased, showing PTC (Positive Temperature Coefficient of Resistance) characteristics. Both showed PTC characteristics when heated regardless of the presence or absence of flush (see Figure 4). When heating the mold, the change in resistance was measured in the low-temperature range (30~60 °C) and high-temperature range (130 °C or above) (see Figure 5). The rate of change in the normalized R value in the low-temperature range was 2.4%. In the high-temperature range, it was 2.3%, and the change rate in resistance was similar across the entire temperature range. In the flush test mold, the flush between the busbar and the bottom insulator was set to 0 mm, 0.1 mm, and 0.3 mm, and power was applied to observe the change in resistance of the CNT web film. The variation rates of CNT web film's normalized R with a flush of 0.1 mm and 0.3 mm were found to be 2.9% and 9.6% in the low-temperature range and 2.7% and 4.3% in the high-temperature range, respectively. In all experiments, the resistance change rate in the high-temperature section was lower than in the low-temperature section. That appears to be a characteristic of the resistance change converging and becoming constant by the aging phenomenon of the CNT web film when heated above a specific temperature. When the flush was 0 mm or 0.1 mm, resistance changes were similar to those in the low- and high-temperature ranges. However, when the flush was 0.3 mm, the resistance change in the low-temperature range was 2.2 times higher than that in the high-temperature range. In addition, when comparing the resistance of each repeated experiment in the low-temperature section, an abnormal phenomenon was observed in which the resistance decreased. When the flush inside the mold is over 0.3 mm, it seems to cause damage to the CNT web film during heating.

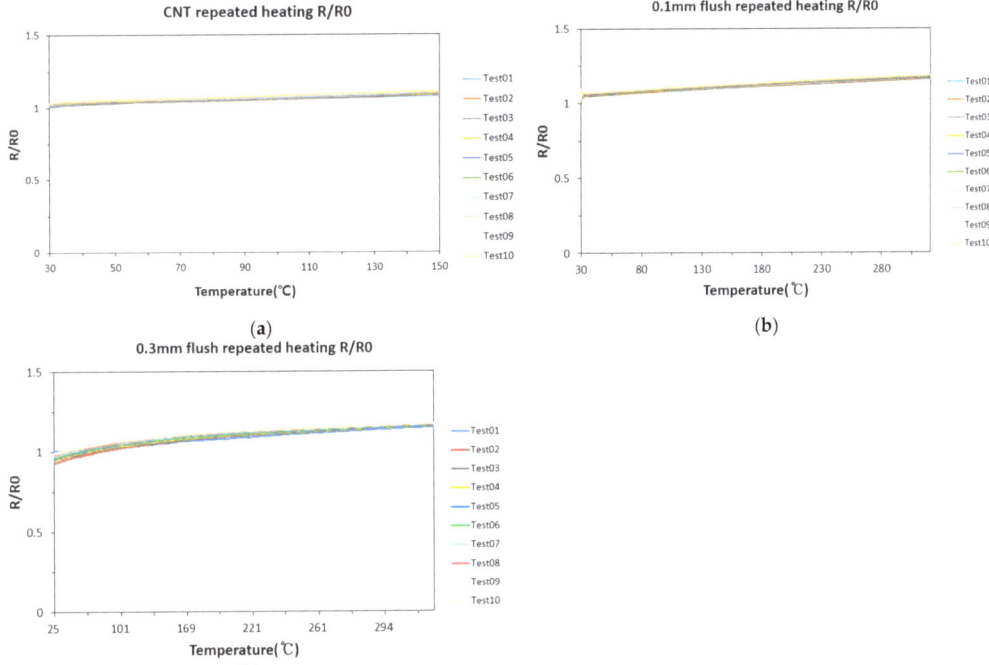

Figure 4. Resistance variation of CNT web film by flush: (**a**) 0 mm flush, (**b**) 0.1 mm flush, (**c**) 0.3 mm flush.

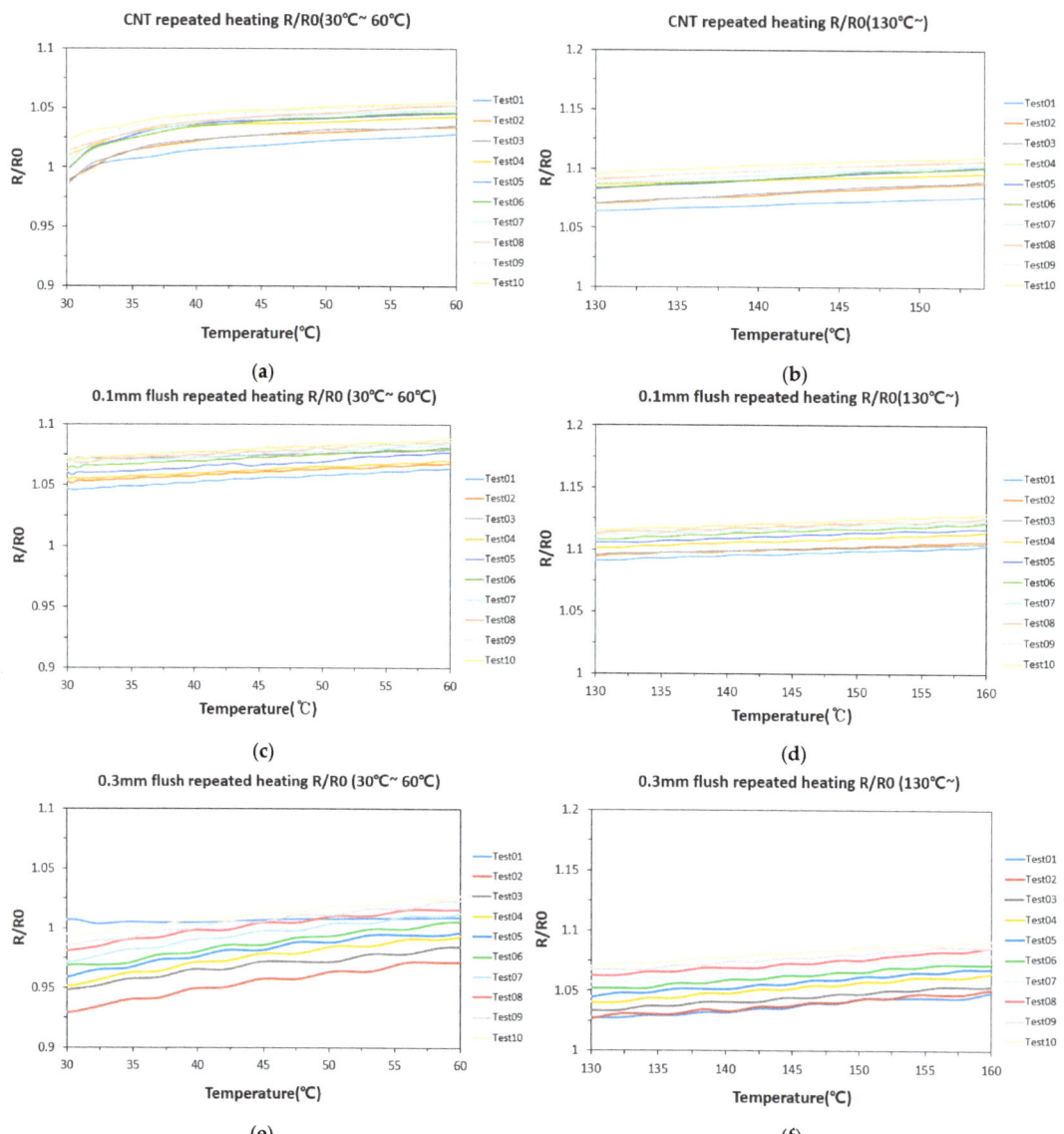

Figure 5. Resistance variation of CNT web film by flush and temperature range: (**a**) 0 mm flush at 30 °C < T < 60 °C, (**b**) 0 mm flush at 130 °C < T, (**c**) 0.1 mm flush at 30 °C < T < 60 °C, (**d**) 0.1 mm flush at 130 °C < T, (**e**) 0.3 mm flush at 30 °C < T < 60 °C, (**f**) 0.3 mm flush at 130 °C < T.

3.2. Raman Spectroscopy Measurements of CNT Web Film

CNT web film was measured using Raman spectroscopy to directly observe the damage to the CNT web film after repeated flush mold heating experiments. As shown in Figure 6, five points of the CNT web film were designated and observed. At the P1 point, the actual contact part and the non-contact part were separated and measured into P1-1 and P1-2 points, and the Raman measurement results are shown in Figure 7. The degree of defect in the CNT web film was confirmed through the D/G peak. The sample's P0, P1-1, P1-2, P2, and P3 points with a flush of 0 mm presented D/G peaks of 0.18, 0.16, 0.18, 0.14, and 0.14 on average, respectively. Each point of the 0.1 mm sample presented D/G peaks of 0.18, 0.18, 0.21, 0.35, and 0.39, respectively. Each point of the 0.3 mm sample presented D/G peaks of 0.23, 0.26, 0.41, 0.25, and 0.31. When there was no flush (0 mm), similar peak values were presented at all points, and no defects appeared. However, the defect caused by the flush showed a maximum peak of 0.41 at the P1-2 point of 0.3 mm. Hence, a non-contact overheating defect occurs when the flush is over 0.3 mm.

Figure 6. Measuring points (**a**) 4 measuring points of CNT web film, (**b**) Detail points in P1.

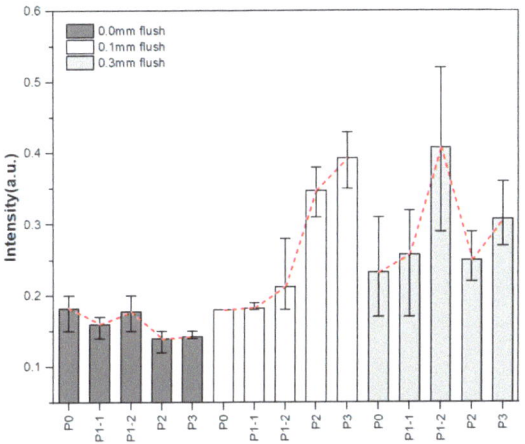

Figure 7. Results of Raman spectroscopy of CNT web film.

3.3. Heat-Transfer Analysis by the Thickness of Layers

The heat-transfer efficiency was compared, as shown in Figure 8, by changing the thickness of each layer in the multilayer structure mold. To improve the heat-transfer efficiency of the multilayer structure mold and find the optimal thickness of each layer, comparisons of heating rates with varying material thickness and simulation analysis were conducted using the Ansys simulation tool. The detailed simulation setup is listed in Table 3. To verify the simulation model before optimization analysis, one-cycle heating performance was verified by comparing analysis and experimental data (see Figure 8e). The simulation model presented a maximum error of 12.6% during heating, but the maximum heating temperature was very similar, with an error of approximately 0.5%. The simulation model was verified with an average error of 9.4%. Based on this simulation model, the heat-transfer performance of each layer in the multilayer structure mold was analyzed. In Figure 8b, it can be seen that as the thickness of the CNT web film decreases, heat-transfer performance reaches its maximums at 10 μm and 5 μm. In Figure 8c,d, it can be seen that the heat-transfer performance increases as the insulator thickness increases and the thickness of the electrical insulator decreases, respectively. The maximum heat-transfer performance was achieved when the insulator thickness was over 5 mm and the electrical insulator thickness was 0.25 mm. Finally, the thicknesses of the multilayer structure mold's CNT web film, insulator, and electrical insulator were selected as 10 μm, 5 mm, and 0.5 mm, respectively. In the case of electrical insulators, thinner thicknesses improve heat-transfer performance, but for safety reasons, a thickness of at least 0.5 mm should be applied for electrical insulation. Additionally, the one-cycle heating performance of the RHCM mold with optimal thickness was compared to the CIM mold applied with cartridge heaters. It was confirmed that RHCM heats approximately four times faster than CIM.

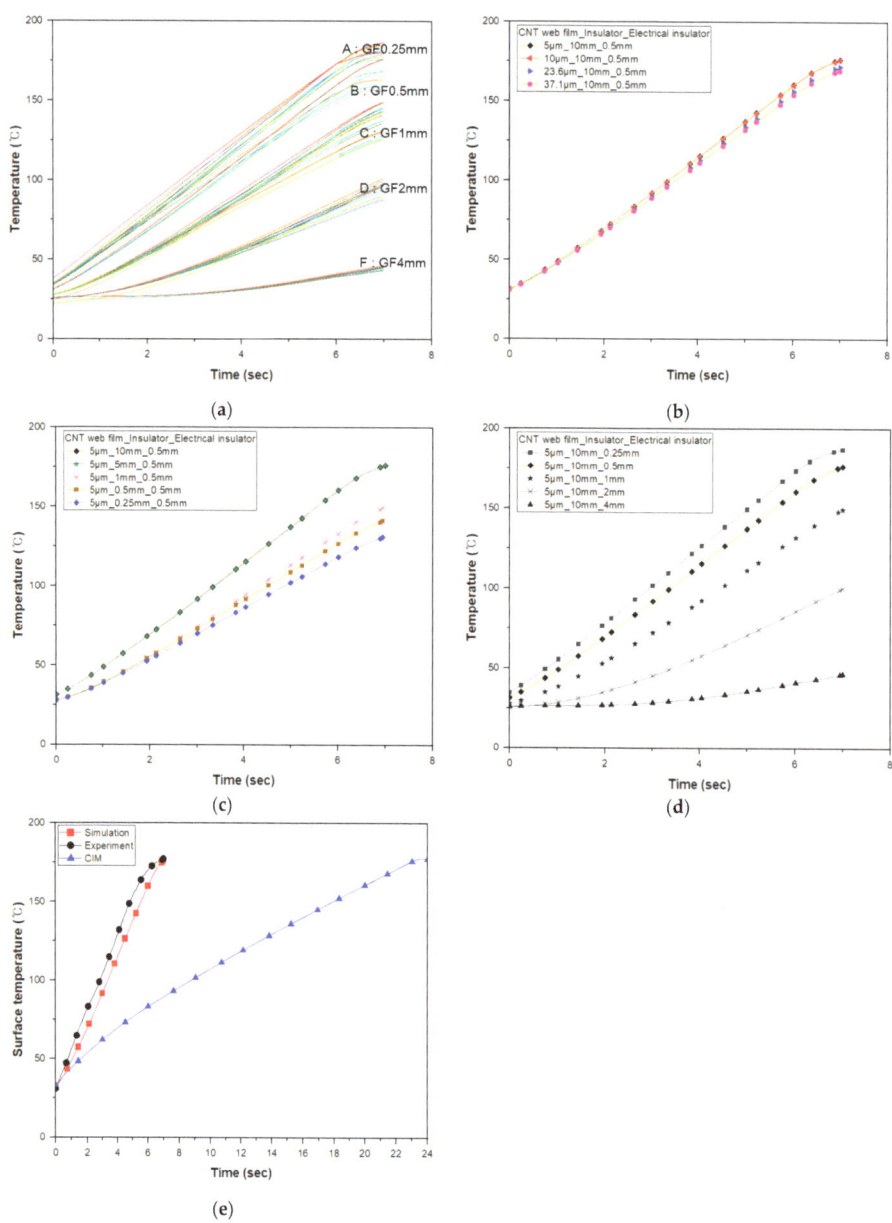

Figure 8. Temperature response of multilayer structure mold: (**a**) total data of various thicknesses, (**b**) CNT web film thickness variation, (**c**) insulator thickness variation, (**d**) electronical insulator variation, (**e**) verification of simulation model and comparison of RHCM and CIM.

Table 3. Multilayer structure mold CNT web film, insulator, and electrical insulator optimizing parameters.

Material	Thickness Levels (mm)					Power Density (W/cm^2)
CNT web film	0.005	0.01	0.023	0.037		57
Insulator	0.5	1	2	4	10	57
Electric insulator	0.25	0.5	1	2	4	57

3.4. Surface Temperature Uniformity

The heat-transfer analysis model was verified by comparing it with heating experiment data, reflecting the thickness of each layer of the final selected multilayer mold. As shown in Figure 9, a similar temperature distribution was observed during heating. According to the analysis model, the maximum temperature reached was 176 °C, while the experimental results showed a similar maximum temperature of about 177 °C. The maximum error between the simulation model and the experimental results was 12%, with the average error staying within 10%, indicating comparable behavior. Similar temperature trends were observed during the heating period, as shown in Figure 9c.

$$T_u = 100 \times \left(1 - \frac{T_t - T_p}{T_p}\right) \qquad (3)$$

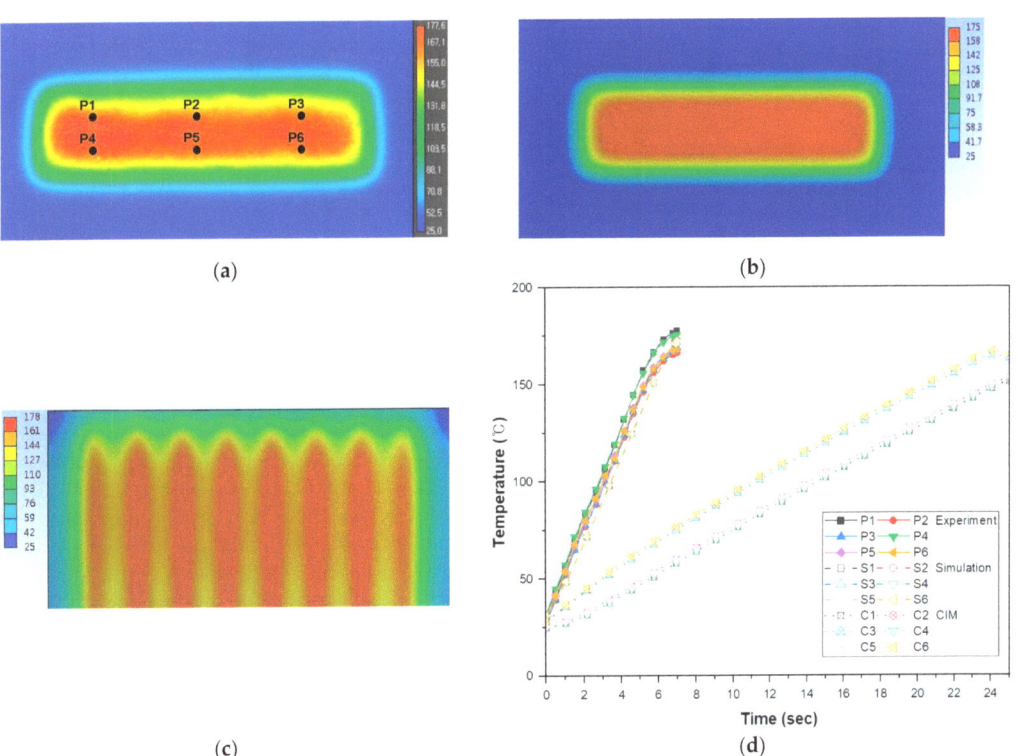

Figure 9. Temperature uniformity of multilayer structure mold: (a) RHCM experiment temperature contour, (b) RHCM simulation temperature contour, (c) CIM mold temperature contour, (d) temperature response of 6 points.

In the experiment, the temperature uniformity T_u is calculated as Equation (3) based on the target temperature of about 170 °C. T_t is the target temperature, and T_P represents the measured temperature at the point. Temperature uniformity was 95.7%, 97.8%, 99.3%, 96.8%, 99%, and 99% at points 1–6, respectively, with an average uniformity of 98% at the highest temperature point. In the CIM process, temperature uniformities at the same point were 83.9%, 85%, 94.5%, 84.1%, 85.3%, and 95.8% at points 1–6, with an average temperature uniformity of 88.1%.

4. Conclusions

Problems that appear in the mold design stage for implementing a rapid heating process using CNT web film as a heat source were identified by designing variables. When applying CNT web film to multilayer structure molds, processing and assembly errors may cause non-contact areas called flush, damaging the CNT web film when heated.

(1) CNT web film was applied by setting flush of 0 mm, 0.1 mm, and 0.3 mm through a flush test mold, and the damage to CNT web film after heating was measured through changes in resistance and Raman spectroscopy.

(2) When 0.1 mm flush was applied, the resistance change and D/G peak did not show much difference from the 0 mm flush sample, confirming that the flush was within the allowable value. However, when applying a 0.3 mm flush, the resistance change rates in the repeated experiment were highest in the low- and high-temperature ranges, and the D/G peak value of Raman spectroscopy was also highest. It was confirmed that it is inappropriate to apply CNT web film as a heat source in a multilayer structure with a flush of 0.3 mm or above. As the flush increases, the non-contact area of the CNT web film becomes more extensive, and it is relatively overheated during heating, confirming that the effect of oxidation is more significant than in other areas. For the stable implementation of a rapid heating multilayer structure mold with a CNT web film, it is necessary to design the flush level of the multilayer structure to be less than 0.3 mm.

(3) Optimization analysis was performed by combining the thicknesses of each material. The thicknesses of the CNT web film were 5 μm, 10 μm, 24 μm, and 37 μm. Insulator thicknesses were 0.25 mm, 0.5 mm, 1 mm, 5 mm, and 10 mm. The thicknesses of the electrical insulator were 0.25 mm, 0.5 mm, 1 mm, 2 mm, and 4 mm. As a result of the analysis, heat-transfer performance increased as the thickness of the CNT web film and electrical insulator decreased, and heat-transfer performance increased as the thickness of the insulator increased. The heat-transfer performance of the CNT web film converged below 10 μm, and that of the insulator converged above 5 mm. Electrical insulators show better performance as they decrease. However, a thickness of at least 0.5 mm was selected for insulation safety. Heat-transfer performance in the direction of the cavity surface varies depending on the thickness of the insulator to block heat-transfer to the back of the mold and the electrical insulator located between the cavity surface and the CNT web film. The heat flow direction was toward the cavity surface when the electrical insulator was thinner than the insulator. That caused maximum heat-transfer performance to be observed.

(4) When comparing RHCM and CIM using cartridge heaters, the heating performance of the multilayer structure mold (RHCM) was heated more than four times faster than with CIM. The maximum heating rates in the RHCM mold and CIM mold were 21 °C/s and 5 °C/s, respectively. RHCM mold temperature uniformity was also higher by more than 10% for RHCM, with an average of 98% compared to 88% for CIM.

The rapid heating injection mold with the multilayer structure designed in this study has the advantage of a faster heating rate compared to the existing rapid heating technique. It also has significant advantages in production and cost, with low facility investment costs. In the future, the main variables of the rapid heating mold required for application to the injection process will be identified and reflected in the mold design to increase the durability and stabilization of the technology.

Author Contributions: Conceptualization, Y.K.; Formal analysis, H.L.; Investigation, H.L.; Methodology, Y.K. and W.C.; Validation, H.L.; Writing—original draft, H.L.; Writing—review and editing, Y.K. and W.C. All authors have read and agreed to the published version of the manuscript.

Funding: This work was supported by the Technology Innovation Program (Grant No. 20004272) funded by the Ministry of Trade, Industry and Energy, Republic of Korea.

Institutional Review Board Statement: Not applicable.

Informed Consent Statement: Not applicable.

Data Availability Statement: The original contributions presented in the study are included in the article, further inquiries can be directed to the corresponding author.

Conflicts of Interest: The authors declare no conflicts of interest.

References

1. Park, K.; Sohn, D.-H.; Cho, K.-H. Eliminating Weldlines of an Injection-Molded Part with the Aid of High-Frequency Induction Heating. *J. Mech. Sci. Technol.* **2010**, *24*, 149–152. [CrossRef]
2. Wang, G.; Hui, Y.; Lei, Z.; Guoqun, Z. Research on Temperature and Pressure Responses in the Rapid Mold Heating and Cooling Method Based on Annular Cooling Channels and Electric Heating. *Int. J. Heat Mass Transf.* **2018**, *116*, 1192–1203. [CrossRef]
3. Chen, S.-C.; Wang, Y.-C.; Liu, S.-C.; Cin, J.-C. Mold Temperature Variation for Assisting Micro-Molding of DVD Micro-Featured Substrate and Dummy Using Pulsed Cooling. *Sens. Actuators A Phys.* **2009**, *151*, 87–93. [CrossRef]
4. Chen, S.-C.; Jong, W.-R.; Chang, Y.-J.; Chang, J.-A.; Cin, J.-C. Rapid Mold Temperature Variation for Assisting the Micro Injection of High Aspect Ratio Micro-Feature Parts Using Induction Heating Technology. *J. Micromech. Microeng.* **2006**, *16*, 1783–1791. [CrossRef]
5. Huang, M.; Tai, N. Experimental Rapid Surface Heating by Induction for Micro-injection Molding of Light-guided Plates. *J. Appl. Polym. Sci.* **2009**, *113*, 1345–1354. [CrossRef]
6. Chen, S.-C.; Chang, Y.; Chang, Y.-P.; Chen, Y.-C.; Tseng, C.-Y. Effect of Cavity Surface Coating on Mold Temperature Variation and the Quality of Injection Molded Parts. *Int. Commun. Heat Mass Transf.* **2009**, *36*, 1030–1035. [CrossRef]
7. Wang, G.; Zhao, G.; Li, H.; Guan, Y. Research of Thermal Response Simulation and Mold Structure Optimization for Rapid Heat Cycle Molding Processes, Respectively, with Steam Heating and Electric Heating. *Mater. Des.* **2010**, *31*, 382–395. [CrossRef]
8. Theilade, U.A.; Hansen, H.N. Surface Microstructure Replication in Injection Molding. *Int. J. Adv. Manuf. Technol.* **2007**, *33*, 157–166. [CrossRef]
9. Chang, P.; Hwang, S. Experimental Investigation of Infrared Rapid Surface Heating for Injection Molding. *J. Appl. Polym. Sci.* **2006**, *102*, 3704–3713. [CrossRef]
10. Menotti, S.; Hansen, H.N.; Bissacco, G.; Calaon, M.; Tang, P.T.; Ravn, C. Injection Molding of Nanopatterned Surfaces in the Sub-Micrometer Range with Induction Heating Aid. *Int. J. Adv. Manuf. Technol.* **2014**, *74*, 907–916. [CrossRef]
11. Chen, S.-C.; Jong, W.-R.; Chang, J.-A. Dynamic Mold Surface Temperature Control Using Induction Heating and Its Effects on the Surface Appearance of Weld Line. *J. Appl. Polym. Sci.* **2006**, *101*, 1174–1180. [CrossRef]
12. Guerrier, P.; Tosello, G.; Nielsen, K.K.; Hattel, J.H. Three-Dimensional Numerical Modeling of an Induction Heated Injection Molding Tool with Flow Visualization. *Int. J. Adv. Manuf. Technol.* **2016**, *85*, 643–660. [CrossRef]
13. Yao, D.; Kimerling, T.E.; Kim, B. High-frequency Proximity Heating for Injection Molding Applications. *Polym. Eng. Sci.* **2006**, *46*, 938–945. [CrossRef]
14. Chen, S.-C.; Chien, R.-D.; Lin, S.-H.; Lin, M.-C.; Chang, J.-A. Feasibility Evaluation of Gas-Assisted Heating for Mold Surface Temperature Control during Injection Molding Process. *Int. Commun. Heat. Mass. Transf.* **2009**, *36*, 806–812. [CrossRef]
15. Yao, D.; Kim, B. Development of Rapid Heating and Cooling Systems for Injection Molding Applications. *Polym. Eng. Sci.* **2002**, *42*, 2295–2481. [CrossRef]
16. Kim, Y.; Choi, Y.; Kang, S. Replication of High Density Optical Disc Using Injection Mold with MEMS Heater. *Microsyst. Technol.* **2005**, *11*, 464–469. [CrossRef]
17. Wang, G.; Zhao, G.; Wang, X. Development and Evaluation of a New Rapid Mold Heating and Cooling Method for Rapid Heat Cycle Molding. *Int. J. Heat Mass Transf.* **2014**, *78*, 99–111. [CrossRef]
18. Jeng, M.-C.; Chen, S.-C.; Minh, P.S.; Chang, J.-A.; Chung, C. Rapid Mold Temperature Control in Injection Molding by Using Steam Heating. *Int. Commun. Heat. Mass Transf.* **2010**, *37*, 1295–1304. [CrossRef]
19. Lee, J.; Turng, L.-S. Improving Surface Quality of Microcellular Injection Molded Parts through Mold Surface Temperature Manipulation with Thin Film Insulation. *Polym. Eng. Sci.* **2010**, *50*, 1281–1289. [CrossRef]

20. Yang, H.; Yilmaz, G.; Han, G.; Eriten, M.; Zhang, Z.; Yu, S.; Shi, M.; Yan, H.; Yang, W.; Xie, P.; et al. A Quick Response and Tribologically Durable Graphene Heater for Rapid Heat Cycle Molding and Its Applications in Injection Molding. *Appl. Therm. Eng.* **2020**, *167*, 114791. [CrossRef]
21. Li, Y.-L.; Kinloch, I.A.; Windle, A.H. Direct Spinning of Carbon Nanotube Fibers from Chemical Vapor Deposition Synthesis. *Science* **2004**, *304*, 276–278. [CrossRef] [PubMed]
22. Kim, H.W.; Ha, J.H.; Song, H.J.; Park, J.H.; Jeong, Y.J. Rapid and Durable Electric Heating Characteristics of Carbon Nanotube Web Film. *Conf. Korean Soc. Precis. Eng.* **2020**, *1*, 799.

Disclaimer/Publisher's Note: The statements, opinions and data contained in all publications are solely those of the individual author(s) and contributor(s) and not of MDPI and/or the editor(s). MDPI and/or the editor(s) disclaim responsibility for any injury to people or property resulting from any ideas, methods, instructions or products referred to in the content.

Article

Prediction of Tooth Profile Deviation for WEDM Rigid Gears Based on ISSA-LSSVM

Yazhou Wang *, Zhen Wang, Gang Wang and Huike Xu

School of Mechanical and Electrical Engineering, Lanzhou University of Technology, Lanzhou 730050, China; wangzhen_lut@163.com (Z.W.); wangg_lut@163.com (G.W.); xuhuike_lut@163.com (H.X.)
* Correspondence: wangyzh@lut.edu.cn

Abstract: This study aimed to develop and validate an improved sparrow search algorithm (ISSA)-optimized Least Squares Support Vector Machine (LSSVM) model for accurately predicting the tooth profile deviation of rigid gears produced by wire electrical discharge machining (WEDM). The ISSA was obtained by optimizing the sparrow search algorithm (SSA) using Tent chaotic mapping, adaptive adjustment strategy, dynamic inertia weights, and grey wolf hierarchy strategy. The effectiveness of the ISSA was verified using four different classes of benchmark test functions. Four main process parameters (peak current, pulse width, pulse interval, and tracking) were taken as inputs and the tooth profile deviations of rigid gears were considered as outputs to develop an ISSA-LSSVM-based profile deviation prediction model. The prediction performance of the ISSA-LSSVM model was evaluated by comparing it with the LSSVM model optimized by three standard algorithms. The prediction results of the ISSA-LSSVM model were $R^2 = 0.9828$, $RMSE = 0.0029$, and $MAPE = 0.0156$. The results showed that the established model exhibits high prediction accuracy and can provide reliable theoretical guidance for predicting the tooth profile deviation of rigid gears.

Keywords: rigid gears; wire electrical discharge machining; tooth profile deviation; least squares support vector machine; improved sparrow search algorithm

Citation: Wang, Y.; Wang, Z.; Wang, G.; Xu, H. Prediction of Tooth Profile Deviation for WEDM Rigid Gears Based on ISSA-LSSVM. *Appl. Sci.* **2024**, *14*, 4596. https://doi.org/10.3390/app14114596

Academic Editor: Marco Troncossi

Received: 8 April 2024
Revised: 22 May 2024
Accepted: 24 May 2024
Published: 27 May 2024

Copyright: © 2024 by the authors. Licensee MDPI, Basel, Switzerland. This article is an open access article distributed under the terms and conditions of the Creative Commons Attribution (CC BY) license (https:// creativecommons.org/licenses/by/ 4.0/).

1. Introduction

Harmonic gear reducers offer numerous advantages, such as a significant transmission ratio, robust load-carrying ability, and exceptional transmission precision. Consequently, they find widespread application in aerospace, robotics, the defense industry, and other high-end precision technology fields [1,2]. Given the precision transmission characteristics of harmonic gear reducers, it becomes crucial to guarantee the accuracy and quality of each mechanism during the manufacturing process. This is necessary to guarantee that the transmission performance of the finished parts aligns with the design requirements. Being the core component of the harmonic gear reducer, the tooth profile deviation of the rigid gear significantly impacts the performance and assembly performance of the harmonic gear transmission system.

Numerous researchers have conducted extensive studies on gear tooth deviation in different machining processes. Guo et al. [3] explored the computation approach of tooth profile deviation in conventional turning, assessed the impact of turning tool rake angle, and proposed a method to improve tooth profile deviation through turning tool grinding. Yuan et al. [4] developed a comprehensive tooth profile deviation model using conjugate surface meshing theory, the Box–Behnken experimental design, and the artificial immune clone algorithm. The model optimizes and actively controls the internal gear power honing (IGPH) process parameters to obtain high gear geometry accuracy. Wang et al. [5] established quantitative mapping models for hob geometry errors and gear geometric errors, revealing essential mapping rules and laying a theoretical foundation for achieving higher precision in roll-cutting gears. Sun et al. [6] provided a forecast model for hobbing gear geometric errors. They used a modified PSO-BP algorithm to analyze the correlation between the hobbing process parameters and tooth shape deviation. Peng et al. [7] analyzed the tooth profile deviation in the hobbing forming process base on the theory of gear meshing, and adjusted the hobbing process parameters for the deviation size. Yusron et al. [8] performed a study analyzing how wire-cutting parameters, including pulse width, open circuit voltage, wire tension, and pulse current, affect the deviation of the straight-toothed cylindrical gear tooth profile through orthogonal experiments. Vishal et al. [9] found that adjusting hobbing parameters can greatly impact the microgeometry deviation and average deviation of gears. By determining the optimal combination of parameters, gear precision can be significantly improved. Mo et al. [10] presented a model to analyze the time-varying meshing stiffness of asymmetric gear pairs, which yields outcomes more similar to primitive meshing by taking into account the tooth shape deviations. They also highlight the significant effect of small shape deviations on gear meshing characteristics. Chen et al. [11] presented a new method to solve the meshing stiffness and analyzed the variation in the stiffness and load distribution ratio with tooth profile deviation during gear meshing. Tsai et al. [12] introduced a mathematical method to investigate the variation in tooth profile deviation that occurs when cutting gears under various parameters using the same turning tool. Their findings indicated that reducing the helix angle or the number of teeth can result in a change in tooth profile deviation.

The existing literature primarily focuses on the gear processing mechanism and uses theoretical modelling and simulation analysis to explore the causes of tooth profile errors. Traditional machining methods, such as hobbing and shaping, have been extensively studied. However, these methods often face limitations in flexibility and precision, especially when dealing with complex gear geometries. Recent advances in gear manufacturing have highlighted the potential of wire electrical discharge machining (WEDM) for improving gear quality and performance. These methods allow for higher precision and the ability to handle intricate designs that are challenging for traditional techniques. R. Chaudhari et al. [13] studied the effect of WEDM process parameters on surface morphology, highlighting its significant impact on gear quality.

Additionally, the importance of free-form milling has been underscored in the recent literature. This method offers a universal tool geometry and the ability to machine various gear types and sizes within one manufacturing system. Studies have shown that free-form milling enhances the quality and performance of gears by providing higher flexibility and precision [14]. Moreover, the emergence of 5-axis double-flank CNC machining for spiral bevel gears presents new opportunities in flank form design and manufacturing, overcoming kinematic restrictions of traditional methods [15].

However, there are limited studies on the impact of actual machining process parameters and changes in tooth profile deviations. In this paper, we investigate the tooth profile machining process of rigid gears, a key challenge in the manufacturing process of harmonic gears. The study utilizes wire electrical discharge machining (WEDM), a machining method that employs pulsed spark discharges from an electrode wire to machine workpieces. Unlike conventional machining technologies that rely on mechanical force and energy, WEDM can machine workpieces with complex shapes [16,17]. Currently, the setting of WEDM process parameters mostly relies on the operator's experience, which is unable to adapt to the processing of variable working conditions and affects the processing quality of the workpiece. Prediction problems have been tackled using a range of algorithms in recent years, including neural networks, random forests, support vector machines (SVMs), and the least squares support vector machine (LSSVM) [18–21]. Neural networks, despite their complex structure, have poor generalization ability. Random forest has drawbacks, including a long training time and poor interpretability. An SVM is primarily used for classification problems and is not well-suited for data prediction. For this particular study, we have chosen to use the LSSVM as the preferred predictive algorithm model. The LSSVM is an efficient machine learning technique employed when dealing with limited sample data analysis. However, it encounters challenges regarding intricate parameter selection and a lack of interpretability [22]. In order to tackle this issue, researchers have been investigating the application of various methods like particle swarm optimization (PSO), grey wolf optimization (GWO), genetic algorithm (GA), and others for the purpose of optimizing parameter selection [23–25]. This practice has led to an enhancement in prediction accuracy. The sparrow search algorithm (SSA) is a commonly used intelligent optimization algorithm. However, as with other algorithms, increasing the number of iterations can result in a reduction in population diversity, leading to a tendency for local optimization. Hence, the objective of this research is to enhance the diversity of the SSA through the utilization of a hybrid strategy. Additionally, the parameters in the LSSVM model are optimized to make it more suitable for predicting the tooth profile deviation in rigid gears with limited sample sizes.

In summary, this paper presents a novel approach to predict tooth profile deviation in rigid gears by proposing an ISSA-optimized LSSVM model. By incorporating Tent chaotic mapping, adaptive adjustment strategy, dynamic adaptive weights, and grey wolf hierarchy strategy to refine the SSA algorithm, the LSSVM model is enhanced. Based on these improvements, an ISSA-LSSVM model is established to accurately predict tooth profile deviation in rigid gears using WEDM experimental data as input.

The study's primary components are categorized as follows: In Section 2, the algorithmic principles and innovations of the research are outlined. Section 3 presents the experimental design and data analysis. The effectiveness and better prediction performance of the ISSA-LSSVM model are demonstrated in Section 4. Finally, Section 5 summarizes the key findings throughout the text.

2. Methodology

2.1. LSSVM Model

With the increase in sample data and the complexity of sample relationships, traditional SVMs tend to lose noise immunity, resulting in a decrease in computational speed. To address this issue, Suykens et al. [26] proposed the LSSVM as an improvement over the original SVM. The LSSVM replaces the inequality constraints in the SVM with equations and utilizes a least-squares linear equation as the loss function. This modification transforms the training process from quadratic programming to solving a system of linear equations, thereby reducing computational complexity and increasing computational speed.

Common nonlinear kernel functions include the radial basis kernel function (RBF), polynomial kernel function, and sigmoid kernel function [27]. The RBF was chosen for this study due to its superior performance in practical applications. The RBF is known for its ability to handle nonlinear relationships and its robustness in various scenarios, making it more suitable for the complex nature of the data in this research compared to other kernel functions such as polynomial or sigmoid functions. The basic principles and operational steps of the LSSVM are described in the literature [28].

2.2. Sparrow Search Algorithm

The LSSVM model relies significantly on the exploration of optimal parameters, including penalty factors and kernel function parameters. Traditional optimization approaches often face challenges in finding the optimal parameter settings due to the complex and nonlinear nature of the LSSVM model. By combining the SSA with the LSSVM, we aim to enhance the parameter optimization process of the LSSVM for improved performance and generalization ability. The synergy of the SSA's global search advantage and the LSSVM's powerful generalization capability facilitates effective parameter optimization, addressing challenges in complex parameter selection and enhancing model performance and stability.

The SSA was developed based on sparrows' foraging and defense strategies [29]. Depending on the main responsibilities of the search process, sparrow populations typically consist of three types: discoverers, followers, and guards. Discoverers, constituting around 10–20% of the population, hold a significant role in locating food sources and directing the collective movement of the entire sparrow population. Discoverers take the lead in the search for food and lead the population to migrate in time when predators are detected. The followers obtain food by following the discoverers. When the follower's position is at the outermost end of the population and food is scarce, it will follow the discoverer's tracks and feed in the discoverer's foraging area. The main responsibility of the guards is to monitor the status of the entire search process and provide early warning information. They monitor the performance metrics, convergence, and other key parameters of the search process, and the guardians send out early warning signals as soon as they notice that the search process is going wrong or needs to be adjusted. The basic principles and operational steps of the SSA are described in the literature [29].

2.3. Improved Sparrow Search Algorithm

In the optimization process, the SSA demonstrates high convergence accuracy. However, in the later iterations, the population diversity decreases, making it susceptible to the issue of local extremes [30]. Therefore, this paper proposes the ISSA algorithm that incorporates the four strategies. The specific strategies are outlined below.

2.3.1. Improved Tent Chaotic Mapping

The initial populations of the SSA are randomly generated, leading to an uneven distribution of sparrow populations in the search space. This lack of population diversity can be addressed by using chaotic mapping techniques. Logistic and Tent mapping are algorithm optimization technologies that are highly regarded among researchers. Tent chaotic mapping, renowned for its simple form, tunable parameters, and reversibility, distinguishes itself among a myriad of chaotic mappings. However, the iteration sequence of Tent mapping may contain small cycles and unstable cycle points. Therefore, a random variation factor rand(0,1) was introduced in the Tent mapping strategy to increase the diversity of the initial population according to the literature [31]. Equation (1) is the improved Tent expression:

$$x_{n+1} = \begin{cases} 2x_n + \text{rand}(0,1) \times \frac{1}{T}, & 0 \leq x_n \leq \frac{1}{2} \\ 2(1-x_n) + \text{rand}(0,1) \times \frac{1}{T}, & \frac{1}{2} < x_n \leq 1 \end{cases} \quad (1)$$

The expression after the Bernoulli transform is:

$$x_{n+1} = (2x_n)\text{mod}1 + \text{rand}(0,1) \times \frac{1}{T} \quad (2)$$

T denotes the number of particles in the Tent mapping. Figure 1 displays the initial distribution of chaotic sequences generated by Logistic, Tent, and improved Tent chaotic mapping in a 2D region. It is evident that the improved Tent chaos mapping exhibits better distribution uniformity.

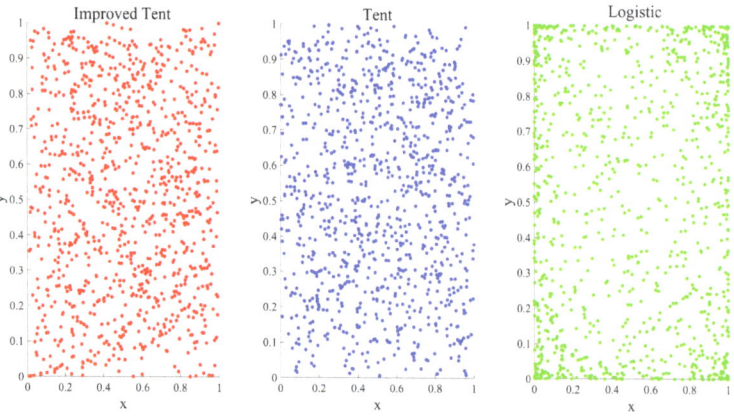

Figure 1. Initial distribution of chaotic sequences.

2.3.2. Adaptive Adjustment Strategy

The proportional balance between the number of discoverers and followers is crucial during the iteration of the algorithm. However, during the initial iteration phase, the limited number of discoverers hampers the effectiveness of a global search. Conversely, as the iteration progresses, it becomes necessary to augment the quantity of discoverers and followers to enhance the precision of a local search [32]. Therefore, the present study proposes an adaptive adjustment strategy for the ratio of sparrow discoverers and followers. This strategy aims to enhance the algorithm's general convergence precision. Equations (3)–(5) reflect the specific form of the strategy.

$$\lambda = 0.15 \cdot \left(2e^{-(2t/K)} - 0.1q\right) + 0.1 \tag{3}$$

$$Dn = \lambda N \tag{4}$$

$$Fn = (1 - \lambda)N \tag{5}$$

In the above expression, λ is a proportion factor with a nonlinear decreasing trend. Dn and Fn represent the number of discoverers and followers, respectively. N is the population size. K denotes the maximum iterations, and t indicates the current iteration number. $q \in [0, 1]$ denotes a randomly generated number for perturbing λ. The performance of this strategy is depicted in Figure 2. After a series of iterations, the discoverer–follower ratio demonstrates convergence. This approach aims to balance early global exploration and later local optimization.

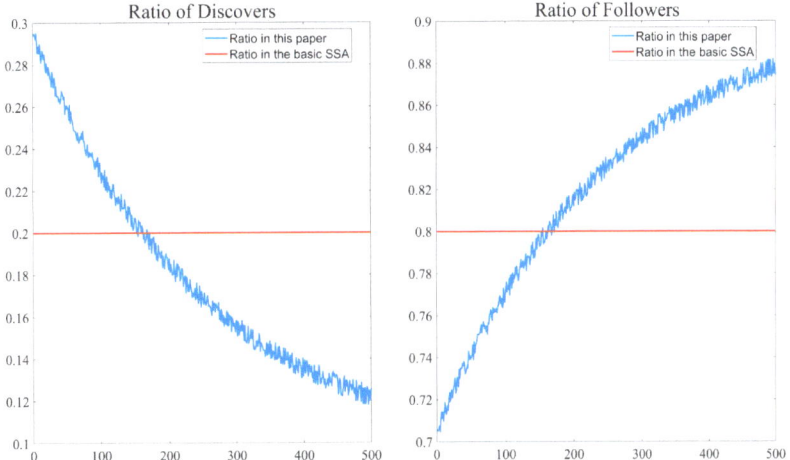

Figure 2. Ratio of discoverers to followers.

2.3.3. Dynamic Inertia Weights

The SSA often exhibits a jumping step during the iterative process, which helps improve the convergence speed. However, this can also lead to a decrease in the diversity of the search process and result in local optima. To address this, a perturbation strategy using inertia weights is proposed in this study. This strategy updates the positions of the discoverers, enhancing their global search capability and promoting information exchange among sparrow populations. The weighting factor ω is shown in Equation (6), and the location update formula for the discoverer is shown in Equation (7):

$$\omega(t) = \omega_{\max} \cdot \left(1 - \sin\left(\frac{\pi t}{2K}\right)\right) + \omega_{\min} \cdot \sin\left(\frac{\pi t}{2K}\right) \tag{6}$$

$$x_{i,j}(t+1) = \begin{cases} x_{i,j}(t) \cdot \omega(t) \cdot \exp\left(\frac{-i}{z \cdot K}\right), & R_2 < ST \\ x_{i,j}(t) + \omega(t) \cdot QL, & R_2 \geq ST \end{cases} \tag{7}$$

where $\omega_{\max}$ and $\omega_{\min}$ are the maximum and minimum values of weight changes; t and K, respectively, denote the current number of iterations and the maximum number of iterations; $x_{i,j}$ represents the current position of the discoverer; $z \in (0,1]$ is a random number; Q is a random number which obeys normal distribution; and L is a $1 \times dim$ matrix with all elements of 1.

2.3.4. Grey Wolf Hierarchy Strategy

In situations of danger, individual sparrows escape in a progressively narrower manner, focusing solely on the best possible solution at the present state without considering alternative suboptimal solutions. This leads to all individuals converging prematurely to the current optimal individual. When the current optimal individual is not the global extreme value, a local solution will emerge. Therefore, this paper introduces a hierarchical strategy in the GWO algorithm that selects the top 3 historically optimal locations $\{x_\alpha, x_\beta, x_\delta\}$ to obtain the potential optimal solution. This strategy enables more flexibility in finding reliable solutions nearby, thus avoiding the SSA from falling into a local optimum. Equation (8) is an expression for the grey wolf hierarchy strategy.

$$\begin{cases} x_{1,j} = x_{\alpha,j}(t) + \gamma |x_{i,j}(t) - x_{\alpha,j}(t)| \\ x_{2,j} = x_{\beta,j}(t) + \gamma |x_{i,j}(t) - x_{\beta,j}(t)| \\ x_{3,j} = x_{\delta,j}(t) + \gamma |x_{i,j}(t) - x_{\delta,j}(t)| \end{cases} \tag{8}$$

where x_1, x_2, and x_3 denote the positions of the remaining grey wolf individuals that need to be adjusted under the influence of α, β, and δ wolves, respectively; $x_{i,j}(k)$ represents the position vector of the current grey wolf individual; and γ is a random variable obeying a normal distribution.

The expressions for the weights θ_i corresponding to α, β, and δ wolves are shown below:

$$\omega_i = \frac{3f_\delta - f_i}{3f_\delta - f_\alpha} \tag{9}$$

$$\theta_i = \frac{\omega_i}{\sum_{j=\alpha,\beta,\delta} \omega_j}, \quad i \in \{\alpha, \beta, \delta\} \tag{10}$$

where f_α, f_β, and f_δ denote the optimal fitness of α, β, and δ wolves.

From the principle of the grey wolf optimization algorithm, it is clear that the closer the head wolf is to the prey, the higher the weight will be. α wolves have the highest status in the pack and provide the main direction of movement for the grey wolf population. β wolves and δ wolves provide the secondary direction to speed up the encirclement and attack on the prey.

The improved expression for the guard's position is presented in Equation (11):

$$x_{i,j}(t+1) = \begin{cases} \theta_1 \cdot x_{1,j} + \theta_2 \cdot x_{1,j} x_{2,j} + \theta_3 \cdot x_{1,j} x_{3,j}, & f_i > (f_\alpha \text{ or } f_\beta \text{ or } f_\delta) \\ x_{i,j}(t) + m \cdot \left(\frac{|x_{i,j}(t) - x_{worst}(t)|}{(f_i - f_w) + \varepsilon}\right), & f_i = (f_\alpha \text{ or } f_\beta \text{ or } f_\delta) \end{cases} \tag{11}$$

where θ_1, θ_2, and θ_3 represent the weights of α, β, and δ wolves, respectively; $m \in [-1,1]$ is a random number; f_i is the fitness value of the present sparrow; f_w is the current global worst fitness value; and ε is the smallest constant so as to avoid zero-division-error.

2.4. Performance Test of ISSA

To assess the effectiveness and innovation of the ISSA, simulation experiments were conducted using four benchmark test functions listed in Table 1 [33]. Specifically, F1 and F2 represent unimodal functions, while F3 and F4 represent complex multimodal functions. The optimization performance of the ISSA algorithm was demonstrated by comparing it with PSO, GWO, and SSA.

Table 1. Selected 4 benchmark functions.

Function	Dimension	Range	F_{min}
$F_1(x) = \sum_{i=1}^{d} \left(\sum_{j=1}^{d} x_j \right)^2$	30	$[-30,30]$	0
$F_2(x) = \sum_{i=1}^{d} \left[100(x_{i+1} - x_i^2)^2 + (x_i - 1)^2 \right]$	30	$[-30,30]$	0
$F_3(x) = \sum_{i=1}^{d} \left[x_i^2 - 10\cos(2\pi x_i) + 10 \right]$	30	$[-600,600]$	0
$F_4(x) = \frac{1}{4000} \sum_{i=1}^{d} x_i^2 - \prod_{i=1}^{d} \cos\left(\frac{x_i}{\sqrt{i}}\right) + 1$	30	$[-5.12, 5.12]$	0

The following are the initial parameter settings for each optimization algorithm. The number of populations N and the number of iterations K remained consistent ($N = 30$, $K = 100$). For PSO, the learning factors c1 and c2 were set to the same value (c1 = c2 = 1.5), with an elasticity coefficient of 0.8. The safety thresholds for the ISSA and SSA were defined as 0.8, and the discoverers and guards accounted for 20% each of the sparrow population. In the ISSA, the maximum coefficient of dynamic inertia weights is 0.9, while the minimum coefficient is 0.6.

In order to minimize the influence of chance events and enhance the persuasiveness of the experiment, the average value and standard deviation were selected to assess the optimization ability and stability of each algorithm. The results of optimizing the benchmark functions using the ISSA, SSA, GWO, and PSO are presented in Table 2. The ISSA demonstrates superior global optimization ability for both unimodal and multimodal functions compared to the SSA, GWO, and PSO. Figure 3 illustrates the convergence curves of each algorithm, showing that the ISSA converges to the global optimal solution faster and performs well across various classes of test functions.

Table 2. Comparison and analysis of ISSA and other algorithms.

F	Parameters	Optimization Algorithm			
		ISSA	SSA	GWO	PSO
F_1	Average value	6.86×10^{-291}	6.62×10^{-221}	0.00218	6.08×10^3
	Standard deviation	0	0	0.00306	2.28×10^3
F_2	Average value	3.17×10^{-6}	1.33×10^{-4}	26.75	2.78×10^2
	Standard deviation	5.83×10^{-6}	2.40×10^{-4}	0.77846	1.48×10^2
F_3	Average value	0	0	6.99	27.20
	Standard deviation	0	0	5.08	7.43
F_4	Average value	0	0	0.00297	4.07×10^2
	Standard deviation	0	0	0.00685	32.34

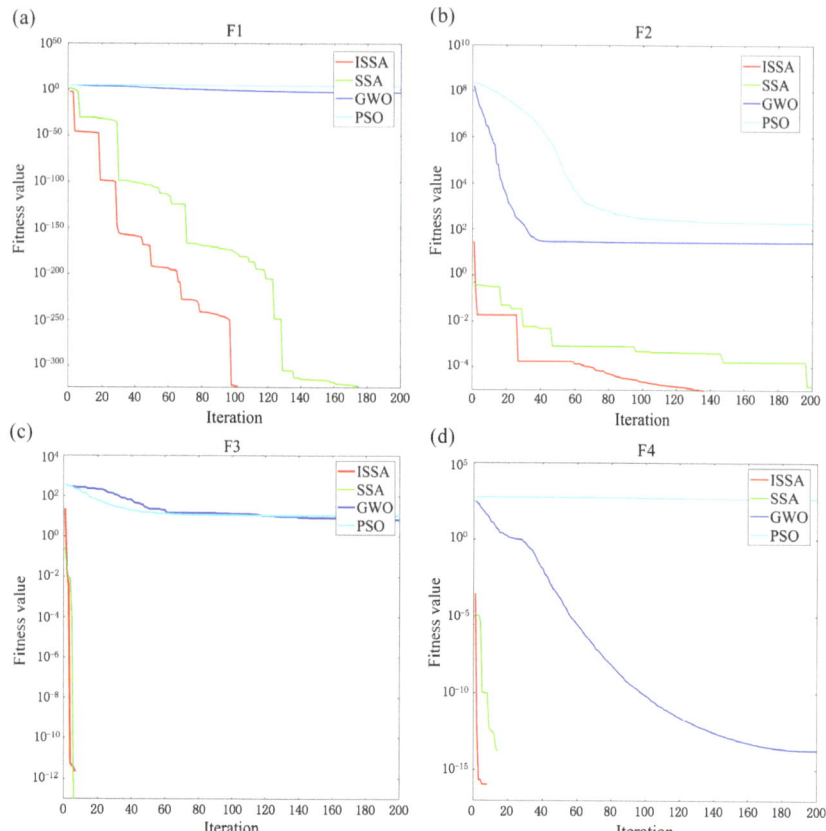

Figure 3. Fitness curves of four optimization algorithms with different benchmark functions. (**a**) F1 function curve; (**b**) F2 function curve; (**c**) F3 function curve; (**d**) F4 function curve.

3. Experimental Section and Methods

3.1. Experimental Conditions

The rigid gears were machined using the FZT-540SF middle-walking WEDM machine manufactured by Fangzhen Company in Jiangsu, China. The structure of the machine and the machining process are shown in Figure 4a,b. In this study, an involute harmonic rigid gear with a reduction ratio of 50 and a module of 0.416 is used as the object of study. Table 3 reflects the basic characteristics of rigid gears. The electrode wire chosen for machining is molybdenum wire (wire diameter ϕ = 0.18 mm), and the working medium utilized is emulsion, considering the gear teeth's characteristics and the machining process. The gear material selected is AISI 1045 steel due to its favorable machinability and mechanical properties, with its chemical composition detailed in Table 4.

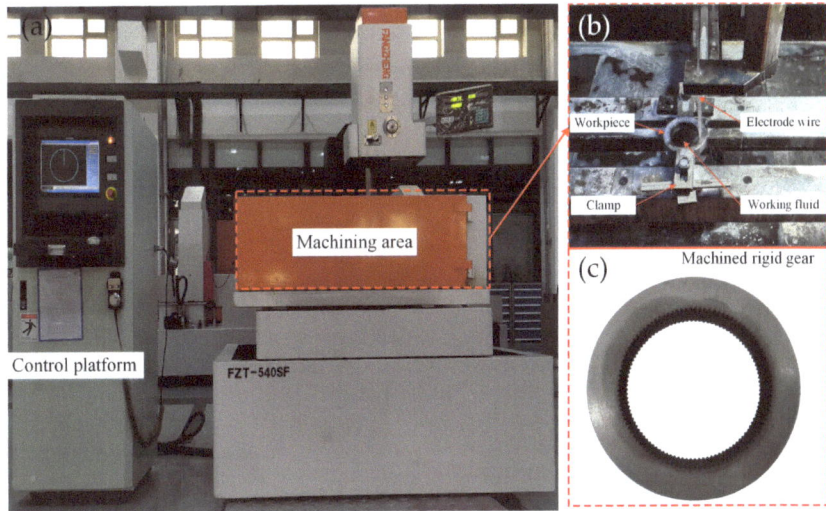

Figure 4. Rigid gears wire electrical discharge machining. (**a**) WEDM machine; (**b**) WEDM process; (**c**) machined rigid gear.

Table 3. Main parameters of rigid gears.

Module (mm)	Pressure Angle (°)	Number of Teeth	Tooth Width (mm)	Tip Diameter (mm)	Root Diameter (mm)
0.416	20	102	13	42.13	43.07

Table 4. Chemical composition of AISI 1045 steel [34].

Composition	Si	C	Mn	Cu	Cr	Ni	Fe
(%)	0.17–0.37	0.42–0.50	0.50–0.80	≤0.25	≤0.25	≤0.25	balance

Due to constraints in acquiring sufficient experimental resources and the time-consuming nature of conducting precise WEDM tests, the number of experimental data used in this study is relatively low. This limitation should be considered when interpreting the results of the evaluation of prediction methods. Nevertheless, the study provides valuable insights and serves as a preliminary assessment for predicting the tooth profile deviation of rigid gears.

3.2. Orthogonal Test Scheme

To accurately predict the tooth profile error of rigid gears and to improve product quality and performance, the WEDM tests were arranged using Taguchi's orthogonal method. The Taguchi method can be used to analyze the effects of test factors on performance indicators through fewer tests and then obtain a better combination of solutions to form optimal production conditions [35]. To investigate the effect of machining process parameters on the tooth deviation of rigid gears, an L16 orthogonal array was used for the wire-cutting machining test. The main factors considered in the test were peak current, pulse width, pulse interval, and tracking. Table 5 displays the chosen four process parameters and the level settings for each parameter.

Table 5. Input parameters and levels.

Level	Peak Current/(A)	Pulse Width/(μs)	Pulse Interval/(μs)	Tracking/(Hz/s)
1	1	8	6	100
2	1.5	16	7	150
3	2	24	8	200
4	2.5	32	9	250

3.3. Total Tooth Profile Deviation Measurement

The machined rigid gear, a small modulus multi-tooth internal gear, is shown in Figure 4c. Small module gears typically have small tooth slot clearance and poor tooth rigidity. Conventional contact measuring instruments are inefficient and difficult to use for measuring small module gears [36]. This study uses a fully automated image measuring machine (MED-5040CNC, Leader Metrology Inc, MD, America) shown in Figure 5 to measure the total tooth profile deviation of rigid gears. This machine utilizes machine vision inspection technology, enabling accurate gear measurement and online detection of gear defects. The measurement results are presented in Table 6, with the total tooth profile deviation denoted by F_α.

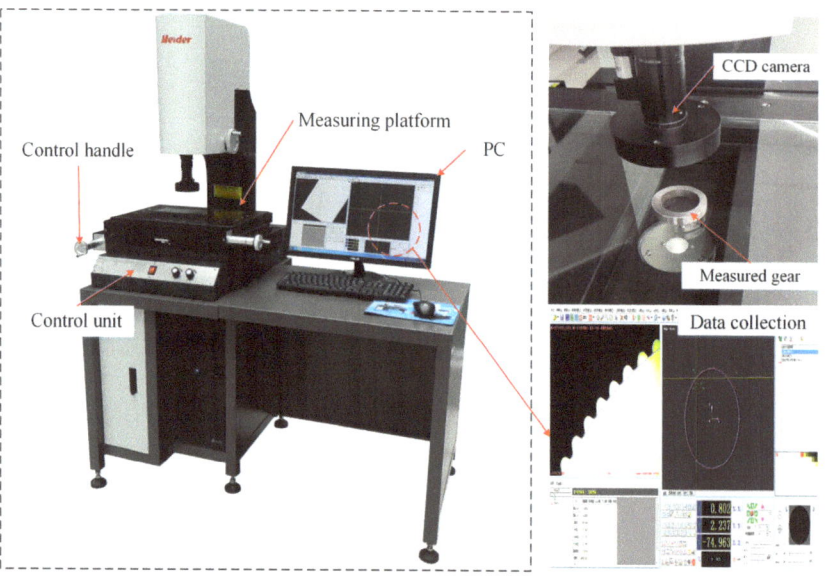

Figure 5. Image measuring machine and measuring procedure for total tooth profile deviation.

Table 6. Orthogonal test results of total tooth profile deviation.

Test Number	Peak Current (A)	Pulse Width (μs)	Pulse Interval (μs)	Tracking (Hz/s)	F_α (mm)
1	1	8	6	100	0.151
2	1	16	7	150	0.149
3	1	24	8	200	0.154
4	1	32	9	250	0.157
5	1.5	8	7	200	0.146
6	1.5	16	6	250	0.155

Table 6. *Cont.*

Test Number	Peak Current (A)	Pulse Width (µs)	Pulse Interval (µs)	Tracking (Hz/s)	F_α (mm)
7	1.5	24	9	100	0.161
8	1.5	32	8	150	0.173
9	2	8	8	250	0.156
10	2	16	9	200	0.165
11	2	24	6	150	0.178
12	2	32	7	100	0.185
13	2.5	8	9	150	0.158
14	2.5	16	8	100	0.171
15	2.5	24	7	250	0.212
16	2.5	32	6	200	0.223

4. Tooth Profile Deviation Prediction Model Based on ISSA-LSSVM

4.1. Model Construction

Utilizing the ISSA, two core parameters C and σ^2 of the LSSVM are iteratively optimized to enhance the model's prediction capability. Figure 6 illustrates the procedure for predicting tooth profile deviation in rigid gears using the ISSA-LSSVM approach.

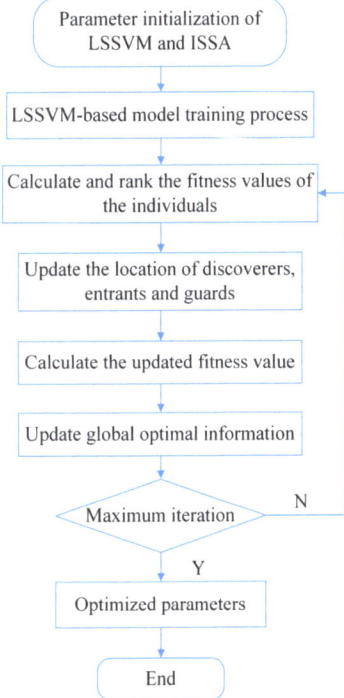

Figure 6. Flowchart of ISSA-LSSVM model prediction.

The concrete steps for predicting tooth profile deviation in rigid gears cover the following stages:

Step 1: Data set division. The WEDM process parameters are used as inputs to the model, and the rigid gear profile deviation is used as the output of the model. Then divide the WEDM test data into training and test sets and normalize them.

Step 2: Initialize the parameters of the model, including the optimization intervals for C and σ^2, population size, maximum number of iterations, and safety threshold. Adjust the proportions of discoverers and followers according to Equations (4) and (5).

Step 3: Select the mean squared error (MSE) as the model fitness function. The MSE is commonly used in the evaluation of regression models to help measure the predictive effectiveness of the model for continuous variables.

Step 4: Calculate and sort the individual adaptation values for all sparrows to determine the current best and worst fitness, along with their respective positions.

Step 5: Update the positions of the discoverer, follower, and guard, respectively. Calculate and update the fitness value of each sparrow and find the best position for the global fitness values through comparison.

Step 6: Determine whether the current iteration number reaches the maximum value. If this condition is satisfied, optimize the model parameters and build a prediction model for tooth profile deviation using ISSA-LSSVM. If not, return to step 3 and repeat the iteration process.

Step 7: Predict the profile deviation of rigid gears using the constructed ISSA-LSSVM model and generate all prediction results.

4.2. Model Setup and Indicators' Selection

The results of the orthogonal experiments were used as the dataset for the model, and it was separated randomly into a training set and a test set (training set–test set = 8:2). To evaluate the performance and accuracy of the rigid gear tooth deviation prediction model based on ISSA-LSSVM, the prediction results were compared with the PSO-LSSVM, GWO-LSSVM, and SSA-LSSVM models. All four models were configured with the same basic parameters: a search interval of [0.01, 1000] for the LSSVM model parameters. The remaining parameters for each algorithm were consistent with those described in Section 2.4.

This paper evaluates and compares the optimization results for four prediction models using three metrics: the $RMSE$, $MAPE$, and R^2. The $RMSE$ quantifies the average discrepancy between the model's predicted and actual values. The $MAPE$ expresses the accuracy of a model as a percentage, indicating how close the predicted values are to the actual values on average. A lower $RMSE$ and $MAPE$ indicate better performance in model prediction. The statistic R^2 reflects the degree of closeness between the data points and the fitted curve, with values ranging from 0 to 1. A higher R^2 value approaching 1 indicates a more ideal fit between the model and the data.

The formulas for each of the three evaluation indicators are shown below:

$$RMSE = \sqrt{\frac{1}{l}\sum_{i=1}^{l}(y_i - f_i)^2} \tag{12}$$

$$MAPE = \frac{1}{l}\sum_{i=1}^{l}\left|\frac{y_i - f_i}{y_i}\right| \times 100\% \tag{13}$$

$$R^2 = 1 - \frac{\sum_{i=1}^{l}(y_i - f_i)^2}{\sum_{i=1}^{l}(y_i - \bar{y})^2} = \frac{\sum_{i=1}^{l}(y_i - \bar{y})^2}{\sum_{i=1}^{l}(f_i - \bar{y})^2} \tag{14}$$

In the above equation, l denotes the number of samples, y_i denotes the total deviation of the actual measured tooth profile, and f_i represents the predicted values. In Equation (12), $\bar{y}$ denotes the arithmetic mean of the true values.

4.3. Model Validation

The performance of the rigid gear tooth profile deviation prediction model based on ISSA-LSSVM is demonstrated by comparing it with other models including PSO-LSSVM, GWO-LSSVM, and SSA-LSSVM. Figure 7 presents the links between real and simulated values, respectively, showing the performance of the prediction models. The results show that the ISSA-LSSVM model closely aligns with the actual prediction curve, with minimal error between the actual and predicted values.

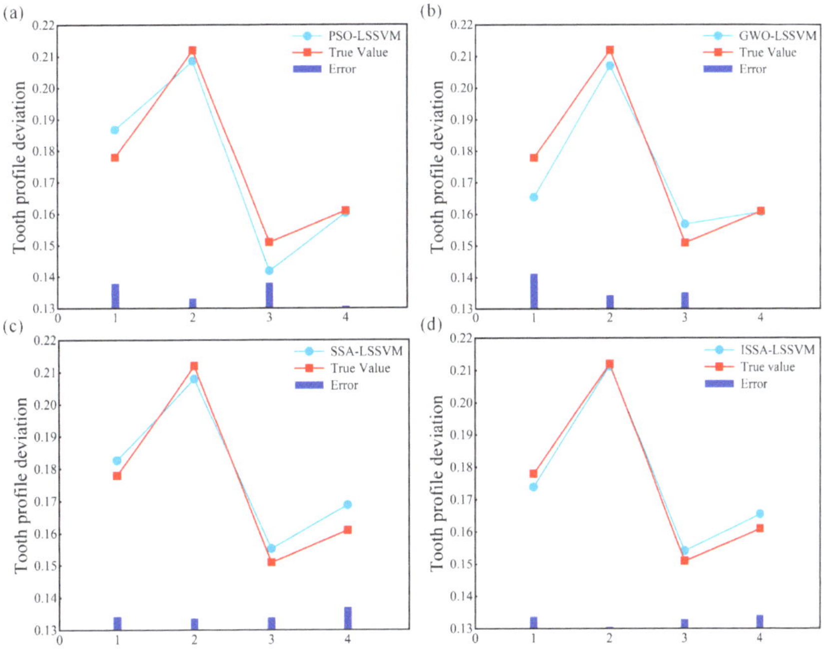

Figure 7. Prediction results and errors for each model. (**a**) PSO-LSSVM model; (**b**) GWO-LSSVM model; (**c**) SSA-LSSVM model; (**d**) ISSA-LSSVM model.

The predictive indicators of the four models are presented in Table 7. The R^2 value of the ISSA-LSSVM model (R^2 = 0.9828) significantly exceeds 0.95, whereas the R^2 values of the other models fall below 0.95. The comparison shows that the ISSA-LSSVM model has the highest degree of fit. Additionally, the *RMSE* and *MAPE* of the ISSA-LSSVM model are smaller than other models (*RMSE* = 0.0029, *MAPE* = 0.0156). In comparison to the SSA-LSSVM model, the ISSA-LSSVM model shows an increase in R^2 value by 0.0389, a decrease in *RMSE* by 0.0009, and a decrease in *MAPE* by 0.0070. The above analyses also validate the feasibility and superiority of the ISSA, which incorporates multiple strategies for improvement. Both Table 7 and Figure 7 demonstrate that the ISSA-LSSVM model outperforms other models in terms of prediction accuracy and stability.

Table 7. Results of the evaluation indicators for the four models.

Model	R^2	*RMSE*	*MAPE*
PSO-LSSVM	0.9307	0.0056	0.0327
GWO-LSSVM	0.9205	0.0071	0.0357
SSA-LSSVM	0.9439	0.0038	0.0226
ISSA-LSSVM	0.9828	0.0029	0.0156

5. Conclusions

In this study, a novel profile deviation prediction model (ISSA-LSSVM) is proposed for accurately predicting the profile error of WEDM rigid gears. The model is utilized to analyze the impact of WEDM process parameters on the profile error of rigid gears and to enable intelligent adjustment of the profile error. The key findings are outlined below:

- The standard SSA is improved by introducing Tent chaotic mapping, adaptive adjustment strategy, dynamic inertia weights, and grey wolf hierarchy strategy, which significantly improve the effectiveness and robustness of the algorithm. The improved ISSA is verified to have better convergence speed and global optimization capability than PSO, GWO, and SSA by four different types of benchmark test functions.
- The prediction results and errors of the ISSA-LSSVM tooth profile deviation prediction model were compared with those of the PSO-LSSVM, GWO-LSSVM, and SSA-LSSVM prediction models on different datasets. The results show that the ISSA-LSSVM prediction model has a higher prediction accuracy and faster convergence speed (ISSA-LSSVM model: $R^2 = 0.9828$, $RMSE = 0.0029$, $MAPE = 0.0156$).
- The developed ISSA-LSSVM model exhibits superior prediction capability and can provide reliable theoretical guidance for predicting the tooth profile deviation of rigid gears.

This research provides an innovative and reliable model for predicting tooth profile deviation in WEDM rigid gears. Despite the promising results, this study has several limitations that should be addressed in future research. Firstly, the dataset used for model training and validation is relatively small and specific to certain types of rigid gears and WEDM conditions. To enhance the generalizability of the proposed ISSA-LSSVM model, it is essential to collect and utilize more diverse and extensive datasets. Secondly, while the ISSA optimization strategy has been shown to be effective, the influence of different parameter settings on the model's performance needs further exploration. Additionally, the current model's applicability to other types of gears and machining methods remains uncertain and warrants further investigation.

Future research could focus on several key areas to further improve and validate the proposed ISSA-LSSVM model. One important direction is the collection and analysis of more diverse and extensive datasets to ensure the model's robustness and generalizability across different types of rigid gears and machining conditions. Additionally, exploring the combination of the LSSVM with other advanced optimization algorithms could potentially enhance the model's prediction accuracy and stability. Furthermore, developing new models or improving existing ones to handle more complex prediction tasks and larger datasets will be crucial for advancing the state of the art in gear profile deviation prediction.

Author Contributions: Conceptualization, Y.W. and Z.W.; methodology, Y.W. and Z.W.; software, Z.W.; validation, Z.W.; formal analysis, Y.W., Z.W., G.W. and H.X.; investigation, Z.W., G.W. and H.X.; resources, Y.W. and Z.W.; data curation, Z.W., G.W. and H.X.; writing—original draft preparation, Z.W.; writing—review and editing, Y.W.; visualization, Y.W. and Z.W.; supervision, Y.W.; project administration, Y.W.; funding acquisition, Y.W. All authors have read and agreed to the published version of the manuscript.

Funding: This research was funded by the Natural Science Foundation of Gansu Province, grant number 22JR5RA268.

Institutional Review Board Statement: Not applicable.

Informed Consent Statement: Not applicable.

Data Availability Statement: Data are contained within the article.

Conflicts of Interest: The authors declare no conflicts of interest.

References

1. Ma, J.; Li, C.; Luo, Y.; Cui, L. Simulation of meshing characteristics of harmonic reducer and experimental verification. *Adv. Mech. Eng.* **2018**, *10*, 1687814018767494. [CrossRef]
2. Song, C.; Li, X.; Yang, Y.; Sun, J. Parameter design of double-circular-arc tooth profile and its influence on meshing characteristics of harmonic drive. *Mech. Mach. Theory* **2022**, *167*, 104567. [CrossRef]
3. Guo, Z.; Mao, S.; Li, X.; Ren, Z. Research on the theoretical tooth profile errors of gears machined by skiving. *Mech. Mach. Theory* **2016**, *97*, 1–11. [CrossRef]

4. Yuan, B.; Han, J.; Tian, X.; Xia, L. Optimization and active control of internal gearing power honing process parameters for better gear precision. *Mech. Sci.* **2022**, *13*, 449–458. [CrossRef]
5. Shilong, W.; Shouli, S.U.N.; Jie, Z.; Ling, K.; Cheng, C. Research on Mapping Rules of Hob Geometric Errors and Gear Geometric Precision. *J. Mech. Eng.* **2013**, *49*, 119–125.
6. Sun, S.; Wang, S.; Wang, Y.; Lim, T.; Yang, Y. Prediction and optimization of hobbing gear geometric deviations. *Mech. Mach. Theory* **2018**, *120*, 288–301. [CrossRef]
7. Peng, B.; Luo, Y.; Wang, H.; Niu, T.; Wang, Y. Investigation on the effects of tooth profile deviation in gear rolling process. *Int. J. Adv. Manuf. Technol.* **2023**, *126*, 1877–1887. [CrossRef]
8. Yusron, R.M.; Prasetyo, T.; Pramudia, M. Investigation of Involute Profile Error on Spur Gear Processed using Wire EDM. *IOP Conf. Ser. Mater. Sci. Eng.* **2021**, *1125*, 012119. [CrossRef]
9. Kharka, V.; Jain, N.K.; Gupta, K. Influence of MQL and hobbing parameters on microgeometry deviations and flank roughness of spur gears manufactured by MQL assisted hobbing. *J. Mater. Res. Technol.* **2020**, *9*, 9646–9656. [CrossRef]
10. Mo, S.; Li, Y.; Luo, B.; Wang, L.; Bao, H.; Cen, G.; Huang, Y. Research on the meshing characteristics of asymmetric gears considering the tooth profile deviation. *Mech. Mach. Theory* **2022**, *175*, 104926. [CrossRef]
11. Chen, Z.; Zhou, Z.; Zhai, W.; Wang, K. Improved analytical calculation model of spur gear mesh excitations with tooth profile deviations. *Mech. Mach. Theory* **2020**, *149*, 103838. [CrossRef]
12. Tsai, C. Simple mathematical approach for analyzing gear tooth profile errors of different gears cut using same power-skiving tool. *Mech. Mach. Theory* **2022**, *177*, 105042. [CrossRef]
13. Chaudhari, R.; Vora, J.J.; Patel, V.; Lacalle, L.N.L.D.; Parikh, D.M. Effect of WEDM Process Parameters on Surface Morphology of Nitinol Shape Memory Alloy. *Materials* **2020**, *13*, 4943. [CrossRef]
14. Sliusarenko, O.; Escudero, G.G.; González, H.; Calleja, A.; Bartoň, M.; Ortega, N.; de Lacalle, L.N.L. Constant probe orientation for fast contact-based inspection of 3D free-form surfaces using (3+2)-axis inspection machines. *Precis. Eng.* **2023**, *84*, 37–44. [CrossRef]
15. Escudero, G.G.; Bo, P.; González-Barrio, H.; Calleja-Ochoa, A.; Bartoň, M.; de Lacalle, L.N.L. 5-axis double-flank CNC machining of spiral bevel gears via custom-shaped tools—Part II: Physical validations and experiments. *Int. J. Adv. Manuf. Technol.* **2022**, *119*, 1647–1658. [CrossRef]
16. Gupta, K.; Jain, N.K. On Micro-Geometry of Miniature Gears Manufactured by Wire Electrical Discharge Machining. *Mater. Manuf. Process.* **2013**, *28*, 1153–1159. [CrossRef]
17. Nain, S.S.; Garg, D.; Kumar, S. Evaluation and analysis of cutting speed, wire wear ratio, and dimensional deviation of wire electric discharge machining of super alloy Udimet-L605 using support vector machine and grey relational analysis. *Adv. Manuf.* **2018**, *6*, 225–246. [CrossRef]
18. Li, Z.; Li, X.; Zhang, H.; Huang, D.; Zhang, L. The prediction of contact force networks in granular materials based on graph neural networks. *J. Chem. Phys.* **2023**, *158*, 054905. [CrossRef]
19. Zhu, C.; Li, G.; Luis, N.V.J.; Dong, W.; Wang, L. Optimization of RF to alloy elastic modulus prediction based on cuckoo algorithm. *Comput. Mater. Sci.* **2024**, *231*, 112515. [CrossRef]
20. He, J.; Cu, S.; Xia, H.; Sun, Y.; Xiao, W.; Ren, Y. High accuracy roll forming springback prediction model of SVR based on SA-PSO optimization. *J. Intell. Manuf.* **2023**, 1–17. [CrossRef]
21. Shi, M.; Tan, P.; Qin, L.; Huang, Z. Research on Valve Life Prediction Based on PCA-PSO-LSSVM. *Processes* **2023**, *11*, 1396. [CrossRef]
22. Feng, Y.; Hong, Z.; Gao, Y.; Lu, R.; Wang, Y.; Tan, J. Optimization of variable blank holder force in deep drawing based on support vector regression model and trust region. *Int. J. Adv. Manuf. Technol.* **2019**, *105*, 4265–4278. [CrossRef]
23. Li, S.; Li, S.; Liu, Z.; Vladimirovich, P.A. Roughness prediction model of milling noise-vibration-surface texture multi-dimensional feature fusion for N6 nickel metal. *J. Manuf. Process.* **2022**, *79*, 166–176. [CrossRef]
24. Zhao, Z.; Chen, K.; Chen, Y.; Dai, Y.; Liu, Z.; Zhao, K.; Wang, H.; Peng, Z. An Ultra-Fast Power Prediction Method Based on Simplified LSSVM Hyperparameters Optimization for PV Power Smoothing. *Energies* **2021**, *14*, 5752. [CrossRef]
25. Wan, P.; Zou, H.; Wang, K.; Zhao, Z. Hot deformation characterization of Ti–Nb alloy based on GA-LSSVM and 3D processing map. *J. Mater. Res. Technol.* **2021**, *13*, 1083–1097. [CrossRef]
26. Suykens, J.A.K.; Vandewalle, J. Least Squares Support Vector Machine Classifiers. *Neural Process. Lett.* **1999**, *9*, 293–300. [CrossRef]
27. Ge, Y.; Zhang, J.; Song, G.; Zhu, K. An effective LSSVM-based approach for milling tool wear prediction. *Int. J. Adv. Manuf. Technol.* **2023**, *126*, 4555–4571. [CrossRef]
28. Yu, C.; Xi, Z.; Lu, Y.; Tao, K.; Yi, Z. LSSVM-based color prediction for cotton fabrics with reactive pad-dry-pad-steam dyeing. *Chemometr. Intell. Lab.* **2020**, *199*, 103956. [CrossRef]
29. Xue, J.; Shen, B. A novel swarm intelligence optimization approach: Sparrow search algorithm. *Syst. Sci. Control Eng.* **2020**, *8*, 22–34. [CrossRef]
30. Dokeroglu, T.; Sevinc, E.; Kucukyilmaz, T.; Cosar, A. A survey on new generation metaheuristic algorithms. *Comput. Ind. Eng.* **2019**, *137*, 106040. [CrossRef]
31. Ouyang, C.; Qiu, Y.; Zhu, D. Adaptive Spiral Flying Sparrow Search Algorithm. *Sci. Program.* **2021**, *2021*, 6505253. [CrossRef]
32. Qiu, S.; Li, A. Application of Chaos Mutation Adaptive Sparrow Search Algorithm in Edge Data Compression. *Sensors* **2022**, *22*, 5425. [CrossRef] [PubMed]

33. Sharma, P.; Raju, S. Metaheuristic optimization algorithms: A comprehensive overview and classification of benchmark test functions. *Soft Comput.* **2023**, *28*, 3123–3186. [CrossRef]
34. Zhao, J.; Wang, Q.; Wang, Y.; Wu, D.; Zhang, L.; Shen, B. Research on the Tooth Surface Integrity of Non-Circular Gear WEDM Based on HPSO Optimization SVR. *Appl. Sci.* **2022**, *12*, 12858. [CrossRef]
35. Erkoçak, Y.; Kayır, Y. Analyzing the Impacts of Cutting Parameters on Cutting Forces in the Taguchi Method for Boring High-Alloy White Cast Irons with CBN Inserts. *Arab. J. Sci. Eng.* **2023**, *48*, 12569–12585. [CrossRef]
36. Luo, M.; Zhong, S. Non-Contact Measurement of Small-Module Gears Using Optical Coherence Tomography. *Appl. Sci.* **2018**, *8*, 2490. [CrossRef]

Disclaimer/Publisher's Note: The statements, opinions and data contained in all publications are solely those of the individual author(s) and contributor(s) and not of MDPI and/or the editor(s). MDPI and/or the editor(s) disclaim responsibility for any injury to people or property resulting from any ideas, methods, instructions or products referred to in the content.

MDPI AG
Grosspeteranlage 5
4052 Basel
Switzerland
Tel.: +41 61 683 77 34

Applied Sciences Editorial Office
E-mail: applsci@mdpi.com
www.mdpi.com/journal/applsci

Disclaimer/Publisher's Note: The title and front matter of this reprint are at the discretion of the Guest Editor. The publisher is not responsible for their content or any associated concerns. The statements, opinions and data contained in all individual articles are solely those of the individual Editor and contributors and not of MDPI. MDPI disclaims responsibility for any injury to people or property resulting from any ideas, methods, instructions or products referred to in the content.

www.ingramcontent.com/pod-product-compliance
Lightning Source LLC
LaVergne TN
LVHW072353090526
838202LV00019B/2536